31° E

A

LAKE RWANYAKIZINGA

Akagera
National
Park

LAKE IHEMA

TANZANIA

KIGALI

Kayonza

—2° S

GESERA

Ngoma
(*formerly* Kibungo)

Akagera

Rusumo Falls

BURUNDI

0               20 Miles

0           20 Kilometers

# ROAD TRIP
# RWANDA

## ALSO BY WILL FERGUSON

# ROAD TRIP
# RWANDA

## A Journey into the New Heart of Africa

# WILL FERGUSON

VIKING

VIKING

an imprint of Penguin Canada Books Inc., a Penguin Random House Company

Published by the Penguin Group
Penguin Canada Books Inc., 320 Front Street West, Suite 1400,
Toronto, Ontario M5V 3B6, Canada

Penguin Group (USA) LLC, 375 Hudson Street, New York, New York 10014, U.S.A.
Penguin Books Ltd, 80 Strand, London WC2R 0RL, England
Penguin Ireland, 25 St Stephen's Green, Dublin 2, Ireland (a division of Penguin Books Ltd)
Penguin Group (Australia), 707 Collins Street, Melbourne, Victoria 3008,
Australia (a division of Pearson Australia Group Pty Ltd)
Penguin Books India Pvt Ltd, 11 Community Centre, Panchsheel Park,
New Delhi – 110 017, India
Penguin Group (NZ), 67 Apollo Drive, Rosedale, Auckland 0632, New Zealand
(a division of Pearson New Zealand Ltd)
Penguin Books (South Africa) (Pty) Ltd, 24 Sturdee Avenue, Rosebank,
Johannesburg 2196, South Africa

Penguin Books Ltd, Registered Offices: 80 Strand, London WC2R 0RL, England

First published 2015

1 2 3 4 5 6 7 8 9 10  (RRD)

Copyright © Will Ferguson, 2015
Photos copyright © Will Ferguson, 2015, used by permission

*Penguin is committed to publishing works of quality and integrity.*
*In that spirit, we are proud to offer this book to our readers;*
*however, the story, the experiences, and the words are the author's alone.*

Maps created by Lisa Jager

Manufactured in the U.S.A.

LIBRARY AND ARCHIVES CANADA CATALOGUING IN PUBLICATION

Ferguson, Will. Author
Road trip Rwanda : a journey into the new heart of
Africa / Will Ferguson.

Includes bibliographical reference.
ISBN 978-0-670-06642-1 (bound)

1. Ferguson, Will—Travel—Rwanda.  2. Authors, Canadian
(English)—20th century—Travel—Rwanda.  3. Rwanda—Social
conditions—21st century.  4. Rwanda—Description and travel.
I. Title.

DT450.44.F47 2015        967.57104'3        C2015-903919-3

eBook ISBN 978-0-14-319619-8

Visit the Penguin Canada website at **www.penguin.ca**

Special and corporate bulk purchase rates available;
please see **www.penguin.ca/corporatesales** or call 1-800-810-3104.

# CONTENTS

# AUTHOR'S NOTE

IN 2006, RWANDA REORGANIZED its administrative boundaries, merging twelve smaller provinces into five larger ones. Regional cities and towns that bore the names of the older provinces had their names changed as well. This can be confusing for visitors, especially those with an interest in Rwandan history. Books and testimonies about the genocide, for example, do not refer to "Huye" but Butare, not to "Rubavu" but Gisenyi. I've employed the older names throughout, while acknowledging the new ones in parentheses. On the maps, I have reversed this, listing the current names followed by *"formerly ..."*

# RUSUMO FALLS

THE BRIDGE AT THE END OF RWANDA crosses the Akagera River in a single, graceful arc: a thin span joining the scrub hills of southern Rwanda with those of northern Tanzania.

Below the bridge, a drama is playing out. The milk-tea waters of an otherwise languid river narrow suddenly into the bottleneck of Rusumo Falls, a tumult more heard than seen. Only a trace of mist hints at the waterfall's presence.

Transport trucks from Tanzania rumble across the bridge, the din from their engines drowning out the sound of water, but Rusumo is always there, just out of sight.

I want to walk out onto the bridge and peer down at the falls but I can't, even though the two Rwandan soldiers posted there—a young man and a young woman in heavy olive-green uniforms, rifles slung over shoulders, faces sheened in perspiration—shrugged and gave me a weary "go ahead" wave when I asked. Just don't go past the middle of the bridge, they advised, because after that I would be Tanzania's concern.

This is the crux of the conundrum I face: I have permission, but I don't. Or rather, I have two conflicting sets of permission, one granted by the soldiers at the bridge, the other being withheld by an officious little man who has disappeared with my passport and papers. Normally, I would say take your cues from the people who are armed—in my experience, an AK-47 generally trumps a stamp pad—but one never wants to underestimate the power of a mid-level bureaucrat to ruin one's day.

So.

I do not walk onto the bridge.

Instead I sit, sticky-shirted in the heat, under the rapidly diminishing slice of shade afforded by the corrugated overhang of the roof at the Rwanda Customs and Immigration—well, *hall* is too grand a word. *Bungalow* is more accurate. It's a squat, cement-walled structure with a warren of offices in the back and a pair of bank-teller-type windows out front where forms are duly shuffled and stamped.

A procession of tired-looking Tanzanian truck drivers, paperwork in hand, moves past me. And is there anything more wilted or damp in this world than the paperwork of a Tanzanian truck driver? At times, this procession becomes a crush of bodies, the air pungent with perspiration, and as the men push through, they give me sympathetic nods and deeply curious looks. A *muzungu,* flesh the colour of boiled pork, forced to wait? Unfathomable.

I appreciate their concern, even if none of the drivers offer to smuggle me across. Under a sack of coffee beans, say.

So I sit here, marinating in the heat, and I wonder what has become of Jean-Claude. I wonder whether he has been arrested. I wonder whether I will be arrested. More importantly, I wonder what we're going to do about lunch.

I'm stuck in a no man's land, the term a tad misleading at a border crossing packed with drivers and vehicles, trucks wedged in every which way like a giant game of Jenga. At the top of the hill, Rwandan taverns are cooing promises of Primus beer and welcoming shade. But I can't retreat and I can't move forward. I can only wait.

As one hour drips by, then another, I make friends with a succession of Tanzanian truck drivers. They speak French, Swahili, and a bit of Kinyarwanda, with a smattering of English thrown in more for style than substance.

Fortunately, I speak Truck Driver, a form of male-speak found in most countries. Using a range of gestures (often involving eyebrows, puffed-cheek exhalations, and the pantomimed fanning of one's brow), we are able to come to an agreement, for example, that it is very hot out. We likewise agree that a beer would be good right about now. We are also in favour of women. Other points covered include: man, is it hot; too hot, really; someone should sell beer down here, they'd make a lot of money; women, eh? Cor!

They ask me where I'm from. Really? They have a cousin/aunt/
uncle/brother-in-law there! Is it hot like this in my country? And can
I sponsor them? Truck driving is hard work, you see. Too hard. And
the women in my country? Are they, *you know,* heh heh? (That last
query is delivered non-verbally for the most part, involving the
further artful use of eyebrows along with a leering grin, a leering grin
being the International Symbol for *Women, eh? Cor blimey!*)

Hiding under a sack of coffee beans is looking better and better.
Maybe I'll become a truck driver's turn boy, one of those assistants
who guide the massive rigs into car parks. Maybe I'll work my way
up to my own rig, become a mythical figure, a wild-eyed muzungu
of the plains, crazy from the heat, who made a fortune selling Primus
beer outside of immigration offices. They'd write songs about me.
Women would run alongside, waving as I passed. Boy, is it hot.
Someone should really sell beer down here. They'd make good money.

Before I can slip dreamily into that other life, Jean-Claude
reappears, mightily irked by the slow-motion ordeal he's been put
through.

He's had enough of the Rwandan customs official, that small
hovering man who has followed him out and is now pleading for us
to wait. This insubstantial gentleman needs to hear from his superiors
in the district office on what to do about us. But today is Saturday,
and no one is answering the phone.

"It is a simple request," Jean-Claude says to him. "Can we go out
on the bridge and take photographs or not?"

But our hovering official doesn't know. He is caught in an
administrative no man's land of his own.

"Are you detaining us?" Jean-Claude demands. "Are you placing us
under arrest? I didn't think so." He turns to me. "Come on, let's go."

We walk out onto the bridge, leaving the anxious clerk behind,
wringing his hands to no avail.

"Did he want a bribe?" I ask.

"This is Rwanda," Jean-Claude says. "We don't pay bribes."

The two soldiers nod as we pass.

Jean-Claude and I walk out to where the river is spilling over the boulder-strewn narrows, water splaying across the rocks. Murky currents. Earth-scented air. A permanent rainbow. *This is where the bodies would have tumbled ...*

As trucks roll by, the bridge bounces with a disconcerting sproinginess.

"I remember that!" Jean-Claude says with a sudden smile. "I remember it bouncing. I thought it was just my imagination!"

He has never seen this bridge before, though he remembers it well. When he crossed twenty years ago, he was hiding under coffee sacks in the back of a transport truck.

"What would they have done?" I ask. "If they had caught you?"

"Oh," he says. "They would have killed me."

He says this without rancour or melodrama, but as a simple statement of fact. *If they'd caught me, they would have killed me.*

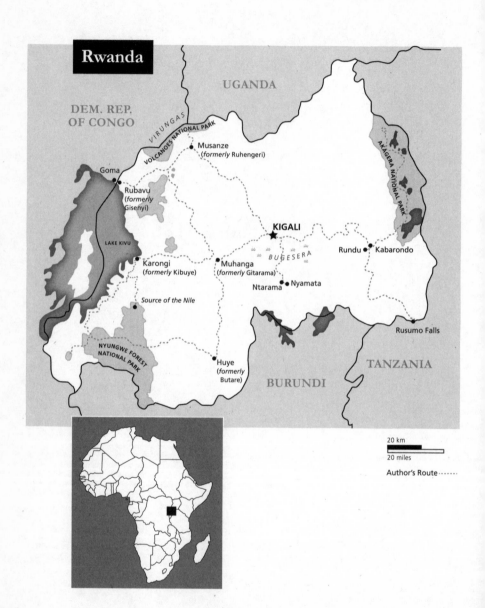

# Rwanda

UGANDA

DEM. REP.
OF CONGO

*V I R U N G A S*

VOLCANOES NATIONAL PARK

AKAGERA NATIONAL PARK

• Musanze
*(formerly Ruhengeri)*

Goma •

Rubavu
*(formerly
Gisenyi)*

**KIGALI** ★

LAKE KIVU

*B U G E S E R A*

Rundu •• Kabarondo

Karongi •
*(formerly Kibuye)*

• Muhanga
*(formerly Gitarama)*

Ntarama • Nyamata

• *Source of the Nile*

NYUNGWE FOREST
NATIONAL PARK

Rusumo Falls •

• Huye
*(formerly
Butare)*

TANZANIA

BURUNDI

20 km
20 miles

Author's Route ------

# PART ONE

## A THOUSAND HILLS

# 1

I FIRST MET JEAN-CLAUDE MUNYEZAMU on a summery field in Calgary seven years earlier. Our children were on the same under-five community soccer team (*"Go Tigers!"*) and Jean-Claude was one of the volunteer coaches, though coaching kids at that age amounted primarily to making sure they were at least running in the same direction. Jean-Claude and I became friends; our wives became friends, our children as well.

When I found out where he was from, one of the first things I asked him—which I cringe at, even now—was "So you're from Rwanda? Are you a ... Tutsi or a Hutu?"

He smiled softly. "Tutsi."

I did a quick calibration in my head: *In Rwanda, did the Tutsis kill the Hutus, or did the Hutus kill the Tutsis?* That's how little I knew. I had only vague recollections of one of the worst mass killings in human history.

At their home in southwest Calgary, Jean-Claude's wife Christine would cook bubbling stews served with *ugali,* a loaf-like communal dumpling torn and dipped. Over tall glasses of ginger-laced tea— a Rwandan specialty—Jean-Claude would urge me to visit his country someday.

"Rwanda is beautiful," he'd say, and Christine would agree. "You have to see it! Take your boys."

"We'll go there together," Jean-Claude said. "We'll bring soccer equipment to donate."

I hesitated, not for reasons of safety—but of sadness. I'd always maintained that a sense of humour can be found in any destination, no matter how bruised, how battered, and that through humour we can find a sense of shared humanity. But Rwanda?

Through Jean-Claude, I'd gotten to know Calgary's Rwandan community, and through them I had gained the smallest glimpse into the terrors of the 1994 genocide against the Tutsis of Rwanda, when over the course of one hundred horrific days, upward of one million men, women, and children were butchered under the racially charged ideology of Hutu Power.[1] More than 75 percent of the Tutsi population inside Rwanda was wiped out and almost all Hutu political moderates executed in what has been described by analysts as "the most efficient and complete genocide of modern times." Also targeted were independent journalists, lawyers, human rights investigators, members of the opposition—anyone on the wrong side of power. But whereas political opponents had been killed for what they believed, Tutsis were killed simply for having been born. This is the key distinction of a genocide. The Tutsis were not targeted as individuals; they were targeted as a group. It was a deliberate, well-planned, organized undertaking. *One million people in one hundred days*. It was a killing rate five times higher than that attained by the Nazis.

A young Rwandan woman in Calgary, speaking softly, told me how she'd survived the carnage as a little girl by climbing under the "buddies." But no—not buddies. In her lovely accent, so rounded and rich, she was referring not to buddies, but *bodies*.

Whenever I describe Jean-Claude as a genocide survivor, he quietly corrects me. "I'm not a survivor, I'm an escapee. There is a big difference." He was never hunted through the marshes, hacked at by machetes. He never hid under the dwindling warmth of *buddies*.

---

1. The number of people who died during the Rwandan genocide is often given, incorrectly, as 800,000. This was an initial estimate made by Human Rights Watch. The International Red Cross and the UN Rwanda Emergency Office put the number at a million, as did Oxfam U.K. A census, taken six years after the genocide, was able to establish the names of 951,018 victims. Of these, 94 percent were identified as Tutsi, which still leaves more than 50,000 Hutus dead, a staggering number in its own right and one worth remembering. A later census placed the number killed at 937,000. Given that in the more remote regions of Rwanda entire villages were exterminated and all records destroyed, the final number is almost certainly higher. It may well have been more than a million. No one can say for sure.

Jean-Claude's mother had died when he was little, so when his father passed away in 1993, Jean-Claude, as a young man of nineteen, knew there was nothing keeping him in Rwanda.

"As a Tutsi, it was oppressive. You were a second-class citizen. You were targeted constantly." Dark clouds were forming. Practice massacres had already occurred in the outlying regions. The walls were closing in, and a sense of dread pervaded every transaction as the radio and newspapers exhorted Rwanda's Hutu majority to "stop having mercy" on the Tutsis. Fortunately for Jean-Claude, he had a brother in Kenya, and that would prove to be his escape hatch. He scraped together enough money to pay a truck driver to smuggle him across the border into Tanzania under a cargo of coffee beans, past armed soldiers and then overland to Mombasa.

The genocide in Rwanda began ten months later.

Jean-Claude Munyezamu had made it out alive. His brothers and cousins, his uncles and nephews, were not so lucky. An older sister and her infant child were rescued by UN peacekeepers from a church just before the killers swarmed in. "She lives with that—with the trauma of that—every day," Jean-Claude told me.

Jean-Claude reached Canada by a circuitous route that took him first through Tanzania and Kenya, and then as an aid volunteer to Somalia and Sudan, until finally—and most daunting of all, perhaps— he landed in Montreal in the middle of February. "When I arrived it was minus thirty-two and I was wearing a hoodie. It was the warmest jacket I could find. I grew up on the equator, and when I got out of the airport it felt like the cold was sucking the air out of my lungs." He laughed. "I wondered if I should not have stayed in Africa."

Granted permanent residency status, he settled in Alberta, worked as a meat cutter, an oil-rig worker, a taxi driver, learned English, and attained his Canadian citizenship. He began volunteering at Calgary homeless shelters and, in his spare time, set up Soccer Without Boundaries, a volunteer-run program for immigrant and refugee children. The goal was to help them integrate into their local communities through an open-door sports program—and it worked.

Very well, in fact. I helped out with his soccer club now and then, was thanked profusely and far in excess of whatever minor assistance I'd provided, and through it got to know parents and children from countries as far afield as—and this is just a partial tally, mind you—Syria, Iran, Afghanistan, Egypt, Lebanon, Somalia, Sudan, Congo, Burundi, Rwanda, Pakistan, Ethiopia, Korea, the Philippines, Uruguay, and Colombia.

Today, Jean-Claude sits on the Premier's Council on Culture. He has received the Queen's Diamond Jubilee Medal for his work with youth. He is married, with three children. A father, a husband, a community organizer, a soccer coach. And a genocide escapee.

# 2

RUSUMO FALLS IS A FATEFUL BOTTLENECK, for it was at Rusumo, where the river narrows, that an obscure German count first crossed over into the Kingdom of Rwanda. This was in 1894. Other explorers had skirted the edge of this remote realm; none had entered.

Rwanda lies in the crosshairs of Africa. Known as the "Land of a Thousand Hills," it is the true heart of the continent, the last region to be reached by Europeans, one never impacted by the slave trade, located along the farthest watersheds of the Congo and Nile rivers.

What the German count discovered surprised him. Here, in the deepest reaches of Africa, was a complex, highly organized, semi-feudal society with a divine king, or *mwami,* in the centre and a network of aristocrats, courtiers, prefects, and vassals radiating outward from his majesty's royal court. It was highly bureaucratic as well, with an administration divided into four levels: prefecture, district, hilltop, and local commune. Every hill had its chiefs, every chief his delegate. Every farm, every home, every house was accounted for.

Rwanda was—and still is—the most densely populated country in continental Africa: fertile soil and a fertile populace as well. The culture was cohesive and tightly controlled, and the people were known throughout the region for being law-abiding and compliant—traits that mark Rwanda, for better or worse, right through to today. A Hutu lawyer, struggling to explain how so many of his fellow countrymen could be incited to mass murder, admitted, "Conformity is very deep, very developed here. In Rwanda, everyone obeys authority."

In many ways, the roots of the 1994 genocide were planted by that first German count pushing across the narrow gap at Rusumo Falls, filling in the last part of the map. Even before the Germans appeared, the mercantile empires of Europe had divided Africa among themselves, drawing presumptuously decisive lines on cartographical charts, claiming tracts of land so vast they defied the imagination. Rwanda was claimed by Germany without anyone from Germany ever having set foot in it; the kingdom was so remote it took nearly ten years before even that first count arrived. Of course, he didn't *tell* the mwami he had come to claim a kingdom. It was a scouting mission as much as anything, an act of stealth, the opening gambit of a slowly constricting campaign.

Although Rwanda was part of German East Africa, German rule didn't last. During World War I, Belgian troops occupied the kingdom, and with Germany's defeat, the colony was handed over to Belgium, which had been ruling the Congo next door in what can only be called a reign of terror. Rwanda was—and still is—one of the most culturally homogeneous nations in Africa: everyone spoke the same language, followed the same religion, shared the same territory. It was certainly more united and homogeneous, both linguistically and culturally, than was Belgium. Or Germany, for that matter.

Society was divided into numerous clans and two main social classes: the minority Tutsis, who were traditionally cattle herders, and the Hutu majority, who were farmers. Rwanda's royal lineage was drawn exclusively from the Tutsis, who made up roughly 16 percent of the population, though some estimates put the Tutsi population closer to 20 percent.[2] A small number of pygmy hunter-gatherers, known as the Twa, lived in the forests, making up less than 1 percent of the population.

The Tutsi herders held a higher social status than Hutu farmers, who were often involved with them in a master–client relationship. (The word *Hutu* signifies "subject" or "servant," whereas *Tutsi* refers to someone rich in cattle.) But the obligations went both ways, and the system was so intricate that it was referred to as "intertwined fingers."

It's important to note that "wealthy" was not synonymous with "Tutsi." Tutsis of high lineage were a minority even among their own people. Most were just as poor and put-upon as their Hutu neighbours, and intermarriage was common enough not to be an issue. It's also important to note that Hutu and Tutsi do not represent different ethnic groups, and certainly not different "tribes." The defining markers of ethnicity—a separate language, territory, religion, or culture—simply don't apply. There was no "Hutuland," no "Tutsiland"; no Hutu language, no Tutsi dialect. The two groups didn't even have distinct surnames, unlike in Northern Ireland, say, where the gaping Protestant–Catholic divide, based on competing histories and differing religious affiliations, is easily divined; in Belfast a "Johnston" or a "Murphy," a "Billy" or a "Seamus," knows immediately which side of the divide the other is on. In Rwanda the categories were more fluid than that; if a Hutu farmer owned enough cattle, for example, he became a Tutsi.

European culture, however, steeped as it was in the proto-fascist ideals of Social Darwinism, was obsessed with notions of race, and in Rwanda the colonial rulers decided that the Tutsi were a separate "race" from the Hutu. This was part of a pernicious strain of historical quackery known as the "Hamitic hypothesis," though *myth* would be a more accurate term.

---

2. The number of Tutsis in Rwanda prior to the genocide is sometimes given, incorrectly, as 9 percent of the population, based on a dubious government census by Hutu nationalists that was then used to limit the quota of Tutsis in schools and public employment.

Baffled when faced with a developed society in the heart of darkest Africa, the Europeans concluded that Rwandan civilization must have come from somewhere *else*. The Tutsis, being taller, lighter skinned, finely featured, and thinner nosed, were considered more "European" in appearance, making them, almost by definition in European eyes, superior to the shorter, squatter, broader faced, darker skinned "Negroid" Hutus. The Hamitic hypothesis posited that the Tutsis were not "real" Africans but rather a lost tribe of Israel, having migrated south from Egypt or Ethiopia as the descendants of Ham, Noah's outcast son. Missionaries embraced this bit of Biblical nonsense, and in doing so granted the Tutsi aristocracy a privileged place in an imperially sanctioned racial hierarchy. Throughout the Bantu region of Africa, this bizarre myth was used to explain—or rather, explain *away*—all signs of civilization, from the use of iron tools to advanced political systems to monotheistic beliefs, but only in Rwanda and neighbouring Burundi did it become so entrenched, so corrosive.

Whether their much-ballyhooed physiological differences—which are not in any way universal; Rwandans themselves are notoriously inaccurate when it comes to guessing who is a Tutsi and who is a Hutu based solely on appearance—were due to generations of dietary divergence or are in fact the genetic relic of some distant and now-forgotten migration is really a moot point. Any separate origins that might have explained the difference in appearance between Tutsi and Hutu are lost in the mists of time. Their language and culture are now the same. It is worth repeating: Tutsi and Hutu are *social categories,* not ethnicities.

Certainly, on either end of the spectrum are people who look more "Hutu" and those who look more "Tutsi," but most exist in the muddled middle. As a vice-president of the former Rwandan National Assembly confessed, "Even *we* can't tell us apart." And these physical differences are shrinking as lifestyles change—a telling detail, suggesting as it does that such traits may indeed be the lingering inheritance of an aristocratic diet over that of the commoners, a distinction between milk-drinking pastoralists and hard-working agriculturalists who consumed more grains and root vegetables. (As a French social geographer has pointed out, the difference in height recorded between Hutu and Tutsi was "exactly the same difference that existed in France between a conscript and a senator in 1815.")

This may seem esoteric, but so much of what followed was predicated on exactly these myths and perceived physical differences. During the genocide, people were killed simply for being tall. And one of Jean-Claude's cousins survived because, being short and heavy-set, he was able to bluff his way through the killers' roadblocks by passing himself off, in an angry huff, as a Hutu.

It was the Germans who first decided that the Tutsis were a more highly evolved "race," but it was the Belgians who brought the idea to fruition, making race *the* defining aspect of colonial policy in Rwanda. In an eerie foreshadowing of Nazi racial studies, Belgian scientists armed with calipers and clipboards set about measuring the nose length and cranial capacity of Africans, carefully recording height and gradations of skin colour and then classifying subjects into two mutually exclusive groups. *"Unlike the Tutsi, the Hutu have a wide brachycephalic skull,"* a typical entry might read. (The black-and-white photographs of these experiments are unsettling, to say the least.) When in doubt, the Belgians counted cows; if someone owned enough cattle he became "Tutsi." In the 1930s, Belgium began issuing racial ID cards marked HUTU or TUTSI, which every Rwandan was required by law to present. In 1994, these same identity cards would become death warrants.

While the mwami himself was traditionally drawn from a Tutsi line, as were his cattle chiefs, the land chiefs were often Hutu and the war chiefs were either. Any given hill might have three different subchiefs overseeing it. Under Belgian rule, that changed. The Hutu chiefs were deposed, one after another, and replaced with Tutsis,[3] and when, as they had in the Congo, the Belgians brought in a system of

---

3. By the end of Belgian rule, 549 out of 559 subchiefs were Tutsi, a massive social shift.

forced labour and mandatory cash crops, the Tutsis were exempted—
just as the Hutu were systematically excluded from positions of power
and privilege.

In imposing forced labour, whether to pick crops, build roads,
drain swamps, or clear land, the Belgians favoured strips of sun-dried
hippopotamus hide as their primary means of persuasion, and the era
of Belgian rule in Rwanda became known as "the time of the whip."
The Hutu bore the brunt of it. Tutsi overseers, meanwhile, were
forced to push the peasantry to greater and greater limits. "Whip
them or we will whip you" was the directive they were given as
Rwanda became one vast work camp. The inner heart of Africa may
have avoided the slave trade of previous centuries, but not its modern
manifestations.

Average Tutsis were hardly pampered. The vast majority remained,
as always, just as poor as their Hutu neighbours. Resentment bubbled
and boiled nonetheless, and so, on the eve of Rwandan independence
in 1962, when Belgium suddenly threw its support behind "majority
rule" (meaning Hutu), payback was inevitable.

Instead of rejecting the Hamitic hypothesis, Hutu nationalists took
it further, citing it as evidence that the Tutsis were foreign interlopers,
a "race of invaders that does not belong in Rwanda." Under the clarion
cry of the Hutu Manifesto, the Hutu peasantry was presented as the
"pure" race of Rwanda, its true inhabitants, an oppressed majority.
Instead of replacing the racial stereotypes of colonial rule, the Hutu
Social Revolution reinforced them, embracing the very myths that
had been used against them.

Rwanda was declared a republic and its monarchy abolished. (A
largely symbolic act, as the king had long been reduced to near-
figurehead status.) The Hutu majority took power—with a vengeance.
The new nationalist government immediately began purging Tutsis
from public office. Racial quotas were imposed, ID cards retained,
and violence against Tutsis actively encouraged. A culture of impunity
took hold, and what had begun as a cry for justice turned into a lust
for revenge; and oh how often are those two ideas—justice and

revenge—conflated. A UN Commission warned early on that Rwanda was now in the grip of a regime that employed measures bordering on "Nazism against the Tutsi minority."

The first massacres aimed at cleansing Rwanda of its Tutsi population had happened even before independence was granted. In the years that followed, the situation only got worse. More than 100,000 Tutsis fled, spilling into refugee camps in Burundi, Uganda, and the Congo. This was only the first wave. The number would eventually top a million as the Tutsi diaspora became Africa's largest and longest-running refugee crisis, one that created a nation-in-exile, a stateless state yearning for return, with the Tutsis as the self-described "Jews of Africa." Sadly, the parallel would not end there.

When Tutsi exiles in Burundi launched a series of raids into Rwanda, crossing the border under cover of darkness to attack military posts before melting back into the night, the Hutu government responded in vicious fashion, butchering Tutsi civilians by the score. In December 1963 alone, more than 10,000 people were murdered. British philosopher Bertrand Russell described the atrocities in Rwanda as "the most horrible and systematic massacres we have witnessed since the extermination of the Jews by the Nazis." As a French witness noted, "The goal was not just to loot but to kill, to exterminate all those that bore the Tutsi designation."

After Rwanda's minister of defence, Juvénal Habyarimana, a northern Hutu, seized power in 1973, the country was drawn increasingly into the French sphere of influence, with France effectively replacing Belgium as the country's primary patron. Under the banner cry of *la Francophonie,* Rwanda was seen as a bulwark against creeping Anglo-American influences in the region, and the French government happily supplied arms, cash, and military training to the Habyarimana regime, racist doctrines and ethnic quotas be damned.

Like the boiling of the apocryphal frog, restrictions on Tutsis increased by increments as the heat was slowly turned up. Access to travel, employment, and higher education was severely limited. Having been excluded almost entirely from political life and the military as well, Tutsis in Rwanda carved out a niche for themselves in the private sector instead. But any success they had was resented—murderously so. Like the Jews in pre-war Germany, the Tutsis of Rwanda were accused of hoarding wealth, of secretly controlling the banking system, of being cunning and conniving, treacherous and traitorous.

And when the refugees outside of Rwanda began pressing the government for the right of return—a right guaranteed under the UN Universal Declaration of Human Rights—Habyarimana replied brusquely that Rwanda "was full," and that they could not come home.

The next time, they would not ask. They would come.

# 3

IN 1988, TUTSI EXILES IN UGANDA formed a rebel army, the Rwandan Patriotic Front (RPF). Several prominent Hutu opposition leaders, having fled the decaying Habyarimana regime, joined their ranks. (Although founded among the Tutsi diaspora, the RPF saw itself as a pan-Rwandan movement whose goal was to topple the Habyarimana regime and end the politics of ethnic identity. Their mantra, often repeated, was "Our fight is with the government of Rwanda, not the Hutu.") Among the leaders was a skinny, relentlessly serious young officer who had grown up in the refugee camps of Uganda across from the misted mountains of Rwanda, *that Promised Land, just out of reach*. His parents had fled the anti-Tutsi violence in Rwanda thirty years earlier, carrying him across as a toddler. He was a descendant of the Tutsi aristocracy, his name was Paul Kagame, and he would change the course of history.

In 1990, the RPF launched a surprise attack from Uganda. The initial invasion was beaten back with the help of French troops and helicopters, but it sent shock waves through the halls of power nonetheless. President Habyarimana had always had an uneasy relationship with the Hutu extremists inside his own party, and in the panicked aftermath of the attack, he lost control of them entirely. Within two weeks of the RPF invasion, government officials were secretly discussing—and organizing—the mass killing of Tutsis.

By 1992, the Belgian ambassador was warning that a secretive cabal within Habyarimana's inner circle was preparing "the extermination of the Tutsis of Rwanda." His report was promptly ignored. French newspapers likewise raised the alarm that Hutu leaders were planning a "final solution" to the ethnic problem—echoing quite intentionally the Nazi wording. In 1993, Paris-based magazine *Libération* alerted readers that "in the far hills of Rwanda ... France is supporting a regime which for two years, with militias and death squads, has been trying to organize the extermination of the minority Tutsis." The coming holocaust was not an unforeseen event; it was well documented, well prepared, and well known far in advance. Genocide is never spontaneous. It takes planning, it takes *intent*.

The RPF, meanwhile, had regrouped. They pushed deep into Rwandan territory, sending hundreds of thousands of Hutu refugees fleeing before their advance. The RPF had expected to be greeted as liberators; instead they were seen as foreign invaders. Amid the stampeding fears of this invasion, a "re-conquest" in the eyes of Hutu extremists, anti-Tutsi sentiment reached its apogee under a racial ideology known as Hutu Power.

An endless barrage of radio and newspaper propaganda portrayed Tutsis as cockroaches—*inyenzi*, a term first used to describe the cross-border raids of the 1960s—and as snakes, racially impure subhumans worthy of eradication. Genocide, after all, is always preceded by propaganda, and in Rwanda the media played a shameful, dishonest role in what followed. The 1994 genocide against the Tutsis was the result of *decades* of indoctrination. Think of what the Nazis were able to achieve—the hatred and vile scapegoating, the yellow stars and horrors of the Holocaust—in just twelve years. Now imagine the propaganda and brainwashing going on for generations, and you will understand how toxic Rwandan society had become.

Gérard Prunier, a French scholar of East African history, notes, "It is not because of its 'primitiveness' that Rwanda could suffer from a genocide; quite the contrary.... In Rwanda, all the preconditions for a genocide were present: a well-organized civil service, a small tightly-controlled land area, a disciplined and orderly population, reasonably good communications and a coherent ideology containing the necessary lethal potential."

Under the tactically precise leadership of Paul Kagame, the RPF had fought its way to the outskirts of Kigali, Rwanda's capital, before falling back. A distraught Habyarimana, with his back to the wall and his options severely limited, had finally given in and signed a wide-ranging peace agreement in Arusha, Tanzania. The Arusha Accords, as they were known, included the right of return for all Rwandan refugees, integration of the RPF into the armed forces, and the creation of a broad-based transitional government that would include moderates and members of the opposition in Cabinet, leading toward a democratically elected parliament. As a sweeping blueprint for change, with extensive political, legal, social, and military reforms, the Arusha Accords would have transformed Rwanda—had they been implemented.

The peace agreement also contained a provision for a UN mission to oversee the transition to democratic rule, during which French troops supporting the Habyarimana regime would be required to withdraw. The RPF had assumed that the presence of UN peacekeepers would protect the Tutsi minority. They were wrong.

Hutu extremists saw the Arusha Accords as nothing less than capitulation, and they denounced Habyarimana as a traitor and an accomplice. Colonel Théoneste Bagosora, a Hutu Power hardliner, had stormed out of the peace negotiations, saying he was going back to Rwanda to prepare *"Apocalypse deux"*—a second apocalypse. Bagosora would prove to be a man of his word.

An internal U.S. intelligence report warned that if the peace process failed, half a million people could die. As it turned out, the report was overly optimistic in its estimate. Even as the Arusha Accords were being finalized, homes in Kigali were being marked with X's. This was merely for a census, government officials insisted. Only Tutsi homes were being marked.

When Canadian general Roméo Dallaire was informed that he would be overseeing a peacekeeping mission to Rwanda, he thought, *Great!*, and then asked, "That's in Africa, isn't it?"

The UN arrived in December 1993 with few supplies and a limited mandate, one that explicitly forbade military intervention. General Dallaire had requested a minimum of 4,500 troops. He received 2,500. They were cobbled together from twenty-four different countries, and included office staff and unarmed military observers: a motley, poorly prepared, minimally equipped assortment of men and women tasked with keeping peace in one of the most volatile regions of the world. This was peacekeeping on the cheap, run on a shoestring, and Dallaire found himself constantly short of fuel, vehicles, ammunition—even food.

Portents soon surfaced. A highly placed informant dubbed "Jean-Pierre" whispered to Dallaire that death lists of Tutsi civilians and Hutu opposition members were being compiled and that illegal arms were being stockpiled in defiance of the Arusha Accords. He warned Dallaire that there were plans afoot to kill Belgian peacekeepers as well, with the Hutu Power extremists reasoning—correctly, as it turned out—that at the first sign of casualties, Belgium would cut and run. (Belgian troops made up the core of the mission, and were the best trained and best equipped; extremists knew that losing them would gut the UN presence.) Dallaire faxed UN headquarters in New York, informing them of the warnings he'd received and saying that he was preparing to raid the alleged cache and seize the weapons. The response was immediate and unequivocal: Dallaire was to do no such thing. Such actions were outside his mandate. He was instead to turn the information over to the Rwandan government—the very people who were stockpiling the weapons. The UN raid never went ahead, and Jean-Pierre was never heard from again.

Incredibly, even as hate radio station RTLM was openly calling for the mass extermination of Tutsis, French weapons kept arriving via various conduits. French troops may have been withdrawn under the terms of the Arusha Accords, but France itself provided arms, cash, training, and logistical support to the genocidal regime before, during, and even *after* the killings. The Habyarimana government had started importing shipments of machetes from China as well, under the guise of "agricultural implements"; these were distributed to Hutu militias and neighbourhood groups. In the lead-up to the genocide, more than half a million machetes were brought in, one for every three Hutu adult males. A propaganda newspaper headline asked: WHAT WEAPON SHALL WE USE TO CONQUER THE INYENZI COCKROACHES ONCE AND FOR ALL? Beside it was a picture of a machete.

On April 6, 1994, President Habyarimana's plane was shot out of the sky.

He was returning from a one-day summit in Dar es Salaam. Also on board were several of the president's key advisers and confidants, his chief of staff, his private secretary, his head of presidential security, and even his personal physician, as well as the president of neighbouring Burundi who had, fatefully, asked for a ride home. Habyarimana had made it clear that upon his return to Kigali he would—*finally*—be swearing in the broad-based transitional government required under the Arusha Accords. Had his plane touched down, it would have signalled the end of Hutu Power.

And so, as the presidential Falcon 50 jet came in low on its final approach to the Kigali airport, ground-to-air missiles streaked into the night sky. The jet exploded in mid-air, with the wreckage crashing into the grounds of the Presidential Palace.

A 2012 French judicial inquiry would determine that the missiles had been fired from inside the Kanombe military base, where Colonel Bagosora had once been in charge of the anti-aircraft battery. Bagosora would have been well-versed in the flight path the president's plane would follow as it went directly over the base, but to this day, no one knows for certain who pulled the trigger. What we do know is that the death of Habyarimana was the signal for Bagosora's apocalypse to begin.

Extremist news editorials and Hutu Power radio broadcasts had been predicting just such an event. The editors at the *Kangura* newspaper had declared that President Habyarimana would be assassinated, not by treacherous Tutsis, but at the hands of Hutu citizens enraged at his betrayal. HABYARIMANA WILL DIE IN MARCH ran one banner headline. They were off by only six days. Soldiers at Camp Kigali had also heard rumours that the president was going to be killed.

On April 3, RTLM radio had predicted, with ominous confidence, that "a little something" would happen in Kigali over Easter. "On April 7th and 8th you will hear the sound of bullets and grenades exploding." They were off by only one day. Within an hour of Habyarimana's death,[4] the systematic slaying of prominent Hutus who'd supported the Arusha Accords had begun. Under the directives of the Presidential Guard, crowds quickly assembled and headed straight for the homes of the ruling party's political opponents. "Things happened very rapidly," Dallaire's chief of staff would later recall. "As if they had been rehearsed."

Colonel Bagosora moved swiftly to install an interim government and eliminate potential rivals. The president's death wasn't merely an assassination, it was a coup d'état, and dawn found the colonel addressing a mob of armed militias near the airport. "Erect roadblocks at the roundabouts, let no one escape," he ordered. "Hunt the Tutsis down, house after house." *"Muhere ruhande,"* he had said, meaning, "Go about it systematically," the way one might pull weeds or clear brush.

---

4. The president's plane was shot down at approximately 8:30 p.m. By 9:15 p.m., UN staff in Kigali were reporting that roadblocks had gone up across the city. There was nothing spontaneous about it.

Among the first to die was Agathe Uwilingiyimana, Rwanda's prime-minister-in-waiting, a moderate Hutu who had been named transitional leader under the peace accords. She was waiting for Habyarimana to return so that she could be sworn in. As a former schoolteacher and minister of education, she'd tried to end ethnic quotas in public schools and had been physically attacked for it. Although Hutu, she had refused to identify herself as such, saying, "I am a Rwandese and I am a person. I have a role to play in my country and it does not matter whether I am a man or a woman, a Hutu or a Tutsi." They killed her in a particularly brutal fashion.

The UN soldiers from Belgium and Ghana who had been sent to protect Agathe Uwilingiyimana were quickly disarmed and taken as captives to the Camp Kigali army barracks, where the Ghanaians were released and the Belgians beaten, then murdered. They were being killed even as General Dallaire sped by en route to a meeting with Colonel Bagosora to negotiate their release. Dallaire would later collect their ten bodies, laid out like sacks of potatoes, at the hospital morgue.

A mass evacuation of expats was soon underway. Within four days, almost 4,000 foreign nationals had been airlifted to safety, and within a week Belgium—just as Hutu Power ideologues predicted—had pulled out of Rwanda, abandoning thousands of terrified civilians who had been under their protection. As soon as the Belgians rolled away, the killers rushed in. It was an ignoble retreat, to say the least.

The killings spread quickly across the country. Roadblocks went up and ID cards were demanded, with Tutsis executed on the spot. (The lack of a card was usually taken as evidence of guilt.) Occasionally, the victims had their feet chopped off first to "cut them down to size," a mocking reference to the tall nature of Tutsis. Machete-wielding members of youth militia groups, many of whom had been trained by French troops and who were known collectively as *interahamwe,* "those who work together," roamed the streets hooting for blood, carrying lists of names. Others, armed with homemade clubs studded by nails, chased their victims from house to house, room to room, as neighbours killed neighbours and coworkers hunted down former friends. Property that belonged to the victims was often handed over to the people who had killed them, giving a strong economic incentive to the carnage as well. The genocide was, in the words of one commentator, "a licence to loot."

Everyone was targeted, even children—*especially* children. "The child of a snake is still a snake!" the propagandists cried, reminding listeners constantly that Paul Kagame had been only two years old when his family escaped to Uganda. They must not make the same mistake again. *"Rip up the weeds by the roots! Wipe them out completely!"* This was the message: *Leave none to tell the story.* Once the genocide got underway, a fearful logic compelled it forward. The necessity for complete eradication took hold; you couldn't allow any witnesses to survive, and you had to implicate every Hutu in the crime. The guilt would be shared; no one would be spared.

Rwanda became an abattoir as UN troops looked on in horror. Thousands of bodies dumped into rivers floated downstream, where they tumbled over Rusumo Falls and eventually washed up on the shores of Lake Victoria to the stunned disbelief of their Ugandan neighbours. Hundreds of bodies, without end. "By early May," journalist Linda Melvern writes, "an estimated 5,000 a day were coming down the Akagera River." And all of it sanctioned by the screeching voices on the radio, exhorting the racially pure Hutu to wipe out the traitorous Tutsi minority.

RTLM became known as "Radio Machete," providing names, addresses, and even licence plate numbers and makes of the vehicles belonging to those "cockroaches" and "collaborators" who needed killing. Radio announcers would direct hunters to the hiding places, to the schools and churches, to the homes of "soft" Hutus rumoured to be giving shelter to Tutsis, marking them all for death. RTLM even sent out calls to bulldozer drivers when it came time to prepare mass burial pits. "The graves are still half-empty! Who will help us fill them up?" the announcers asked, appealing to the population to work ever harder. In Rwanda, radio was like the Voice of God, and it was common to see Hutu militias manning the barricades with a bloodied machete in one hand and a portable FM radio in the other. As Dallaire noted, "The *génocidaires* used the media like a weapon." The radio and the machete: these were the two primary tools of the genocide, one to give the orders, the other to carry them out. (Given the role the media played throughout the genocide, heavy restrictions now exist in Rwanda forbidding any hint of "divisiveness." Rwandans are not as enamoured as we in the West are with the notion of an unfettered, unbridled media—understandably so, perhaps.)

Even as the Belgians were pulling out, Dallaire was asking for more troops, arguing that with just 5,000 soldiers and an expanded mandate he could stop the slaughter. He received neither. Instead, the UN voted to slash Dallaire's mission, reducing it by 90 percent to a token force of just 270 "observers." Journalist Scott Peterson, on the ground through much of it, noted that "Rwanda was the first ever case in which the UN responded to a crisis by *reducing* its commitment." (In the end, Dallaire managed to keep 470 personnel, due largely to the unflinching support of countries like Ghana and Tunisia, who stood firm. The men and women of Ghana's peacekeeping force in particular almost singlehandedly salvaged the mission.)

The United States had just suffered a humiliating defeat in Somalia, and the Clinton administration had no stomach for further humanitarian interventions in Africa; the photo ops were bad. Do you remember those images of the bodies of dead American soldiers being dragged through the streets of Mogadishu? Rwanda paid the price for that. The White House refused even to use the word "genocide" when referring to what was happening; the most they would admit was that "acts of genocide *may* have occurred." When a reporter tartly asked, "How many 'acts of genocide' does it take to make a genocide?" the administration refused to answer. Had the U.S. acknowledged that a genocide was occurring, the UN Security Council would have been required to act under the terms of its own Convention on the Prevention and Punishment of the Crime of Genocide. Instead, the United States, backed by Great Britain, blocked all attempts at expanding the mission.

A panel of military experts later concluded that Dallaire had been correct in his assessment: 5,000 troops early on, with minimal air cover and a more robust mandate, was all it would have taken to prevent at least half of the deaths that occurred; 500,000 people might have been saved. Dallaire laid the blame squarely on three members of the Security Council: the U.S., the U.K., and France. "The blood is on their hands," he wrote.

Outgunned, outmanned, and often surrounded, the beleaguered UN peacekeepers—unable to stop the killings—focused instead on protecting those already under their care while negotiating prisoner exchanges and arranging temporary ceasefires. Although the mission itself is considered a failure, more than 16,000 lives were saved by Roméo Dallaire's small band of blue berets.[5] Among them: Jean-Claude's sister and her baby boy.

# 4

PRIOR TO THE GENOCIDE, Rwanda was known, if at all, as the site of Dian Fossey's groundbreaking research into the endangered mountain gorillas of the Virunga rainforests. In trying to come to terms with Rwanda, I found myself at one point chapter-hopping among three different books: *Gorillas in the Mist,* Fossey's celebrated account of her time in Rwanda; *Conspiracy to Murder,* Linda Melvern's powerful rendering of the genocide; and *Rwanda, Inc.* by business analysts Patricia Crisafulli and Andrea Redmond, subtitled *How a Devastated Nation Became an Economic Model for the Developing World.*

I felt like one of the blind sages of Indian lore, groping my way toward an understanding of an elephant in the dark: here the wall of

---

5. Some sources put that number even higher, at 30,000.

its flank, there the tree trunks of its legs, the serpent of its trunk, the fly-whisk of its tail. How to reconcile these radically different versions of a country that has become a shorthand for failure, on par with Waterloo or Vietnam? *We don't want this turning into another Rwanda,* we say now. But to which Rwanda are we referring? Given the country's remarkable turnaround, shouldn't we hope for more nations in Africa to follow Rwanda's lead, for more countries to become "another Rwanda"? Or is today's Rwanda the oppressive dictatorship that its exiled critics claim?

The 1994 genocide ended, as all genocides do, not through economic sanctions or UN resolutions or heartfelt good intentions, but through armed intervention. When the killings began, the RPF called off its ceasefire and fought its way into Kigali, forcing the génocidaires to flee westward into Zaire (as the Congo was then known). It took three months, but the government finally fell. The RPF had defeated an armed force twice its size, one backed by sophisticated French weaponry and—in the earlier stages and the latter—French troops as well.

To the victors came not the spoils, but the wreckage of a failed state. The RPF had taken control of a ruined city. A ruined nation. Corpses clogged the rivers and the irrigation ditches, and lay rotting in heaps in schoolyards and soccer fields. A terrible silence had descended upon the country.

Canadian journalist Hugh McCullum, in Rwanda during the genocide, recalled the challenges the country now faced: "Nearly a million people had been killed, about three million were refugees and another two million were internally displaced. Africa's most densely populated country had become a ghost state.... The RPF was faced with a bankrupt, depopulated, frightened and traumatized population with none of the infrastructure of government in place."

The Central Bank had been ransacked and its treasury looted, Rwanda's entire reserve of hard currency seized by the departing regime when it fled. The basic institutions of society—sanitation, electrical grids, medical care, policing, judiciary—were either crippled or nonexistent. When the RPF swore in a broad-based coalition government required under the Arusha Accords, Rwanda had no money, no working telephone lines, no electricity, no working offices. The World Bank reported that after the genocide Rwanda was now the poorest nation on earth.

The turnaround since then has been nothing short of miraculous. Indeed, the very seeds of Rwanda's rebirth lay in its destruction; the genocide had left the country bare, a tabula rasa waiting to be rewritten.

If there is one lesson that African history teaches us, it is this: *The Western model doesn't work here*. And if madness is doing the same thing over and over and expecting different results, the West's approach to Africa has been marked by madness. Following the apocalypse of 1994, desperate to rebuild, Rwanda looked east, not west. Where had similar countries been devastated, reduced to rubble and abject poverty—only to pull themselves out of the ruins? The answer: Asia. Japan after Nagasaki and Hiroshima; South Korea and Taiwan after civil war, invasion, and partition. Or how about the emerging Southeast Asian markets of Indonesia, Malaysia, Singapore, Vietnam, and Thailand, which have taken off over the last twenty years, following Japan and South Korea's lead? If Asia could do it, why not Africa? If Singapore, why not Rwanda? It was Asia, after all, that was once the world's economic basket case, not Africa. It was Asia that was considered hopeless: overpopulated, underdeveloped, and culturally unsuited for modernity—or so we were told. (The same Confucian values used to explain why Asia could never compete economically with the rest of the world are now being cited to explain why Asia has been so remarkably successful. Academics are nothing if not pliable.) In 1969, Africa's GDP per capita was higher than Asia's. South Korea's GDP was once at the same level as Sierra Leone's. Not anymore.

In light of this, Rwanda has modelled its recovery on the Asian example. Geographically, Rwanda—a small, landlocked, mountainous country—is the "Switzerland of Africa," which is exactly how early European travellers described it. But socially and economically, it is rebranding itself as "Africa's Singapore": a tightly controlled, politically stable, economically innovative, autocratic democracy dominated by a single party. (In the last election, the ruling RPF won 41 of 53 elected seats.) If Rwanda's success baffles Western commentators, it is precisely because it is not predicated on a Western model.

In defiance of African stereotypes, *Economist* magazine has heralded Rwanda as one of the most business-friendly countries in the world, one "blessedly free of red tape," noting that "no African country has done more to curb corruption. Ministers have been jailed for it." Corruption has long been the bane of African political culture, and Rwanda has tackled this head-on. By 2013, Transparency International had ranked Rwanda as the least corrupt nation in Africa and in the top fifty nations globally. Its ranking has fluctuated since then but is still considerably higher than that of many European states. *Greece, Italy, I'm looking at you.*

Even the doom-and-gloom stalwarts at the World Bank, a group not known for their rah-rah boosterism of African economies, placed Rwanda among the top ten nations in the world in which to start a new business.

I could go on—and I think I will.

The World Bank also ranks Rwanda among the world's top nations when it comes to the *ease* of doing business, which includes registering property, obtaining permits, paying taxes, trading across borders, enforcing contracts, and more. To help this along, the Rwanda Development Board (RDB) has set up a "one-stop" centre for processing all the permits and paperwork required to incorporate. In Rwanda, a new business can usually be registered and fully ready in as little as six hours and for a nominal fee, free if it's done online.

The RDB itself is modelled directly on the Singapore Economic Development Board, a government department designed to seek out and actively encourage foreign partnerships in hospitality, manu-facturing, and infrastructure. Even the country's new nickname, "Rwanda Inc.," suggesting as it does government and business working closely together, with private and public sectors in sync (rather than in opposition to each other), draws to mind Asian parallels and similar references to "Japan Inc."

The country's long-term goals include turning Rwanda into a regional financial hub, parlaying its reputation for stringent business practices and a lack of corruption into establishing itself as a banking destination as well. A *financial* Switzerland, in other words.

On a smaller scale is the "value added" axiom Rwanda has adopted. (This use of simple guiding principles, rules of thumb rather than sweeping ideological agendas, is also very Japanese/Korean/Singaporean in its approach.) Instead of shipping raw materials out of the country, the goal now is to add value to them beforehand. For example, whereas Rwanda had once exported raw coffee beans to other countries, where the crops were then washed, sorted, and resold at a much higher price, Rwandan coffee companies, with government backing, have now built more than 240 washing stations across the country, where the beans are cleaned and outer hulls removed. The final product is sorted by grade and quality before it's shipped, all of which greatly adds to its value. The result? A 33 percent increase in income from coffee exports in a single year.

Rwanda is still one of the world's poorest countries, with an annual budget heavily dependent on foreign aid and an economy still overly reliant on subsistence farming. But with the government's Vision 2020 blueprint, the aim is to transform Rwanda into a middle-income, knowledge-based economy, one that is competitive regionally and globally. Vision 2020 presents a wide-ranging and ambitious agenda, one focusing on poverty reduction, gender equality, compulsory education, universal health care, skills-based training, and local development initiatives.

Here are some more highlights, presented in convenient bullet form:

- Over the last five years, more than one million people in Rwanda have been lifted out of poverty—in a country of 11 million. By 2020, it's projected that more than 70 percent of the population will be above the base poverty line.

- The economy has been growing by an average of 7 percent a year and has almost doubled in size over the last ten.

- Where literacy rates were at barely 50 percent prior to the genocide, today 97 percent of children are enrolled in primary education, which in Rwanda runs from Grade 1 to 9. According to UNICEF, these are the highest enrolment rates in Africa, with more than 70 percent of the students completing Grade 9. Rwanda now spends more on education than it does on the military. University enrolment is nearing 80,000, compared to just 3,000 before the genocide.

- Early childhood mortality has been reduced by 80 percent, one of the steepest declines ever recorded. The UN credits Rwanda with having saved 590,000 children between 2000 and 2015.

- Ambitious immunization and anti-malaria campaigns, together with a community-based health insurance system and a rapidly rising life expectancy (average life expectancy in Rwanda is now 65 years, up from 48 in 1990), have earned Rwanda accolades from the World Health Organization. And although Rwanda continues to suffer from a serious shortage of doctors and other health care workers, more than 97 percent of the population now has medical coverage, the highest in Africa. A quarter of the national budget goes to health care, which is again the highest proportion of any state in Africa.

- Rwanda has also received awards from the UN for addressing issues of gender-based violence and women's rights. The country's innovative "one-stop" centres for

women, offering legal, health, reproductive, and protective services under one roof, have been rightfully
lauded, as has Rwanda's use of microloans for widows
and women in poverty to help them launch small
businesses. *With just a little bit of capital and some
training, they will make their own opportunities:* this is
the guiding principle, the rule of thumb, behind these
small loans. It might just as easily be applied to Rwanda
as a whole.

I could go on—but I won't.

I do realize that Africa is littered with similar "blueprints for
success" and "visions for a brighter tomorrow," but Vision 2020 is no
chimera: Rwanda is meeting its targets, is on track, and is even ahead
of schedule in several areas. Still overly reliant on foreign aid, true,
but working hard to change that.

The Rwandan approach, a seemingly contradictory combination
of progressive social programs and centralized decision making,
coupled with radically *de*centralized governance, is based on a
staunchly pro-business philosophy in which enterprise is rewarded
and rules are respected. Socially progressive *pro*-business policies?
Centralized decentralized decision making? It's enough to make your
head spin—*if* you were to try to force it into a pre-set political
philosophy. But instead of "left wing" or "right wing," Rwanda has
been pre-eminently pragmatic. An example: In Singapore, gum on
the sidewalks was becoming a problem, so chewing gum was outlawed.
Simple, yes? Likewise Rwanda's ban on plastic bags. These non-
biodegradable tumbleweeds seen clotting up fence posts and littering
the windblown cityscapes of Africa are illegal in Rwanda. And the
laws are taken seriously. Walk down the street swinging a plastic bag,
and you risk arrest and a fine of $150. Shop owners foolish enough to
stock plastic bags face jail time. In Rwanda, it's paper or cloth only,
with polythene bags confiscated at the airport with a seriousness
usually reserved for baggies filled with weed. There. Problem solved.

Rwanda's approach to homosexuality is equally revealing. Unlike in neighbouring countries such as Tanzania, Burundi, and Uganda, or Cameroon and Nigeria, where gay citizens can be imprisoned, beaten, and even threatened with execution, Rwanda's post-genocide constitution explicitly recognizes all citizens as having equal rights and the same legal protections. When influential evangelical church leaders in Rwanda tried to pressure the government into introducing harsh anti-gay laws similar to those recently passed in Uganda (where tabloid newspapers began publishing the names and addresses of "notorious homosexuals" to be ostracized and attacked, in much the same way that Hutu Power newspapers in Rwanda had once published lists of Tutsis), the government of Rwanda refused. They knew too well the consequences of targeting one segment of society, of singling out one specific group of people.[6]

In Rwanda, the ethnic ID cards are long gone, and it is now prohibited to publicly identify or denounce someone as "Tutsi" or "Hutu." In private, among friends and family, you may refer to yourself however you like, but the public sphere is a different matter. The official policy is now "one people, one language, one culture, one Rwanda." And in much the same way that Germany, France, and other European nations introduced laws prohibiting Nazi symbols and any denial of the Holocaust after World War II, Rwanda has brought in strict laws concerning genocide denial. Fomenting social divisions or propagating a racial ideology is treated very seriously. And just as, after the catastrophe of Mussolini, Italy made it a crime to publish or promote any "apologia for fascism," in Rwanda the ethnically based doctrine of "Hutu Power" is outlawed.

It is important to remember that Hutu Power is an *ideology*, not an ethnic identity. So when misguided commentators in the West lecture Rwanda about the need for "reconciliation" between the government and supporters of Hutu Power, try replacing the phrase

---

6. Uganda would eventually rescind its anti-gay laws in the face of international pressure and European aid embargoes.

"Hutu Power" with "Nazi propagandists," and see how far you get. When people speak about reclaiming Hutu identity (as opposed to a pan-Rwandan identity), keep in mind that this divide was entrenched for generations and always in opposition to that of "Tutsi." Try floating the idea of reintroducing yellow stars for Jews and see the type of reaction this garners, or try arguing that it's your ethnic right as an Aryan to promote a pure-race ideology. The West routinely demands a malleability in Rwandans that they would never expect of themselves.

From poverty reduction to increased literacy, from economic growth to environmental reforms, from women's rights to universal health care, Rwanda's recovery has been remarkable, and the person responsible for much of it is the same person who ended the genocide: the controversial and always divisive Paul Kagame.

As the RPF commander who spearheaded the advance that toppled the Hutu Power government, President Kagame is loved and loathed in equal parts. Hailed as a hero, denounced as a dictator, he is a polarizing figure, inevitably described as a "strongman," but one who is nonetheless credited with bringing about Rwanda's extraordinary reconstruction.

Addressing an American university, the perpetually dour and stick-thin Kagame (he always reminds me of a high school chemistry teacher who's called you into his office because he's disappointed with your grades) repeatedly stressed, "There is no magic formula." Instead, he spoke about the importance of individual Rwandans working with each other in a *collective* commitment. He was invoking the Rwandan tradition of communal effort, of obeying authority, of following the rules—the same traits the génocidaires had employed to such devastating effect—to help rebuild the country. The goal is to use these cultural mores for constructive rather than destructive purposes, in much the same way that Germanic traits of meticulousness and efficiency, which the Nazis exploited so well, and the Japanese sense of collective identity and a strong work ethic, which the Imperial army took advantage of, would later be harnessed for *economic* rather than militaristic aims. If countries like Germany and Japan, Korea and Vietnam, have turned themselves around—helped by generous dollops of foreign aid, it should be noted—why not Rwanda?

Social mobilization, cultural homogeneity, effective bureaucratic organization, and an emphasis on group obligations over personal entitlements: the "Rwandan miracle," as it is known, is very much in the Asian tradition. In words that could easily have come from the podium of any Japanese post-war leader, Kagame insisted that "national prosperity will be achieved only through a people's capacity to work together, to find common ground, a common cause, a common purpose. There has not been *a* Rwandan miracle, as such," he noted, "but millions."

It was time to see this miracle firsthand.

# 5

I ARRIVED IN KIGALI INTERNATIONAL AIRPORT to the cool embrace of an equatorial night, surfing my way into the main terminal with a crowd of passengers who were apparently under the impression it was a footrace to the baggage carousel.

Jean-Claude had arrived a few days earlier, and he greeted me with a handshake and a hale "Welcome to Rwanda!"

Older travel accounts describe the Kigali airport as cavernous and half-empty, but those days are long gone; the airport has burst its seams like stuffing from a pillow.

"They are building a new one," Jean-Claude shouted as we manoeuvred my bags through the full-court press of passengers at the terminal. (Entire families, it seemed, had come out to greet arriving relatives and see others off.) "It will be south of the city. Much bigger. Much better."

The relocation was overdue. Rwanda had clearly outgrown its original airport, and in more ways than one: this was the landing strip President Habyarimana's plane was approaching when it was shot down, the missiles fired from a military base that still sits beside it. It was from that base that the first killings had been unleashed as well; the neighbourhoods around the airport were among the first to be "ethnically cleansed" of Tutsis. So this airport, in a very real sense, was ground zero of the genocide.

Outside, Jean-Claude led me across the parking lot to where a Toyota 4x4 was jammed into an undersized stall.

"Land Cruiser GXR," he said. "I picked it up from the rental office this morning."

It would be our home on wheels, our refuge, our albatross, our means of escape, and our dauntless beast over the course of the next three weeks.

Inching out of the airport with Jean-Claude at the wheel, we were soon swept into the street lights and leafy darkness of Kigali at night. The silhouettes of tall buildings were arranged along the crest of hills above us like giant chess pieces: the square rooks of hotels, the ornately curled knights of foreign embassies, and the rounded bishop of a new convention centre, a striking-looking structure, imminent and still hidden under scaffolding—the urban equivalent of gift-wrap.

Kigali is draped across a loose federation of hills, and the city's main thoroughfares often run along high-wire ridges before dropping suddenly into the valleys below. This layout—the dip and drop, the ridges and sloping descents, the whorls and loops—makes driving through the city akin to navigating a fingerprint.

Jean-Claude flung us into a valley and then down a curved street— all streets in Kigali curve; finding a straight one would be a feat— before a final funhouse drop brought us to the Republika Café.

The Republika, with its large deck and glowing patio lights, is a local landmark. "Very good food," Jean-Claude assured me.

It didn't hurt, of course, that the owner was stunningly attractive.

Regal and welcoming, Solange Katarebe is a towering beauty of a woman. Formerly a director of Rwandan Tourism and National Parks and now an entrepreneur, Solange was one of the many confident, smart, and engaging women we would encounter over the next few weeks: running enterprises, overseeing government departments, finalizing business deals, managing conservation programs, running hotels. If the country was firing on all cylinders, it was women who were often as not priming the pumps, gunning the engine.

Nor was this wishful thinking on my part. By law, one-third of all national representatives in Rwanda must be women; in actuality, the number elected is even greater. It currently sits at 64 percent, the highest in the world, making Rwanda the only parliament on earth where women outnumber men. A third of the Cabinet is female, including the ministers of agriculture, energy, health, labour, and foreign affairs.

Rwanda's new constitution also sets a minimum of 30 percent women on the boards of all publicly listed companies. Half of the country's fourteen Supreme Court justices are women, and the World Economic Forum's "global gender gap" report—an evaluation based on economic participation and opportunity, educational attainment, health and survival, and political empowerment—ranks Rwanda in the top ten nations *worldwide* for women.

Which is to say, Solange was no anomaly.

She wafted from table to table, laughing, chatting, topping up drinks, waving for new ones, and revising tabs accordingly. The beef skewers were dripping with flavour, and Jean-Claude and I raised a toast to the start of our journey, me with Primus beer, Jean-Claude with bottled water. (Jean-Claude doesn't drink alcohol, something I would learn to begrudgingly accept and eventually forgive.)

"Finally!" Jean-Claude said. It seemed we had been talking about this trip since before we met.

The flickering lights of Kigali formed constellations on the hills across from us, and the beer was as sweet as summer air.

*Finally.*

# 6

JEAN-CLAUDE WAS LIVING IN KENYA when the genocide began.

A teenager on the cusp of his twentieth birthday, he was, as he puts it, "No longer a boy, but not quite a man." Having crossed the bridge at Rusumo Falls, he'd made his way to the humid port city of Mombasa looking for his brother, only to find out that his brother was no longer there. Rwandans living in the city helped Jean-Claude track him down.

"My brother Saïd was in Nairobi, was working as a truck driver. He had been hired by the UN, or maybe Red Cross or CARE International—I don't remember which—to deliver supplies to Somalian refugees. There was civil war in Somalia and the refugee camp, it was near the border."

This was around the time of Black Hawk Down, when U.S. forces were running for cover, disengaging themselves with unseemly haste from further humanitarian interventions in Africa. Somalia was notoriously dangerous and unstable.

"My brother said, 'Wanna come?' I said, 'Sure!' So I jumped in and off we went. It was a long trip. Very long. This was my first time to see the desert, first time to see camels too. Everything was so different from Rwanda. It was all sand; there was no trees, there was no nothing. And flat. We drove, like, five, six days to get to that place and there was nothing there. Just people. These refugees had not even tents. I was puzzled. How can they live in this environment? I couldn't believe anyone could survive in that area. You know, I felt sorry for them."

While Saïd arranged for the cargo to be unloaded, Jean-Claude made friends with some of the children in the camp.

"I showed these kids how to make a soccer ball from plastic bags. There was so much rubbish and plastic blowing around, so what you do, basically, is you take one plastic bag and you put it inside another, then another. There was this kind of twine, you know when they ship stuff, to tie it? I showed these kids how to use that to tighten the plastic, to make it like a real soccer ball. Once I did that, the kids flocked at me. Every child wanted to have their own soccer ball. So I showed them how to make more and more." He smiles even now at the memory of it. "We couldn't talk to each other, we didn't speak the same language. But through soccer, we could become friends, and I said to myself, 'You know what? I think I will come back.'"

And even though Jean-Claude and his brother were robbed at gunpoint by desert bandits on their way home—"They took my shoes! And those were nice shoes. They were Mizuno running shoes. I hated losing those shoes"—Jean-Claude knew he had found his calling. He returned on his own to the Somali camps, this time as a volunteer with an NGO connected to CARE International.

"This American woman at the NGO, she wanted to set up schools for the kids. She needed to identify who used to be a teacher back in Somalia and also to see how many children there was, how many were alone, how many had no mother, no father. So I thought, 'We can use soccer to find this information.' Instead of going to these thousands of people in the camp, calling, 'Parents, bring your children!' the children will come to us. We organized them into teams, according to ages, same as how you would organize a soccer league. I was cataloguing the children's names, where they are from, did they have family, parents. And these kids? They were having fun playing soccer. I stayed in that camp probably for a month. It was very hot. Daytime, it was in the forties. Nighttime, was cold. Then the rainy season came and we couldn't get out! We got stuck for almost two more months in that camp." He laughed. "Even today, I still know many Somali words."

When Jean-Claude returned to Kenya, he found that Saïd had left again, this time for Congo.

"He went to Congo, and I went to Sudan, almost by accident. There was a French organization, maybe Swiss. I went to their headquarters in Nairobi looking for a job, and when I was there, I overheard someone was talking about how they needed a driver to go to a refugee camp, is called Kakuma. It was in northern Kenya near the border with Sudan. So I said, 'Hey, I can drive!' They said, 'Really?' I said, 'Yeah.'"

We were sitting in a café in Kigali, and the waiter brought me a cup of coffee, spiced with ginger. Jean-Claude asked for pineapple juice.

"But didn't you have to pass a road test?" I asked. "Or have some sort of licence for that?"

"Oh, they were desperate. They needed someone to go right away, so my driving test was this: I sat in a car with the guy and he said, 'Okay, drive.' We drove to an industrial area where this truck, maybe one-ton, was parked. We filled it with diesel and he gave me some money and he said, 'Okay, you are going to Kakuma.'"

It was 1,200 kilometres from Nairobi to the Sudanese refugee camp.

"I did it in two days. I was bringing, I think, medicine and something to do with sheeting. I was not supposed to bring back that truck, just leave it there and return by bus."

But then luck intervened. When Jean-Claude arrived, he discovered that the same American woman he'd worked with in the Somali camp was there. She was delighted to see Jean-Claude and asked him to stay and set up another soccer program to help her catalogue students and identify youth at risk. "I've been trying," she told him, "but I can't do it. Organizing teams and making plastic-bag soccer balls is harder than it looks."

So once again, Jean-Claude began manufacturing soccer equipment out of scrap materials and calling kids in for the games. The camp was in the Turkana region, near the arid reaches of southern Sudan.

"It was like there was no border between Kenya and Sudan at that time. In the camp, it was not a good life, it was very bad. They ate poorly compared to the Somalian refugees I saw before, were malnourished compared to the Somalian kids, and I found this work was very tough. They were living kind of makeshift lives. Some built shelters with dry branches, some with just pieces of whatever they could find, with nothing on top. And there were scorpions. Everywhere! I was nervous to sleep there at night."

Jean-Claude later crossed into South Sudan as part of a Red Cross aid convoy. "We went to Lokichogio, to a camp where there was a vaccination program." Again, Jean-Claude used soccer to draw the refugees out. "I started organizing teams for the kids. But before they could take part, they had to have a vaccination. That was the rule. Worked very well. Not only for vaccinations. You know, there is value to feeling you are part of a team. Kids are kids everywhere, and soccer is a language they understand."

Jean-Claude's experiences in Sudan contrasted sharply with those in the Somali camps. "South Sudan was hostile. It was a broken-down society. People had no sense of social obligation. There was no one in the community you could trust, no one you could respect. In Somalia, you could go to see the elders or the imams at the mosque when there was a problem. In Sudan, it was a kind of anarchy. They saw death for a long time those people, first fighting against the north—the Arab region who had dominated them so badly, like slaves really—and then fighting each other. It was a kind of tribal war, one tribe killing another. In Somalia, this kind of anarchy had not started—not yet. But in Sudan, if you were Dinka, you were Dinka. You had nothing to do with the Nuers. The Nuer was your enemy to the very end. That was the one rule they had. The only one. For anything else, there was no rules."

After his tour of duty as a volunteer in South Sudan, Jean-Claude returned to Saïd's apartment in Nairobi, feeling concerned about the animosities he had witnessed in the camps. "I made friends in Sudan, was worried about what would happen to them." But that would pale in comparison to what was coming in his own country.

On his first night back in Kenya, the genocide in Rwanda began.

"It was 5:30 in the morning, and my neighbour Esmaili, he was Congolese, he knocked the door and woke me up. He said, 'Did you hear the news?' I said, 'What news?' He said, 'The president of Rwanda, he has died, together with the president of Burundi. His plane was shot down.' And I thought, 'Oh my God.' I knew this was going to be bad. This is what everybody was preparing for. This is what the radio was predicting. I remembered my Hutu neighbours in

Kigali—those youth militias—saying with a big grin, 'We're gonna kill you guys, all of you!' It was not a secret. When they returned from their training camps, they said, 'We're gonna finish you off. You Tutsis, none of you are gonna be left. You are planning to kill us, you are planning to kill the president, but we are gonna kill you first.' So when I heard what had happened, I thought, '*This is it*. This is what they were preparing for.'"

The Rwandan diaspora in Nairobi gathered at a church called Sainte Thérèse, trying amid the panic and rumours to sort out what was happening back home. Some thought the crisis would soon pass. Others feared the worst. Very few were sanguine at the prospects; the future seemed to have opened up like a dark maw.

"There was some, was studying in Kenya. Their families, all of them, were back in Rwanda. These students felt cut off. Afraid. One said, very quietly, 'I was talking to my mom right now on the phone and she said they killed our neighbours next door, and now they were coming to our house and then—and then the phone cut off.' When we heard that, everybody kind of was in shock."

Many of these students and expats were now stranded, alone and without funds, and without family to turn to.

"They became homeless in an instant. Many of them came to stay with me and my brother. Anyone who doesn't have somewhere to stay, they came to stay with us. There was a time we were seven people in that one-room apartment! Seven with one table to share." He laughed. "And it was a small apartment even when it was just me and my brother. But you know, my brother never minded, even though he was the one paying the rent. I remember that, how kind he was."

As the genocide unfolded on television, Rwandans huddled around their TV sets, watching in disbelief and horror.

"We could recognize people on TV. We could recognize neighbourhoods. There was one family I knew, was living near the soccer stadium. They had a house there. I knew this family very well and I saw their house is being looted on television, saw someone carrying their mattress. And I knew this person, too." Jean-Claude leaned in and looked me in the eyes, still baffled by it, twenty years later. "The last person you would expect to loot, to steal, was that guy. He was working for the government, for the civil service, a middle-class guy. When I saw him carrying a mattress on his head, stealing from his neighbours, I knew right away that my friends were dead. This guy, he had a machete in his belt. And I thought, *'My country has gone mad.'*"

"Did you call your family? Your brothers, your sister?"

"They didn't have a telephone. I tried to phone our neighbour, someone who might know what is happened to my family, but it was impossible to find any information. In my mind, everything went in slow motion. The United Nations had evacuated some Rwandese to Kenya, and they were living in these makeshift tents at the Nairobi airport, so I went there to see if I could find news. I recognized people I knew and I could see they were in shock. I don't know how to say it, except they were *blank*. Some were the only survivors, the only ones who made it. *'They killed my whole family. I escaped by jumping the fence at the airport, but my children couldn't get over the fence and my wife … I don't know where they are.'* Everybody had different stories, everybody had a broken heart. You would find Hutus also who were fleeing the war with their whole family, including this one guy who had been a minister in the government, a moderate Hutu. He went to Switzerland, I think."

"A Hutu among the Tutsis? Was there tension between those who'd escaped?"

"Of course. Imagine someone has lost her entire family and here is a government minister with all of his. Imagine you have lost every one of your children, but here is someone who has all of hers. It was very tough." Jean-Claude finished his pineapple juice, placed the empty glass on the table in front of him. "I knew: *I have to go back.*"

"To Rwanda?"

"To Rwanda."

The RPF had taken control of the eastern regions, were routing the armed forces and youth militias of a collapsing regime. The tide had turned, and the génocidaires knew it.

"I had to go. I felt a kind of guilt of not being there, for being safe when everyone else is in such danger. I thought, 'If I can get to Kigali, maybe I can find my sister, my brothers, my cousins, my family.'"

Jean-Claude took a long-distance coach to Uganda and from there made his way to the border.

"I crossed over at a place called Katuna, between Uganda and Rwanda. The RPF, they weren't letting many people come into the country, saying it's too dangerous—unless you had some training to help people, were a nurse or something. There were so many injured people, if you could say 'I know how to put on a band-aid,' oh, they took you right away. They called you doctor and sent you in. For me, I saw there was so many cars stuck at the border with no people to drive them. Some cars, they were there since 1990. So I told them, 'I can drive any type of thing. Motorcycle, sedan, one-ton truck. Anything, I can drive it. Let me.' So this guy talked to another guy, he said, 'Okay, see that truck over there?' It was a pickup truck, a Daihatsu. Was blue, but had been painted black to camouflage it—black, but you could see the blue showing through. It was a big truck. And he said to me, 'You are going to take that truck to Kigali.'"

This was at a time when there was still fighting in the capital. I asked Jean-Claude, "What was your reaction, when they told you where you would be going?"

"I said, 'Thank you.'"

"And the cargo?" I asked.

"Nothing. Was empty. But they needed vehicles near the front, near the fighting, to move the men in and the injured out, to move supplies around."

And so, barely twenty years old, Jean-Claude Munyezamu set about driving a pickup truck into a war zone.

"I had three people squeezed in beside me. Two was military, one was civilian. They had their radio on, were listening the whole time. We drove toward Kigali, and when we reached that place called Nyachonga, is maybe forty kilometres from Kigali, I started seeing signs of the genocide. The fields were very green. Nothing had been harvested. The roads were quiet. Everywhere, it was kind of peaceful and very silent, because the Hutu militias had fled and the RPF had already moved on. But when we get to Nyachonga … You know, the interahamwe used to have a major roadblock in that place."

There was a long pause. So long, I thought perhaps he had finished telling his story.

"There were so many bodies, Will. You can't imagine. You really can't. Lying in fields. Beside the road. Piled on top of each other. It looked like piles of laundry. I slowed the truck down, and when I realized what it was, I said, 'Oh no, oh no.' The others in the vehicle, they looked at me and said, 'You came from where?' I said, 'I came from Kenya.' And they said, 'Prepare yourself. This is nothing. You're gonna see much worse than this.'"

On the table between us, wet rings marked the places where Jean-Claude had rested his glass. He drew his finger through them, watched the lines disappear.

"And they were right," he said. "It got worse. Much worse."

As they neared the outskirts of Kigali, Jean-Claude could see tracer fire across the skyline, could hear the clatter of gunfire, the subterranean thump of mortar shells hitting unseen targets.

"We passed abandoned checkpoints, saw people chopped. Some, they had no heads. Some, no feet. Some were just pieces of bone and skin."

It was July 3, 1994. Kigali had fallen to the RPF, but pockets of resistance remained, among them the feared Presidential Guards who were making a last stand, holding on till they too were forced to retreat, leaving behind only death and the wreckage of a ruined state.

"As we drove through the city, I thought, *'Rwanda is finished.* This is not a country anymore.' I thought maybe this is how the Roman Empire ended. Maybe this is how Egyptian civilization ended. Maybe they just killed themselves."

Any sense of victory was muted.

"You would see these young RPF soldiers, boys who had been fighting since 1990 to reach Kigali, and you would see them, sitting on the doorsteps of their burned homes looking defeated with their rifles propped up beside them, heads down, like this. Their eyes were empty. I don't know how to describe it. Just empty. Many of these soldiers, they were my age. Some had been fighting since they were sixteen. I spoke with a few of them; they said it felt like they fought for nothing."

Jean-Claude spent two weeks in Kigali his first time back. "The pickup truck I was driving, it had no owner, so this vehicle became mine while I was there. We were looking for people's relatives and other survivors—we collected so many children who were in the bushes or hiding with Hutu neighbours. I found out my sister Claudine was still alive."

Along with their brother Emmanuel, she had taken refuge at Sainte Famille church in the middle of Kigali. She had her youngest child, a baby boy, with her.

"My brother Emmanuel tried his best. He tried to protect Claudine, tried to protect her baby."

Crowding in with 8,000 other desperate people, Emmanuel and Claudine found themselves surrounded by taunting interahamwe militias who tormented them for weeks on end under the sadistic watch of Father Wenceslas Munyeshyaka. A Catholic priest who liked to swagger about with a pistol strapped to his hip, he provided "death lists" to the militias and Presidential Guards, who would then raid the church to drag out targeted Tutsis and Hutu moderates. It was a slow, incremental slaughter. Twenty people killed one day. Forty the next. The church had become a concentration camp, and Father Wenceslas began forcing young girls and women into providing sex in exchange for their lives.[7]

---

7. After the genocide, Father Wenceslas fled to France, where he continued to work in the clergy. Tried and convicted in absentia by a Rwandan court, he was eventually arrested in France under a warrant issued by the United Nations International Criminal Tribunal in Arusha and charged with crimes against humanity, including rape and murder. Released on a technicality, he was re-arrested and then just as quickly re-released. He has yet to go to trial. As of this writing, he is still enjoying his freedom and still ministering at a parish in Gisors, Normandy. The Catholic Church continues to cover his legal costs.

Caught in the crossfire, the church grounds were later hit by RPF shells, killing a dozen more.

"My sister was still nursing her baby. When the UN arrived to evacuate people, they started with the women and children. My sister was in the first convoy. I think it was the only convoy that got through."

His brother Emmanuel didn't make it.

"He put my sister and her baby on the truck, and he said, 'Go. I will follow. I will find you.'"

But as soon as the trucks left, the massacres began anew. Thousands died at Sainte Famille under the raptorial gaze of Father Wenceslas. Among the dead, Jean-Claude's brother Emmanuel.

"We don't know where his body is. When the killers were done, they brought in those excavators to dig a mass grave and they dumped the bodies in it. Later, the RPF exhumed the bones, but we don't know which ones are his."

"You found your sister?"

"I did."

"And how was she?"

He thought about this a moment. "Shattered."

# 7

KIGALI IS NO LONGER the hollow shell of a city that the RPF inherited or that Jean-Claude drove through in a daze, bodies still littering the streets.

Those same streets are now very safe, very clean—famously so. Travellers in Africa are always taken aback at how *tidy* Kigali is. Glass towers are spinning themselves into existence on the dizzying pirouette of construction cranes, but even with the city's population topping a million and growing daily, there are no sprawling slums, no shantytown ghettos stretching into the distance, no garbage pickers living on smouldering hills of trash. This is urban Africa reimagined, something jaded old African hands complain about. Kigali is too clean, they say. Too well-mannered, too manicured. In a word—too *livable*. Even its layout, with clusters of business centres arranged on separate hilltops, gives the Rwandan capital the feel of a much smaller city. A collection of towns, as it were.

Jean-Claude and I would use Kigali as our base, falling back to the city between extended excursions to the remoter regions of Rwanda, and it was always a pleasure to return. Through a contact of Jean-Claude, we'd rented a spacious, fifth-floor apartment in Kigali's Kacyiru district in a building owned and operated by Rwanda's national pension fund. (I liked that the rent we paid went to the Rwanda Social Security Board rather than a private company.) My bedroom looked out over the city, leafy green even in the dry season. Although Kigali, like most of Rwanda, is high enough to be outside the more serious malarial zones (the mosquitoes that carry malaria prefer warmer, lower-lying climes), I still took my anti-malarial pills every morning and slept beneath a cascade of silk netting every night, feeling not unlike a drowsy Southern belle.

I would often wake in the early hours as dawn was tiptoeing in.

I would slip free of my netting and pad down the hall to the kitchen to brew a cup of coffee and take it out on the balcony, where I would watch Kigali stir and come to life.

The city revealed itself in layers, shapes appearing like memories in the morning mist. Flowers and ferns. Eucalyptus trees, silhouetted above the rooftops. It was as though they'd built a city in the middle of a garden.

The haze would give way to light, veils removed one by one to the crescendo of birdsong: whistles and cheeps, melodies musical and not-so-musical. Some echoed the sound of water dripping, others were like question marks given voice. Some birds cooed, some chuckled. Some had songs halfway between a sigh and a sob. It was a far cry from the feuding magpies and cacophonous crows back home. One treetop resident, in the foliage directly below our balcony, would call out, "Wait a week! Wait a week!" and I would think, *Wait a week for what?*

Kigali is a city of brisk mornings, of early risers. It's purposeful. Older ladies in bent-back postures appear at first light, sweeping the sidewalks by hand, and the *whisk, whisk, whisk* of their straw brooms feels unnaturally loud in the fragrant hour. On the packed clay of the alleyway below, a security guard tries to coax a kiss from his would-be girlfriend. She declines and walks away, head high, only to stop and throw a smile back his way before she disappears. Just enough to encourage him to try again tomorrow.

Children walk down the alley to school: girls singing their way to class, boys tromping behind, all of them colour-coded by uniform, laughing and shouting, hurrying along. The parade peaks ... then peters out. There's a long pause, and then a single ten-year-old boy comes running, shirt untucked, flip-flops slapping air, books bouncing.

Every morning I watched the same flow of students pass by, and every morning I saw the same boy, always running, always late. I think about him sometimes, even now. I wonder if he ever made it to class on time.

# 8

KIGALI'S TOWN CENTRE is as lumpy as the rest of the city. This country is famous for its hills, granted, but somehow I thought they'd have staked out at least one flat piece of land to balance their high-rise hotels and office towers upon. But in Kigali there is no flat piece of land; you're always walking up or walking down, except perhaps along the marshy flats of the river below. That stretch is prone to flooding, though, and—until fairly recently—crocodiles.

Strapped into our Toyota 4x4, we followed the contours of Kigali into the downtown core as motorcycle taxis—"taxi-motos"—bobbed in and out with a boldness that bordered on bravado. Their minibus competitors, farting along merrily and weighted down with customers, vied for position. Everything was in motion, even the buildings it seemed. New shops were popping up even as we passed; it was like a time-lapse film on double-speed. One such establishment advertised itself proudly as "The New Better Shop," and the name stuck with me. Seemed redundant on first glance, but no. There is *new,* but not necessarily better. There is *better,* but not necessarily new. But this is Kigali—and everything was *new better.*

Jean-Claude marvelled at this on the drive in: the wide paved thoroughfares, the polished shimmer of new businesses. "It's amazing," he said, hands on the wheel, eyes cranked to the skyline (disconcertingly so, I admit). No matter. Even distracted by the city, he threaded his way through with aplomb.

We changed some money, purchased pay-as-you-go cell phones and refillable bottles of filtered water: the usual accoutrements of modern travel. The streets of Kigali were heaving with commerce. The entire city seemed filled with a sense of possibilities being seized. Rwanda, I'd been told, is a nation of incipient entrepreneurs, and this fact jostled up against me at every turn.

Rwandans are also famously beautiful, famously handsome—and

slightly haughty, it must be said, at least here in the capital. This is the image Rwandans have across East Africa: long-limbed, elegant, and ever-confident—and oh, how often those last two go together. Much as I hate to propagate stereotypes, I had to concur.

"Is there a convention of supermodels in town this weekend?" I asked.

Jean-Claude laughed.

Ugandan comedian Anne Kansiime opened a recent show in Kigali by saying, "You know, back home in Uganda I'm actually very beautiful—and surprisingly tall. Here, it is a different story." I had sympathy for Ms. Kansiime. I'd never felt more dishevelled or stumpy than I did shuffling about the streets of Kigali.

Glass office towers, reflecting a blue deeper than the sky they were catching, lined up alongside low-riding shops and overladen stalls. Two versions of Kigali, wedged against each other, often occupying the same space: the Kigali of clay walls and small shops, and that of glass-tower bank centres. Beauty salons and auto parts. Storefront racks of bright-yellow soccer jerseys (*"Go Amavubis!"*). Trays filled with children's toys. Soft drinks and running shoes. Fanned displays of magazines. Plumbing gewgaws and electronic gadgets were piled up on sidewalk stalls as the city's street hawkers moved through, selling phone-card top-ups and Holy Bibles of various value: white leather deluxe, red vinyl pocketbook, and everything in between.

Several new department stores had opened, and in the downtown Nakumatt we came across HD plasma TVs for sale alongside a wide selection of—Jean-Claude couldn't believe this—treadmills.

Treadmills?

"Now, that—*that* is a good sign!" he said. You know an economy is taking root, you know people truly have disposable income when, in the words of Jean-Claude, "they can waste their money on a walking machine. This is Kigali!" he exclaimed. "Who needs a treadmill? You are *always* walking. Up and down, every day, even on a short trip to the store."

In a lane behind Nakumatt, Jean-Claude bumped into someone he once knew, a soft-spoken older businessman named Paul Ruhamyambuga. He was, I later learned, something of a local legend in Kigali.

While the rest of the city—indeed, the country—still lay in ruins, Mr. Ruhamyambuga was already imagining its restoration. In a public display of confidence, he built the City Plaza office building amid the rubble, sending a message to investors, to the world—but most importantly, to the people—that this was *not* the end. A new city would rise.

The Jean-Claude he'd known had been a gawky teenager living in Kenya. "The same, but different," Mr. Ruhamyambuga said, laughing with genuine warmth on meeting the Jean-Claude of today, the Jean-Claude who'd returned. While the two of them spoke in Kinyarwanda, sharing confidences and small remembrances, I looked up at the tinted glass of the City Plaza office tower with its clamorous jumble of small shops crowding in below.

Jean-Claude turned to me and said, "I remember when this was the tallest building in Kigali."

Once a landmark of the recovery, the City Plaza is now just one building in among the shinier, higher hilltop towers of this new and better Kigali. *You'd hardly have known there was ever a war …*

# 9

FOLLOWING THAT FIRST FORAY into Rwanda after the genocide, Jean-Claude returned to Nairobi, bringing news to families of their loved ones back home.

"Not all the news was good," he notes.

There was still a pressing need for vehicles and supplies back in Rwanda, and Jean-Claude made the run between Kenya and Kigali ten times or more, ferrying people and goods back and forth, helping to gather children and reunite families—there are people he helped who stay in touch with him to this day. His journeys had a dash of Mad Max about them. "The situation was still very unstable," he said. "Many of the side roads were filled with landmines. The remote villages were still being attacked."

But a different sort of adventure was about to begin, although Jean-Claude didn't know it at the time. During evening services at Nairobi's Good Shepherd church, he spotted a strikingly beautiful young woman named Christine Karebwayire. She was new to the city, studying at the technical college, and was living nearby with her aunt.

Christine was born into the diaspora. Her parents had fled Rwanda in 1959—during the *first* genocide against the Tutsis. They'd settled in Burundi and then later in Tanzania, though it might as well have been in Limbo. Although successful in their new life, they were still stateless citizens occupying a liminal world.

"In Nairobi, the Rwandan community was holding an overnight service once a month," Jean-Claude explained. "It would start maybe at nine o'clock, with greetings and testimonies. Every new person who came, they introduced themself. It was mostly social. It was kind of like open-mike night. I knew almost everybody who was Rwandese living in Nairobi. At that time, I was among the longest-running members of that congregation, so when I saw

Christine, I thought, 'Oh my goodness, who is this?' I never seen her before."

Not all of Christine's extended family had left Rwanda. Her uncle was a prominent church official, Canon Alphonse Karuhije, dean of Kigali's Anglican cathedral. Denied the rank of bishop by a Hutu rival, he was killed on church grounds during the genocide after being betrayed by a fellow priest.

His wife, Christine's aunt Thacienne, had escaped the carnage by the slimmest of margins: having gone to visit family in Tanzania over Easter, she was out of the country when the president's plane was shot down. Canon Karuhije had driven his wife and their five children to the border crossing at Rusumo Falls, had said goodbye, then taken a bus back to Kigali while she continued on with the children. He was returning to the city to oversee Easter Mass. His family would never see him again.

Christine's aunt, now widowed, was in Nairobi awaiting sponsorship from the Anglican Church for her and her children to go to Winnipeg. Christine was staying with them while she studied at the college, hoping someday to become a nurse.

"Was it love at first sight?" I asked Jean-Claude.

"You know," he said, "I wasn't thinking that way. At this time, I was taking care of some children who had been separated from their mother, and I was paying school fees for other ones. I had too many things going on, too many responsibilities."[8]

He remembers the car, though. Vividly. "Christine's aunt still had her husband's sedan, the one she drove out of Rwanda. Was a Peugeot 505. French-built. Very good car."

Her aunt needed a mechanic, Jean-Claude helped her find one at a good price, and soon he was spending time with her and her niece.

"Cars and soccer," I said. "Seems like half your life has been tied to those two, JC."

---

8. Christine tells a different version. "He was following me around everywhere!" she says.

He laughed. "I think so."

When Christine's aunt left for Canada with her children, Christine moved into an apartment with five other students to continue her studies.

"I used to tease her because she grew up in Tanzania, so she spoke Kinyarwanda mixed with Swahili. Sometimes she didn't know that it wasn't correct. She would use a Tanzanian word and I would tease her about this, saying, 'What is that? That is not Kinyarwanda.'" (Note the disingenuous use of the past tense on Jean-Claude's part. He *still* teases her about this.) "So what's happened is, we became kind of friends. We started hanging out together, then it started to be kind of dating.[9] I remember our first date. It was in the afternoon and she came from school to meet me, still in her school uniform. We went to a fish and chips place, and then after we took a bus to the zoo." He smiled. "It was a good day."

"Do you remember which animals you saw?"

He thought about this. "No. Not really."

A simple story of boy meets girl, except that it was set against the backdrop and fallout of an African holocaust. The courtship of Jean-Claude and Christine was a reminder of what the Polish journalist Ryszard Kapuściński, who covered countless wars and rebellions in Africa, described as "this beautiful and heartening thing, this obstinate, heroic human striving for normality." The normality of spending time with someone you like, of going on a date. Of taking a bus together, of visiting a zoo.

And then the unexpected: Jean-Claude received sponsorship from a Catholic diocese in Montreal, which meant he would be leaving Africa for a new life in Canada. He promptly asked Christine to marry him.

"And?"

"She said no."

"What? Why?"

---

9. Not sure what "kind of dating" means.

"That's what I wanted to know! I asked her why and she said, 'I'm not ready to get married. I'm gonna finish my studies. I'm gonna be a nurse.' So I said, 'You can still be a nurse, only now you will be a nurse who is married.' But she said, 'Oh, I think that would be very hard. Let's just continue to be friends instead.'"

But then Christine made a serious mistake. She talked to her friends. She told them Jean-Claude had asked for her hand in marriage and that she'd declined.

"She told the other girls?"

"Of course she did! Can you imagine *any* girl, a boy asks her to marry him and she says no, and she's not gonna tell her friends about it? Of course she told them! Soon everybody in the Rwandan community knew."

"And?"

"My supporters, they began to lobby on my behalf. They told her, 'You are crazy! You should have said yes!'"

His supporters also advised Jean-Claude, on the sly, to maybe try one more time. And so, just before he departed for Montreal, he asked her again. This time she said yes.

Christine came to Canada six months later, having finished her schooling. She moved first to Winnipeg to live with her beloved aunt and then to Calgary to marry Jean-Claude. The ceremony was at a local church, with Christine resplendent in her wedding gown. I've seen the photos; it's clear why Jean-Claude was so smitten.

There was a Rwandan aspect to the ceremony as well. "I bought her family a cow," he said. "Is a tradition in Rwanda. The groom presents one to the bride's family. So I sent a cow to her family in Africa."

"What, like by Fedex?"

He laughed. "No, I sent the money to buy one. Was an Ankole cow—they call it the 'Cattle of Kings.' Very elegant animals."

Here was the trajectory of lives lived and roads intersecting, of a wedding dress and a kingly gift, and it all started with a truck rumbling across that bridge at Rusumo Falls with a teenage stowaway on

board, heart pounding, hidden under heavy sacks of coffee, escaping
a coming apocalypse.

# 10

THE BOULEVARD THAT RAN PAST our apartment in Kigali, palmy in
every sense of the word, lacked even the faintest speck of litter. Widows
and elderly women are allotted specific sections of major streets, are
paid a stipend to keep them clean—and Lord help you if you
absent-mindedly drop a candy wrapper on their stretch of pavement.
I'd been warned several times that the whisk brooms these ladies
wielded could also be used in a pedagogically punitive manner.

Jean-Claude and I went for a walk along this ridge-top boulevard
one morning, with Jean-Claude pointing out the flora along the way:
avocado trees and pears, hanging heavy with fruit; jacaranda with
their piñata-like pods ready to burst in a spray of flowers.

"My father," Jean-Claude said, "his passion was trees. He knew
everything about them. With his brother Adalbert he grafted oranges
and lemons onto the same plant. One tree with two different fruits,
the neighbours were amazed."

Jean-Claude's grandfather had been a member of the Royal Army
of King Rwabugiri and was on hand when the German count crossed
into the Kingdom of Rwanda and made first contact.

"My grandfather, his name was Rugaju, and he was sent east with
the son of the king, the prince, to keep the Germans in check. The
Germans were already in Tanzania—Tanganyika, they called it back
then. My grandfather's main assignment was to keep the Germans
from crossing into Rwanda."

The Akagera River marked the outer limits of the kingdom, and
the mwami set up a military outpost not far from Rusumo Falls.

Jean-Claude's grandfather was granted land in a nearby village. This was where Jean-Claude's father was born.

"My family still has land in that area, it's still our village. You know, in Africa, everyone, even if they are born and raised in the city, they will have a traditional village that they call home. Mine is in the east, in Rundu village."

Jean-Claude's father, Ferdinand, was a scholar and a botanist whose talents were recognized early on. "He was sent to Tanzania to learn how to plant coffee plantations when that was first being introduced into Rwanda. He was among the first people to learn how to do that, and he travelled all over the country doing those kinds of work, teaching people how to plant coffee beans and then later eucalyptus."

His father settled in Kigali with his brother Adalbert, down by the river in a neighbourhood now known as Gisozi.

"My father and Uncle Adalbert were the first people to live there."

As a leading arborist, Jean-Claude's father was something of a Johnny Appleseed as well, planting trees tirelessly across Rwanda. "There are forests even now," Jean-Claude said, "that my father planted. When I pass by them, I can still see my father moving about very carefully, examining each tree, nodding. He was a very thoughtful person. Conversations with him were always about serious matters. My uncle Adalbert, he was more open. I think he knew how to talk to children better than my dad. My uncle lived next door. I had many cousins."

Jean-Claude and I walked along the spacious sidewalks of Umuganda Avenue as early-morning pedestrians clipped past at a brisk pace in crisp white shirts. Minibuses veered in and out, stopping to pack more passengers in or unload others. The city was like a giant clock winding *up* rather than down.

"My neighbourhood, the place I grew up, it's over there, on the other side." Jean-Claude pointed across the rolling heights of Kigali to a hill opposite, layered with homes. In between, sloping into the valley and then swooping back up the other side, were the rooftops of other homes, so close together as to be overlapping.

We'd reached the Kacyiru roundabout, tidy and well-tended. A circular garden flowing with traffic, it once marked the frontline in the Battle of Kigali, with RPF soldiers hunkered down on one side, exchanging gunfire with members of the elite Presidential Guards on the other. For three months this roundabout had been in the middle of a war zone. *If no one had told you …*

On a whim, Jean-Claude suggested we walk to his old neighbourhood, through the streets below us, across the river, and then up the other side.

"Hmmm. Looks far," I said.

"Yes, but I know a shortcut. I remember a certain way to go."

So we left the wide boulevard of Umuganda Avenue, with its fountain-pen palm trees and its rise-and-shine, starch-shirted commuters, and plunged into the residential area below. A steep path led us into a labyrinth of low-lying clay-brick homes, tightly packed. Every building seemed to be propping up the one next to it, and the lane we were walking down was narrow enough at times that I could have run my hands along both sides.

We had entered a different Kigali. Smaller, clustered, more intimate. The smell of lye soap and wet charcoal: pots scrubbed and cooking fires doused. The raspy cry of a rooster. A young mother tossing wash-water from a basin onto the ground as her toddler, as toddlers are wont to do, toddles by, beaming at the power of his own locomotion. She begins laying out her hand-wrung laundry on a thorny hedge to dry, keeps a sideward eye on us as we pass. An elderly lady in a patterned apron and matching head scarf sweeps an already clean threshold of hypothetical dirt. (The entire neighbourhood being made of clay, sweeping for dust must be more an existential than a pragmatic endeavour.) She looks up at us, is startled into a smile, eyes lost in a nest of wrinkles, as we squeeze by.

A cadre of young men striding uphill stop as well, taken aback by the sight of us coming down; it was as though Jean-Claude and I were blithely cutting through their living rooms, which in a way I suppose we were. Troops of schoolchildren, startled in mid-gambol, stood gape-eyed and O-mouthed, with the bolder among them venturing a quick "Good morning, teacher. How are you? I am fine" as we passed. Learning English in the classroom has given Rwandan students the habit of addressing English speakers, regardless of who they are, as "teacher." This is usually delivered in a single impressive burst: *"Goo'moaning'teacha'howreyoomfine,"* after which they scramble back to the laughter and breathless congratulations of their peers. *"Muzungu! Muzungu! He talked to a muzungu!"* It would be the highlight of their morning, would grow with each telling I'm sure. Some of the smaller children, always with the most encrusted noses it seemed, stopped to force moist handshakes on me, to which I always obliged. Mental note: *Buy hand sanitizer.*

*Muzungu* is a Swahili word, borrowed by the Rwandese. I assumed it meant "handsome fellow" or "look yonder at that dapper chap!" because wherever I went, I heard it time and time again, heralding my arrival, departure, existence. The response in Kigali was mild. They see muzungus all the time—not in their local neighbourhoods, maybe, but downtown, fanning themselves in front of banks and hotels, counting bills at the money-changers, looking sweaty and perplexed. Outside of Kigali, however, the refrain of "Muzungu!" would increase dramatically, become almost constant, a sort of background chorus. (When I say to Rwandans, "Muzungu must mean good-looking, right?" they always get a pained look on their faces. "No, no, no," they explain, "it means white person," as though I were so dense I hadn't figured that out. So then I have to explain I was only joking, which elicits even more brow-knitting concern. At one point, I tried doubling down—"Muzungu means super-sexy movie star, right?"—but the response was the same, "No, no, no, it means ...")

Our path through the maze of clay-walled homes grew steeper with every ankle-rolling step, turning my initial canter into an extended downward stumble as I tried not to trip myself into an uncontrolled forward rush.

We came out of this rabbit warren of homes onto the side of another, lower thoroughfare. "I remember this road!" Jean-Claude said. "It's paved now. And wider. But it wasn't like this when I was growing up. It used to be so dusty. We would be choking in the dry season."

Memories came quicker now. On passing a newly built gas station, Jean-Claude read the sign and said, "I know him! I know the owner. I knew him as a boy. He taught himself mechanics in his backyard. He has done very well." And as we drew closer to the river: "We used to play along these banks, in those marshes. There were only three cars in our neighbourhood. None of this was paved."

The marshlands of Jean-Claude's youth have largely been filled in. "There was more water," he said, somewhat sadly. But there is always more water in our childhood. More water and taller buildings.

We walked across the busy Kinamba overpass, vehicles clipping by in both directions, and Jean-Claude said, "This is where my cousin died. They threw her over the side with the other Tutsis. She was a long time dying. They could hear her crying for two days is what I'm told."

During the genocide, this overpass was the site of one of the most notorious roadblocks in Kigali. Here, Hutu Power youths tormented and targeted specific people early on, before the more widespread indiscriminate killings began. As the weeks went by, the dead piled up below, began to decompose in the heat; no *buddies* saved her.

Jean-Claude's old neighbourhood of Gisozi was on the other side of this overpass, and as we pushed our way through a crowd of workers trundling toward a nearby lumberyard, the air became spiced with the scent of sawdust and cut wood. The road angled uphill and we walked, leaning into our ascent, until we came to a potholed, packed-clay lane branching off from the main road.

"This is the street," Jean-Claude said. "This is where I grew up."

His old neighbourhood was now a construction site. The past was under repair, but a few of the older buildings still stood, acting as wary benchmarks on a vastly changed map. It took some time, but with the help of a few young men who lived on the street, we did manage to find a remnant of Jean-Claude's family home. "Just this part," he said, laying a hand on its whitewashed texture. A corner incorporated into another building. "These two walls, these were part of our house."

Jean-Claude was four or five when his mother died.

"I try to find her face, but I can't. I remember her clothes and her voice—I remember how she spoke, very calm, very kind—I remember her calling my brother when he was outside, telling him that the supper was ready. I remember her sending me to get him. I even remember she was feeding me with a spoon when I was little and how this food that she cooked, we call it *igihembe,* kind of like a lentil, was so tasty. I remember all of those things, but I can't remember her face."

She died in Uganda. She had family there, and when she became ill they sent for her, because Uganda, as a former British colony, had more advanced medical care.

"She went to Uganda," he said. "And she never came back."

Jean-Claude was playing outside with his older brother the day he found out.

"It was raining and we had to come inside, and when we did there was so many people there, aunts and uncles, neighbours. They went very quiet when we came in and my dad called us into the room, me and my brother, and he said, 'I just want to tell you that your mother has passed away.' But I didn't know what that means. I was thinking, 'Okay, so am I gonna see her now?' After that, I asked my cousin and she explained to me. She said, 'It means you will never see her again. They are going to put her in a box in the ground.' That was when I knew my mother was gone and wouldn't be coming back … My dad was a single parent from that moment until he died."

Jean-Claude's mother had been his father's second wife—he was separated from his first—and the house was filled with the comings-and-goings of step-cousins and assorted siblings.

"I was the second youngest. There were four children from the first marriage, five with my mom."

"A big family."

"Yes. Always there were people in this house. It was very crowded, but was fun."

While we stood looking at the remaining walls of Jean-Claude's childhood home, he recited the names of various brothers and sisters, "Claudine, Marie-Gorette, my brother Elisé, Denise, Jean-Baptiste, Emmanuel," speaking more to himself than to anyone.

By this point, we were surrounded by young men in undershirts and flip-flops: temporary workers from the looks of it, pants caked with dry mud. We'd attracted a gathering of schoolchildren as well. They followed us down the lane, walking when we walked, stopping when we stopped, looking where we looked. "Scoot! You'll be late for school," Jean-Claude admonished, but school pales in excitement to having a real! live! muzungu set loose in your neighbourhood. At one point a sedan angrily pushed its way through the crowd, the driver casting disapproving glares our way.

The young men who had helped Jean-Claude locate the partial walls of his old home wanted to be paid for their assistance. Jean-Claude scoffed at this. "For helping someone, you think you deserve money? Do you think that is the correct way to act?" He asked them this in Kinyarwanda. Admonished, they stared at their feet with hang-dog expressions.

Jean-Claude looked back at that last remaining piece of his childhood.

"Time to go," he said after a moment.

Now, the problem with walking *down,* into a valley, say, is that eventually you have to walk back *up,* and I was already tired. The sun was itching its prickly heat along the nape of my neck and my throat had grown starchy with thirst.

No matter. "We'll follow the river, then cross back farther down, at the next bridge. We can go up the other side over there." Jean-Claude pointed out the route we would follow. It would allow us to avoid having to backtrack and would turn our cross-city hike into one extended loop.

Thus began the long trudge back, as on a treadmill.

The road that ran alongside the river, paved as well and busy with traffic, took us past the marshy meadows that formed a bowl in the bottom of Kigali's many hills.

"The Red Cross owns all of this," Jean-Claude said. It would have been prime real estate, save for the constant flooding and the boggy soil, to say nothing of the crocodiles. (Kigali's crocodiles had departed, but one never knows.)

In a grassy field, a scrawny dog was cavorting with a cow and her calf—at least, that's how the dog saw it, nipping and yapping, in and out of the fray, tail wagging. For the cow it was more akin to harassment; she lowered her head repeatedly, trying to butt the dog clear, but the mutt would scramble aside, sporting that loopy grin dogs wear when caught up in their own hijinks. A tired-looking man in a floppy hat with a long branch resting on his shoulder, a cattle herder by the looks of it, was even now making his way across the field to end the "fun."

Dogs are a rare sight in Rwanda, but it wasn't always so. The country once abounded in them, but in the aftermath of the genocide, Rwanda's dogs began running in feral packs, attacking the wounded, eating the dead, chewing on the bones. The advancing RPF instigated a cull, shooting dogs on sight. Today, Rwanda has fewer than almost any country in Africa, maybe the world.

Something stops Jean-Claude cold.

In an irrigation ditch he sees a tattered red jacket, clogged in the mud.

Jean-Claude stared at it, didn't move, barely breathed. Then: "I'm sorry. It's just—for a moment I thought ..."

I knew what he thought. He thought it was 1994 all over again. He thought it was a dead body, decomposing. But there were no bodies in the water. Only a discarded jacket. We walked on in silence before Jean-Claude spoke.

"That's what they looked like," he said quietly. "The bodies. They looked like piles of old clothes."

Old clothes and dogs dining on human flesh.

We crossed a bridge to the other side of the river, started our ascent. Along the way we passed a Twa pottery market. The Twa, or "pygmies" as they are known in the West, are the invisible people of Rwanda. Where the Tutsis were cattle owners and the Hutu farmers, the Twa were hunter-gatherers. They lived in the nation's forest fringes, distinct from Rwanda's other two solitudes, but during the genocide the Twa were often targeted, too, for no other reason than, Well, why not? Since we're killing minority groups anyway …

The Twa remain on the periphery of Rwandan society, even though the national government, to its credit, has launched a development program aimed at addressing this imbalance. A purpose-built "cultural village," where Twa arts and customs are preserved, albeit in a vaguely dioramic form, has been built near Lake Kivu, and new pottery markets, such as the one Jean-Claude and I passed, have been established. Twa pottery is rightly famous, and the line of oversized urns—made of clay, strong and delicate at the same time—attested to their skill. I desperately wanted to buy some but couldn't imagine how I'd ever get them home in one piece.

Large homes crowded the incline as we walked up, up, up. The lingering effects of jet lag and my own deskbound, ass-in-chair lifestyle were catching up to me as I struggled to suck air into my lungs with less and less success. My chest wouldn't inflate all the way.

It was a thigh-straining walk, with long zigs and slow zags, and when we finally stopped for something cold to drink at a roadside stall—I staggered up to the counter waving a fistful of Rwandan francs, gasping for *amazi* (a word I would use often)—a pair of passing motorcycle taxi boys took pity and pulled over. They were looking for a fare, of course, but I imagined they were also concerned about my well-being. I was just about to pant, "Gentlemen, I will gladly pay whatever it takes to get me to the top of the next hill, here is my wallet, take from it whatever amount you wish," when Jean-Claude intervened, magnanimously waving them off. We were fine, he explained. We didn't need a ride.

As the taxi-moto boys pulled away with a suit-yourself shrug, Jean-Claude saw the stricken look on my face. "Don't worry," he assured me, "we're almost there." And by "almost," he meant another forty-five minutes of slow, steady walking.

My chest-whistling soundtrack had cast a pall over the proceedings, for I knew full well that in just a few weeks' time we'd be hiking the towering rainforests of the Virunga volcanoes in search of Rwanda's famed, and famously remote, mountain gorillas. If a stroll through the streets of Kigali knocked me out, it didn't bode well. I decided to blame it on the altitude. The country's average elevation is 2,725 metres above sea level—and the lairs of the mountain gorillas are higher still, often 4,000 metres or more. Kigali itself was a "mile high," as they say.

"Once I (*wheeze*) get acclimatized (*wheeze*) to these higher elevations, I'll (*wheeze*) be fine (*wheeze*)," I said.

By the time we got back to our apartment, my lungs were burning from oxygen deprivation and the noonday sun had singed my skin, leaving it an amusing shade of rosé. It had been a three-hour "stroll" by my count.

# 11

SOLACE MINISTRIES RAN A GUEST HOUSE across the alleyway from the apartment building we were staying in. (Our balcony looked down onto their courtyard.) Solace Ministries also provided a lunch and supper buffet, and when Jean-Claude and I were in Kigali, we often took our meals there, a breezy commute of about ten steps, out the back gate and across the clay-packed alley. Slices of fruit, rich Rwandan coffee, cheese and pastries, omelettes made to order. And when Jean-Claude was away in the evenings, visiting his sister or old acquaintances, I would go on long walks through our neighbourhood that always seemed to end at Solace in time for coffee and cake.

At Solace Ministries, women gather to share their stories. Soft-spoken tales of siblings slaughtered, of husbands hacked down, of mutilations and machetes, of rape and the children born of rape. The woman who ran the office at Solace told us we could sit in and listen if we liked, that we were welcome to hear their stories, but it felt too intrusive. I watched from the wings instead, and even though they spoke in Kinyarwanda, the pain in their voices was unmistakable.

It was a daily *aide-mémoire* of what survivors still face. Every day, Jean-Claude and I would pass the hall of widows and every day were reminded of the ineluctable logic of hatred. Of hatred, taken to its natural conclusion. Of hatred incubated, encouraged, allowed to run free.

Sometimes the longest walk of the day was the ten steps across the alleyway to Solace.

# 12

BEYOND ITS GARDEN-LIKE ROUNDABOUTS and well-swept streets, the scars of the genocide are still evident in Rwanda's capital. You need only to look.

From the shell-pocked walls of the nation's parliament buildings (where the bullet-hole points of impact have been left as a reminder of the Battle of Kigali, a street-by-street campaign marked by stalemates and sudden sallies, reminiscent of the Siege of Leningrad) to the splattered plaster at the military barracks where the ten Belgian peacekeepers were killed, the capital at times feels like an open-air memorial.

The Belgian monuments, one for each of the soldiers, are understated and poignant, but with a simmering anger in evidence. The families have never forgiven General Dallaire for not storming in and taking the base by force, a wholly unrealistic option considering that the captured Belgian peacekeepers were being held in what was essentially a military fortress with more than 1,500 armed soldiers on hand, well-equipped and fully armed. (The UN, by contrast, had barely forty-seven rounds per person, which would have lasted three minutes at most in a pitched battle.) But no matter. Grief is never rational, and the families of the dead peacekeepers have written their anguish onto the walls of the building where the massacre occurred, maintained now as a memorial by the Belgian embassy.

On a chalkboard inside, preserved under plexiglass, is the heartfelt but misguided *j'accuse:* "General Dallaire—have you no eyes, no heart?" The families might have better focused their anger on the French government of François Mitterrand, which trained and armed the very soldiers who murdered their sons and husbands, or perhaps have looked more critically at Belgium's own colonial legacy, in both Rwanda and the Congo, but that would be to diminish the pain of those who lost loved ones—a pain shared, quite literally, by *millions* of Rwandan women, children, men.

Scars on buildings, scars on skin.

The man Jean-Claude rented our vehicle from had a thick line running across his neck, ear to ear, like a rubbery rope: the distinct slash of a machete.

Scars of the flesh and of the spirit.

The scars that remember, the scars that remain.

Rwanda's national genocide memorial is just up the road from Jean-Claude's childhood home. If, as Stalin infamously noted, one death is a tragedy but a million is just a statistic, the Kigali Genocide Memorial Centre strives to put a human face on those numbers, tries to stop them from becoming a mere tally, numbly recited, emptied of meaning.

Inside are snapshots and photographs. Candid moments, class photos, wedding portraits, Sunday schools, and graduations. The faces of families, of children, of mothers, husbands, lovers. Gone.

Acts of kindness and bravery are commemorated as well: an elderly Hutu woman named Zula Karuhimbi bluffed her local band of killers with nothing more than confidence and a reputation for being a crank. Seventy-one years old, Zula had given refuge to more than twenty frightened Tutsis in her rundown home, including infants. When the interahamwe militias showed up, armed with machetes and demanding she step aside so they could search her hovel on rumours she was harbouring Tutsis, she said, "Be my guest." But be warned, she added. *"I have supernatural powers."* The killers scoffed, but as an old woman living alone, Zula already had a disquieting reputation. She was known to work with traditional medicines. Was she also a witch? Probably not. But did they really want to take the chance? Zula, diminutive, defiant, looked the killers in the eyes, stared down any doubts they might have had, told them, "If you want to die, go inside. I have powers, and evil spirits will swallow you up." Not one of the mob was brave enough to risk it. They swaggered off, vowing to come back later—but never did. The Tutsis hiding inside survived.

Dismas Mutezintare singlehandedly saved 400 Tutsi children and adults at an orphanage. Where is his Hollywood movie? A Muslim man named Yahaya Nsengiumva saved thirty. When asked why, he said it was simple: "The Koran tells us that saving one life is like saving the whole world."

But the saddest room in all of Rwanda is the Children's Room at the Kigali museum. If you were to roll all the pain, all the senselessness of what happened, into a ball the size of your fist and lodge it deep in your stomach, you will feel it here, in this room. It is calm and softly lit.

*Fabrice Murinzi Minega*

| | |
|---|---|
| Age: | 8 |
| Favourite sport: | Swimming |
| Favourite sweets: | Chocolate |
| Best friend: | His mum |
| Behaviour: | Gregarious |
| Cause of death: | Bludgeoned with club |

There are no bodies in this room, no human remains, only the illuminated photographs of children lining the walls. And beneath each photograph, an introduction.

*Aurore Kirezi*
Age:                        2
Favourite drink:            Milk
Favourite game:             Hide-and-seek with her big brother
Behaviour:                  Very talkative
Cause of death:             Burnt alive at the Gikondo Chapel

Here is a photo of a little boy running in short pants, his name is Patrick; the little girl in a pretty dress beaming at the camera is Aurore. Here is Chandelle on her birthday, Hubert on his bicycle.

*Fabrice Cyemezo*
Age:                        15 months
Favourite food:             Rice with milk
Favourite animal:           Cat
Enjoyed:                    Making gestures
Favourite word:             Auntie
Cause of death:             Killed at Muhoro Church

Looking back on the events of 1994, Rwandan poet and genocide survivor Félicien Ntagengwa penned words that often appear at memorials, above doorways, on altars: *Iyo uza kwimenya / nanjye ukamenya / ntuba waranyishe.* "If you really knew me, and you really knew yourself, you would not have killed me."

# 13

AS JEAN-CLAUDE AND CHRISTINE settled into their new life in Calgary, a baby boy soon followed. Jean-Claude was working as a meat cutter at the sprawling Cargill plant in High River, which made for a long commute down a winter highway in a rattling second-hand Hyundai.

"But they were paying me nine bucks an hour!" he told me with a laugh. "For an immigrant from Africa, nine bucks an hour right away? I thought, *'This is good!'*"

We were sharing ugali dumplings at a roadside café as Jean-Claude reminisced about his days in High River, half a world and a lifetime away, it seemed.

"This meat-packing plant, it was *huge*. Like its own city. Very clean, very efficient too. Cows came in one side alive and left the other side wrapped, sorted, packed, and ready to be shipped. Nothing was wasted. Me? I was fine until I visited the kill floor, where the cows are cut and drained. I saw them being pushed in through that little gate and the cows were pushing back, fighting to avoid it. It was terrible. They *knew*. It was very hard for me to watch because, you know, for Rwandese, cows are kind of like a treasure. Not sacred like in India, but sort of. We don't eat them, we keep them. So for me, it was difficult." Suddenly nine dollars an hour didn't seem like very much. "I worked at that meat plant for three years. I still don't eat hamburgers even now."

Getting Jean-Claude to grab a beer and a burger had been pretty much out of the question back in Canada, even though I'd explained to him several times how beer and burgers were two of our national food groups. Now I knew why.

It was during his time as a meat cutter that Jean-Claude began volunteering at Calgary homeless shelters.

"I wanted to meet people. I was studying at the college, but my English was not improving as much as I wanted. It was strange.

Working at the Cargill meat plant, there was no way you can tell you are in Canada. Almost no one was speaking English. During lunch break there was the Vietnamese table, there was the Filipino table, the Sudanese table, the Ethiopian table. One guy is from Congo, another one is from Haiti, another from Sierra Leone. And so on. No one was integrating; it was like they were in separate worlds."

So he began volunteering at Mustard Seed, a downtown Calgary shelter.

"I was naive. I couldn't see how anybody can be homeless in Canada. How can someone be poor in such a country like this? But at Mustard Seed I met many people, good people, some had bad luck, some had problems with drugs or abuse, some had been in jail. They all had a story to tell and I would listen, try to help."

Jean-Claude managed to get one fellow, a former accountant who'd had a mental breakdown and become homeless, a job as a meat cutter at the Cargill plant, even driving him to the interview in High River.

"This guy, he said to me, 'Jean-Claude, why should I bother, no one is gonna hire me,' and I said, 'Of course not! Not if you look like that!' He was a mess. I told him he had to shave and shower and get cleaned up, and I got him a suit from Goodwill for his interview. He was a very smart man, and seeing him in a suit, he was like a different person. When he got his first paycheque he bought me lunch. He said, 'Getting a paycheque makes you feel worthwhile, makes you feel like a human being.' Later, I found out he has left the meat-cutting plant and is working as an accountant for a big company. He called me and he said, 'Guess what!' You know, Will, sometimes just a small thing can change everything."

Jean-Claude went on to volunteer at Inn from the Cold, which provided families with hot meals and holiday dinners. They even helped kids with their homework.

"These events were very fun, like a family atmosphere. We even had movie nights in the basement of a community hall. There were other kids to play with, so they didn't feel alone in their situation. For a moment you could see that these children are able to forget they are homeless or sad."

Jean-Claude eventually left the Cargill meat-processing plant and signed on as a community resource worker for people with mental disabilities. "Helping with their banking, driving them to shopping or the swimming pool, that kind of thing. This work was very satisfying. I enjoyed it so much, but the pay was too low and I couldn't support my family on it." So after a lucrative but exhausting tour of duty in the Alberta oil patch—"Very tiring, very dirty, and I was away from home too much"—he began driving taxi instead.

"First I was a special needs driver, taking kids with disabilities. Was very rewarding, but I had to switch to regular fares. The hours were more flexible."

He needed to take care of his own children while Christine studied for her certificate in practical nursing. And yet, even with this, he still found time to volunteer as a coach at our local soccer club. (Meanwhile, I feel good about myself if I drop a toonie into a Salvation Army tin at Christmastime.)

It was around this time that Jean-Claude also noticed something about his local neighbourhood. It had extensive subsidized housing for lower-income families and refugees, but not much else. "Children from everywhere," as he put it. "With nothing to do."

Many of the families had come to Canada from the same refugee camps in Sudan and Somalia that Jean-Claude had visited years before, or had escaped persecution in Syria and Ethiopia, violence in Colombia and Afghanistan, poverty in the Philippines. The parents were often working two jobs and had no time to think about how to involve their children in the community.

"So these kids, they were just hanging around. In the park or on the street, every night, every weekend. I wondered, when they go to school on Monday and the other children say, 'Oh, I went skiing' or 'I went swimming,' what will they say? When the teacher asks, 'What did you do on the weekend?' what will they tell her?"

So one Saturday, Jean-Claude dragged out a bag filled with second-hand soccer balls and plastic cones and began pacing out a field in their local park. The Saturday Soccer Club was born. It was free and it was fun and everyone was welcome, no matter their age or ability—but they had to be respectful and they had to take the club seriously. The boys and girls in the Saturday Soccer Club ran drills, practised scrimmages, worked on their passing, their shooting, their set plays. Soon he had more than a hundred children involved, with an entire team of volunteers overseeing it. Jean-Claude can be very persuasive, and before long he had FIFA-trained youth coaches volunteering their time, too. Other clubs donated shoes and shin guards, and a local car wash sponsored their jerseys.

The Saturday Soccer Club ran all year, indoor and out, and as talented players emerged they were snatched up by competitive leagues (which gladly waived their fees). Soccer is a sport that crosses international borders. Whether you are from Colombia or Egypt, Syria or Congo, Somalia or Sudan, everyone speaks the language, everyone knows the game.

Valerie Fortney, columnist with the *Calgary Herald*, wrote a feature article on the club, and soon the kids were mini-celebrities, appearing in the *Calgary Journal*, too, as well as on CBC and Shaw TV. The club has grown. It's now called Soccer Without Boundaries and is in the process of attaining full charitable status (so if you're looking for a place to make a donation, hint hint).

Jean-Claude was awarded the Queen Elizabeth II Diamond Jubilee Medal for his work and was asked to join the Premier's Council on Culture specifically to look at how to integrate new Canadians into their community through similar programs.

"And now," Jean-Claude notes proudly, "when the teacher asks the kids, 'What did you do on the weekend?' they tell their teacher, 'I played soccer. I'm on a team.'"

# 14

WE HEADED SOUTH FROM KIGALI amid the city's morning crush. Everyone was yielding to everybody and nobody was yielding to anyone: a paradox worthy of Zeno. It was less a rush hour than an ongoing, imminent multi-car pileup that never *quiiiite* happened. Car horns bleating. Diesel engines roaring. Pedestrians dodging through. At one point an oncoming truck veered directly into our lane, lights flashing, horn sounding, before swinging back onto its side of the road. Head-on collision averted? Check. Muzungu in cardiac arrest? Ditto.

"He should have been more patient," Jean-Claude advised.

A gurgling noise came from the back of my throat, which Jean-Claude took as assent.

"Exactly," he said.

The motorbike bravado boys were out in full force, performing their usual acts of death-defying derring-do with a studied nonchalance. As we passed yet another young man with yet another young woman hanging onto him, Jean-Claude said, sort of wistfully, "It must be a wonderful job, driving a taxi-moto at that age. Never boring."

We'd already noticed how, when they had a particularly pretty passenger on board, the boys would handle their bikes more jerkily than usual, gunning and braking in sudden lurches and stuttering false starts, causing the young women in question to squash up against them on the slow-down and then hold on even tighter on the acceleration.

"It's not entirely innocent, is it?" I said, and Jean-Claude agreed.

Were I still a young man, unencumbered by notions of my own mortality, driving a motorcycle taxi up and down the hilly curves of Kigali would be a fine way to earn a living. There was apparently only one female taxi-moto driver in the city—the papers had done a story on her—and we did see the occasional old guy (by which I mean "over thirty"), but generally this was a young man's sport. Who else would be mad enough to weave through oncoming traffic like that?

I'd also come to realize that Rwanda's ubiquitous traffic police, paced out every four feet or so, were mainly ornamental. They stood on guard, ever vigilant, rifles at the ready—doing absolutely nothing. Even when we passed a truly spectacular snarl-up that was crying out for a bold stride and a sternly raised hand, nothing happened. Not that it mattered. Trying to control the flow of vehicles in Kigali would have been like trying to control a flash flood. And anyway, directing traffic didn't seem to fall under their auspices. Case in point: the snarl-up I just mentioned. A giant backhoe had slipped off a flatbed truck and was now sitting half on the asphalt and half on the flatbed's fallen gate. Leaning at a severely lopsided angle, shovel raised like the Karate Kid in mid-pose, it looked ready to topple over at any moment. Traffic had ground to a halt in both directions, and the backhoe's operator had climbed in and was now—rather cleverly, I thought—trying to use the backhoe's own digger to push the machine up, to pivot the rig back onto the truck. Unfortunately, it wasn't working. If anything, it was causing the backhoe to teeter even more precariously.

Fortunately, a crowd of onlookers had gathered to provide the driver with helpful advice. Their suggestions went oddly unappreciated, though, to go by the operator's muttered invective as he yanked first one lever, then another. The heavy treads of the backhoe were starting to chew up the asphalt. Surely, I thought, this is where Kigali's traffic police will spring into action! This is what they'd been training for, waiting for! But no, they just watched like everyone else. Forget the machine guns, I thought. Give them whistles.

The traffic, like water, finally found its own way past, flowing through a nearby gas station parking lot as the crowd of onlookers grew ever thicker and ever more helpful.

The plan had been that Jean-Claude would drive in the cities and I would take over once we got on the highway. That scheme, concocted so confidently over road maps back home, quickly changed. Rwanda, as noted, is the most densely populated nation in continental Africa. There are 11 million people crowded into a country the size of Vermont, and at any one time 10 million of them are walking alongside the road you happen to be driving on. Including the highways.

Even as Kigali fell away, the pedestrians never faltered. The pavement was pullulating with them: men in shimmering suits, schoolchildren en route to class, women with woven baskets high on head, moving by with a consummate ease, and all of them using the highway like a hallway, walking beside traffic, into traffic, *through* traffic.

I had a sickening feeling in my gut. "Jean-Claude," I said, "I can't do it. If I get behind the wheel, I'll kill somebody, I know it."

"Don't worry," he replied. "I enjoy driving."

I felt terrible for having welched on our agreement, though Christine would later laugh off my guilty apologies. "He was relieved you didn't try to drive," she told me. "He doesn't like other people driving. He's a terrible passenger."

I still felt bad, though.

Villages in Rwanda tend to cluster around any excuse for a community—a local market, a rural intersection, a water pump, a slightly wider stretch of road—and although most were of the same "clay boxes packed in tightly" arrangement, the shops themselves were often painted in cymbal crashes of colour. This was a side benefit of Rwanda's booming telecommunications market. Everybody in Rwanda, it seemed, from modest goat herder to titan-like business tycoon, owned their own cell phone, and several large service providers had staked their claim on Rwanda's burgeoning IT sector—visually, as well. In much the same way that Pepsi and Coca-Cola provide signs for small-town corner stores back home, with their product name prominently displayed, Rwanda's cell phone companies will happily paint any shop, anywhere, in any village, be it a butcher's, an apothecary, or a beauty salon, so long as it's adorned with their brand name and, just as importantly, decked out in their company's colours: red for Airtel, blue for Tigo, yellow for MTN, and green for Tigo's money-transfer service. Painted top to bottom, you will find solid-yellow beauty salons, blue bicycle repair shops, and green drugstores endlessly repeated in blocks of colour: *red, blue, yellow, green; red, blue, yellow, green.*

Rwandan villages used to be rather drab, Jean-Claude said. "Just brownish-red clay. Very dull and dusty." But their shopping areas had now been transformed into cubist compositions, lively and bright. (I don't know who is winning the business war, but Tigo seems to be winning the paint war. Blue was generally the preferred colour.)

Jean-Claude and I had MTN phones, so our team colour was yellow, though I do confess I preferred the rich red of Airtel, at least when it came to storefronts. If nothing else, the competition among Rwanda's cell phone providers had been a boon for paint supply companies. Memo to self: *Buy stock in Rwandan paints.*

As we drove on, the grassy bogs of the southern marshes opened up in front of us. If you imagine Rwanda as a tablecloth, and picture a hand pushing across it, the north and west would be where the fabric folds in on itself, bunching up, forming pleated hills and highlands. The southeast corner of the tablecloth would be flatter, lower, less wrinkled.

We'd entered the papyrus swamps of the Bugesera, where some of the most prolonged and horrific massacres of the genocide occurred. Here, in the Bugesera marshlands, the killings stretched on and on into endless days of hunter and hunted, predator and prey. Even today, tillers turn up human bones in the muck.

The Bugesera is also where French journalist Jean Hatzfeld compiled his heartbreaking trilogy of testimonies gathered from survivors and killers alike: *Into the Quick of Life, The Strategy of Antelopes,* and *A Time for Machetes,* that last collection also published under the title *Machete Season: The Killers in Rwanda Speak.*

It's a murky landscape, the Bugesera, lush and treacherous at the same time, a grassy wet terrain of hillocks and soft recesses, where thousands upon thousands of women and children fled only to be hunted down, tormented, tortured, chopped.

"The club is more crushing, but the machete is more natural," one of the killers, a farmer, later explained. "The Rwandan is accustomed to the machete from childhood. Grab a machete—that is what we do every morning. We cut sorghum, we prune banana trees, we hack out vines, we kill chickens ... In the end, a man is like an animal: you give him a whack on the head or the neck, and down he goes."

"We no longer saw them as human beings," another killer recalled. "They were abandoned by everyone, even God."

And though it's difficult to imagine, those who took cover in the sparse forests above the swamps fared even worse. Exposed, trapped on all sides, they were easier to surround, easier to catch. On Kayumba Hill, they started out with 6,000 and ended with twenty.

The daily massacres lasted for weeks on end, became almost routine. The Hutu men would gather in their local town square or soccer field each morning, plan their day, arrange to flush out a certain area or to chase the Tutsis into an ambush, and would then set off in columns, singing.

"We could hear them coming," one survivor recalled.

At night, after the day's killings, the interahamwe and others would celebrate with home-brewed beer, driving minivans fluttering with flags up and down the village streets as though they'd won a soccer championship.

"They were slaughtering our cattle and having barbecues every night. We could hear their songs, could see the smoke rising up from the feasts they were enjoying while we crawled about in the mud digging up root vegetables in the dark." When the wind shifted, the Tutsis in the swamps could catch the smell of meat being grilled.

Descriptions of the starving and ragged people who came out of the marshes after the RPF arrived and the killers had fled often emphasized their animalistic appearance. This was something the killers commented upon as well, even though, as one of the survivors noted bitterly, "We were not the ones who acted like animals."

# 15

SUGAR CANE AND MARSHY PLAINS. Papyrus islands in a sea of reeds. A secretive river twists through; we caught glimpses of muddy water in the grass, snaking around this hillock and that. There is beauty here as well: sun-dappled Monet arrangements of lily pads; flamingos lifting off, improbably white against the green; pelicans taking flight; storks in still water.

The clay-hut homes we drove by looked spectral, seeping smoke from every crack, every open paneless window.

"Cooking fires," Jean-Claude explained. "Gets very smoky inside. Lots of bronchial problems."

We passed banana-burdened bicycles shepherded by gaunt men, faces thinly stretched, peddlers in every sense. Vignettes appeared and were gone: a procession of brightly wrapped women, gourds perfectly balanced, walking to their local market like a royal cortège. A little boy with a goat on a tether pulls—and is pulled in turn.

We have come looking for a pair of churches, at Ntarama and Nyamata. A red earth road branches off from the main highway, and Jean-Claude follows the ruts past one crossroads tavern named Le Calme Bar, another named Rendez-vous.

An old man offered us a broken smile, more gum than tooth in his grin. He was leaning on a staff and wearing a traditional floppy-brimmed hat that marked him as a Tutsi cattle herder. *Had he survived in the swamps? In the hills?*

When the killings started, Tutsis crowded into the small red-brick church in Ntarama, seeking sanctuary under its sheet-metal roof. This was God's house. They thought they would be safe here, that the sanctity of the site would protect them. But they were wrong. The killers allowed the Tutsis to gather, encouraged it even. It would make it easier to kill them when the time came. There would be no need to run them down in the marshes, no need to track them through the boggy grass. In Ntarama they would be corralled into one spot, like livestock. Nor did they need ID cards to separate Tutsis from Hutu; in villages like Ntarama, everyone knew everyone. These were their neighbours.

Jean-Claude pulled over and parked, and we walked up a grassy path to where the church stood in a shaded grove of trees. On the front of the building, blister marks from the grenades were still visible. Sledgehammered holes in the walls showed where the killers had punched their way through the bricks, with scorch marks fanning upward from the openings, making the church look like a kiln. It brought to mind images of Auschwitz. Of ovens.

The people inside had fought back with what few weapons they had, with bricks and stones and their bare hands. The killers had grenades and machetes and clubs impaled with nails. Then the Presidential Guard arrived. Those few who managed to break through the circle fled to the marshes, where fresh horrors awaited.

Inside Ntarama church, a broken cross leans through a window. ID cards marked TUTSI, a handful of coins, a pair of eyeglasses, and a few discarded shoes were scattered in front of the altar. Caskets draped in cloth were lined up on the bench-like pews. These caskets held the symbolic remains of a hundred victims, representing just a small portion of the 5,000 who died here. Above the coffins the rafters were hung with the matted clothing of victims, a memorial more haunting than any statistic.

Behind the main building were the church kitchen and the Sunday school. Piles of debris. Flip-flops. Broken plates. A wall where the children were killed. *"The child of a snake is still a snake!"* Toddlers and babies-in-arms, battered into nothingness, followed by immolation. A large cooking pot, brittle from the fire, lay heaped amid the everyday aspects of life. Mouldering blankets, foam mattresses, a fallen kitchen cabinet, a child's slipper, a hairbrush, a ladle—all of it rendered in grey by fire and dust. The bodies have been removed, but the rest remains as it was twenty years before. Outside, the rest of Rwanda marched ever onward, but here the past was ever-present. In the stillness, time had slowed to a trickle.

Before I left for Rwanda, I met with Lynn Gran. She was with the Nature Conservancy of Canada but had previously worked for Oxfam, which was among the first NGOs to enter Rwanda immediately after the genocide.

"No one wanted to go, so I volunteered," she said. "To this day, I really don't know why. I had a six-year-old son and a two-year-old daughter back in Canada."

Lynn crossed into Rwanda under harrowing conditions and was taken to a church just like this one. When she arrived, the bodies were still piled up inside.

"I didn't want to be there. It felt too personal. But I was told, 'You are here to bear witness to what happened.' The iron gates of the church were mangled—you can imagine the force used to blow it open and how it would have felt to be inside. When we entered it was dark, and I had to stand a moment to let my eyes adjust. The smell was overpowering. Bodies were heaped everywhere, in the pews, on the floor, with their clothes decomposing. As I moved through the dark, I tripped, and when I looked down it was a woman's leg. I started to cry. I started to cry and I couldn't stop."

There were children's toys and human heads on the altar.

"They'd beheaded them and then lined them up and left them there. I'm not a religious person. Spiritual, I suppose. Not religious. But when I was in that church, I knew."

"Knew what?" I asked.

"That I was in the presence of evil."

# 16

THE HUB TOWN for the Bugesera region is Nyamata. Once a grim spot with a grim reputation—dripping on the edge of malarial swamps in the wet season, choking on dust and drought in the dry—Nyamata today is a city revived. Many of the marshy meadows have been reclaimed. The major roads are paved, and trade is humming.

Nyamata may have the widest main street in Rwanda. It forms a spacious boulevard lined with shop fronts and idling buses, with taxi-motos and their lower-end bicycle equivalents. Loud ad hoc market negotiations flared and faded. Escalating arguments, sudden laughter. Women splitting the crowds, moving through, baskets on head, babies on back. Twenty-four-hour gas stations chugging out petrol, pharmacies and finance centres, taverns and beauty salons, cobblers and charcoal vendors, butchers and bakers and—somewhere in there, I'm sure—candlestick makers, or kerosene sellers at least, which would be the Rwandan equivalent. We parked and waded through the streets, past the Heroes Pub and the Red Lion Tavern, the internet cafés and auto-parts emporiums—all sporting fresh paint—down to a soft bower where the girls sashayed and the young men ached.

There were rows of lively little taverns, all leading to the same small square with its plaque reminding us that in Rwanda you cannot escape 1994, even on a boy-beguiling promenade or a sit-and-stretch park bench. This town—this park—was once a hub of a different sort, the epicentre of Bugesera's genocidal pogroms, a focal point and meeting ground for the killers.

*We could hear them singing as they gathered, singing and beating their drums as they came toward us. One day they followed one path, the next day another. They grew silent only when they were about to attack, as they did not want to give away their positions.*

The killers burned even the photo albums after they'd looted a house, wanting to erase not only the people who had died there but any trace that they had ever existed. Had the RPF advance been delayed even a week longer, it is likely there would have been not a single Tutsi left in the Bugesera—and no witnesses either.

Today, convicted killers wander the streets of Nyamata freely, as they do elsewhere in Rwanda. A presidential pardon released thousands of lower-ranked génocidaires from prison, for reasons not so much of mercy as mathematics.

In the aftermath of the genocide, an International Criminal Tribunal for Rwanda (ICTR) was set up in neighbouring Tanzania to prosecute the key figures involved in the genocide. Colonel Bagosora, for one, was captured in Cameroon trying to cash traveller's cheques he'd looted from the Rwanda state treasury. He was then transported to the ICTR, where he was charged and convicted in the murder of the ten Belgian peacekeepers, as well as in the death of Prime Minister Agathe Uwilingiyimana and others. (He was also indicted for the assassination of President Habyarimana, but the evidence wasn't conclusive enough for a conviction.)

The overwhelming majority of cases, though, were tried in Rwanda. More than 120,000 people were held in squalid, unsanitary conditions in a prison system designed for 15,000. Rwanda's decimated judicial system was overwhelmed. At one point, it was estimated that it would have taken 200 years to process all the cases before the courts.

It soon became clear that to execute everyone responsible would have required a genocide of its own. During the RPF advance, thousands of people accused of being involved with the killings had been summarily executed in extra-judicial killings (which led to at least 400 RPF soldiers being arrested), and in 1998 twenty-two of the Hutu Power ringleaders were marched out to face firing squads. But passing a death sentence on 120,000 people? That was not an option. Instead, Rwanda did something remarkable: it abolished capital punishment and reinstituted traditional *gacaca* or "patch of grass" courts instead, wherein the lesser accused and their victims' families would meet face-to-face under the direction of locally chosen judges. Punishment would be decided by the community, and confession and repentance would mitigate sentencing. The goal was truth and reconciliation; it was an imperfect solution to an almost intractable problem.

In 2003, President Kagame went even further, signing the first in a series of sweeping presidential decrees that would see more than 30,000 rank-and-file génocidaires released. Often only contrition, "re-education," and regular community service were required to make amends for their crimes—much to the anguish of survivors, who were now forced to live alongside the men who had killed their families or done horrible things to them and their loved ones. These survivors are re-traumatized every time they pass one of their former tormentors on a cattle path or run into them at the market or in a bar, drinking banana beer in the darkened corners, watching.

In Nyamata, the church lies in a quiet area on the outside of town. It's larger than the one in nearby Ntarama, though it shares the same modest brick-wall and sheet-metal-roof design. As in Ntarama, thousands of frightened people crammed themselves into the church here when the madness began. Like those who had sought refuge at Ntarama, they thought the killers wouldn't attack a house of worship. And like those who sought refuge in Ntarama, they were wrong.

Inside the shadow-box interior: an altar cloth draped in the sepia stains of dried blood; a baptismal font pocked with bullet holes; a punctured ceiling letting in spikes of sun with Mary in the half-light, hands held out somewhere between embrace and surrender. Our Lady of the Sorrows.

At Nyamata, the clothes of the victims have been left on the pews. Mounds of mouldering cloth, twenty years later: it is a visceral image, a fist constricting around your heart. A heart wrapped in thorns. The taste of rust permeates. Scattered across the altar are the rosaries and hymnals of the dead, and everywhere, those death-sentence identity cards marked TUTSI.

Behind Nyamata church, in underground crypts that smell of earth and old root cellars, the recovered skulls and accompanying bones of 10,000 dead have been exhumed and are now lined up on shelves. When you descend the narrow stairs into the claustrophobic confines of these vaults, you expect it to be eerie, but it isn't. It's not fearful. It's sad, devastatingly so. It's a sadness deeper than hymns, heavier than dirt, as numbing as novocaine.

Standing in the sunlight again, Jean-Claude and I were quiet for a long while.

I didn't know what to say, and when Jean-Claude finally spoke, his voice sounded distant and faint, like someone on the other side of a wall. "The new airport they're building, it will be near here."

I nodded.

"It will be better. When it's finished."

I nodded again.

We'd seen signs of the coming boom on our drive in: pre-emptory hotels in place, incongruous four-lane thoroughfares running through banana plantations. Once the Bugesera International Airport opened, this region would become a key commercial zone, charged with energy. As we drove back through the falling dusk toward the lights of Kigali, all I could hope was that once the businessmen and tourists began pouring in, to be shuttled by sedan and air-conditioned coach from Rwanda's sleek new airport to the conference centres in the capital, some of them would find the time to make a small detour to the churches nearby at Ntarama and Nyamata, to stand awhile among the ghosts of Rwanda's past.

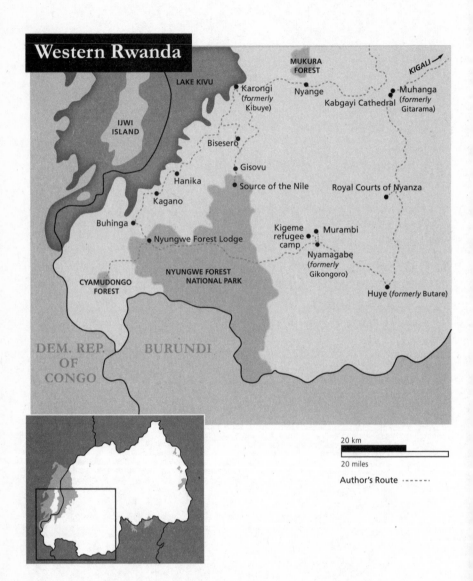

Western Rwanda

MUKURA FOREST

KIGALI

LAKE KIVU

Karongi (formerly Kibuye)

Nyange

Muhanga (formerly Gitarama)

Kabgayi Cathedral

IJWI ISLAND

Bisesero

Gisovu

Hanika

Source of the Nile

Royal Courts of Nyanza

Kagano

Buhinga

Nyungwe Forest Lodge

Kigeme refugee camp

Murambi

Nyamagabe (formerly Gikongoro)

CYAMUDONGO FOREST

NYUNGWE FOREST NATIONAL PARK

Huye (formerly Butare)

DEM. REP. OF CONGO

BURUNDI

20 km

20 miles

Author's Route

# PART TWO

## "WE ARE ALL RWANDANS"

# 17

THE TRANSPORT TRUCKS THAT BLAST past us on blind corners advertise the specific leap of faith they are making. On the back, sides, and front of their vehicles: ornate messages written in florid curlicues and rooster-plume hues.

Jean-Claude helped decipher the religious affiliations as they blurred by.

"*Bwana Asifiwe,* that's Swahili," he said, shouting to be heard. "It means 'Praise the Lord,' so we can tell that driver is a born-again Christian. And that one is in Kinyarwanda. *Imana Niyonkuru.* It means 'God Is Great!' So we know that truck driver is Muslim."

Minibus drivers had their own theological good-luck slogans, often in English and painted in the same plum-berry purples and parrot greens: ONLY GOD and TRUST GOD and GOD IS KING and THE LORD IS GOD.

*Trust God,* I thought. *But maybe check the brakes while you're at it.*

One minibus was aptly named "Patience." A tanker truck rumbled by with its motto, written in French, proclaiming JESUS IS MY SAVIOUR, while the taxicab following in its slipstream boasted a cheerfully informal THANKS GOD.

Other forms of faith vied for our attention as well. Amid the entreaties to Jesus, God, and Allah were trucks and minibuses emblazoned with the names "Messi" and "Iniesta," "Rooney" and "Ronaldo." Appeals to the soccer gods of Barcelona and Manchester, Arsenal and Madrid, they were given the same divine radiance.

"A different type of saviour," I shouted.

Jean-Claude laughed. "That's true. Soccer is like a religion here, especially the English Premier League. The players are like saints. And I don't know which faith is stronger!"

We were heading west, out of the city. The motorcycle taxi boys had given way to heavier traffic, but the pedestrians remained undaunted. Women in bright patterns, hips swaying, with gourds and gunnysacks balancing on their heads, glided through, avoiding oncoming vehicles with a matador's ease. A roadside cobbler worked on a pair of men's shoes while the customer, in suit and tie, stood patiently in stocking feet on a piece of cardboard.

From Kigali, the road dipped into a marshy flood plain, then climbed back into the hills—up, up, up. My ears popped, then popped again. Every bend in the road had a sign warning of a sharp turn ahead, but I didn't know why they'd bothered; they could simply have posted one sign at the start with "etc." written underneath it. This was less a highway than a series of corners joined together.

*Land of a thousand hills,* and we were going to cross them all.

We occasionally got stuck behind the black-cloud coughs of a transport truck trailing bicyclists who had hitched rides on the back like suckerfish on a shark, one hand on the vehicle's rear bumper, the other on their handlebars. These bicyclists would often have passengers—and sometimes these passengers would have babies wrapped tightly onto their backs. It was like watching a Flying Fellini circus act. Jean-Claude always held back in case one of the bicycles fell in front of our tires.

"The truck drivers don't mind when bicyclists catch a ride like that," Jean-Claude assured me. "It's like giving someone a lift. With so many steep hills, you have to."

The highway curved through contoured heights, layered in green. Rice paddies filled the valleys below, stirring up memories of Indonesia, of southern Japan. It was all very familiar. And for good reason: agronomists from Asia had been brought in to improve rice cultivation. With so much of the population still supporting itself through subsistence farming, local governments were looking to increase crop diversification as well. They were also investing in programs to prevent soil erosion and loss of forest habitat. It was the start of what's being heralded as Rwanda's Green Revolution.

Homes scaled the steep slopes above us in acts of architectural audacity that defied both gravity and common sense. The sheet-metal rooftops were like mirrors in the heat, reflecting the sun so sharply that it hurt your eyes to look at them. These were the rooftops of the new and improved, cement-walled homes that were going up across Rwanda, replacing the crumbling mud walls and clay roof tiles of another era. The new buildings, simple designs reminiscent of Monopoly pieces, were part of a massive public housing initiative. It is one thing to admire the folkloric appeal of traditional mud-dried homes, another to live in them. Asking Africans to preserve these is like asking North Americans to remain in sod huts.

A light rain had settled the dust and brought out the greens in the fields. Pineapples and plantain. The silvery grey of eucalyptus. In the fall-away glens below us, the treetops swayed like feather dusters.

Markets, large and small, passed by as the traffic pushed us through a series of ridge-top villages, with the street stalls and storefronts crowding in against each other. *Red, green, yellow, blue.* Children broke like birds around us, running alongside our vehicle, flippity-flop, yelling, *"Muzungu, muzungu!"* I held my hand outside the window, let the wind carry it, riding updrafts.

We came through a narrow cleft in the hills and dropped suddenly into Gitarama.

Gitarama City (or Muhanga, as it is now known) feels like a simplified rendering of Kigali: same hills (only hillier), same incongruous office towers arranged on the hilltops, same hairpin turns buckling through, same kinetic energy—just tighter, more compact. The same women, umbrellas raised to the heat, bundles on head and babies on back, moved through with the same poise, only more so. (There being fewer sidewalks in Gitarama, the streets required even more pirouetting, traffic-avoiding matador moves than Kigali.)

Gitarama was the home of Rwanda's first president, Grégoire Kayibanda, co-author of the Hutu Manifesto. It was here that the leaders of the Hutu Social Revolution declared Rwanda a republic, and it was here also that Kayibanda died, assassinated in slow motion. Overthrown in a military coup, Kayibanda was locked inside his house with his wife and left to starve to death by his successor and former protégé, Juvénal Habyarimana.

Today, anti-corruption billboards in Gitarama City exhort the population to stay united, work together, get tested for HIV. Other billboards featured strongly worded warnings about gender-based violence, reminding husbands, YOUR WIFE IS NOT YOUR PROPERTY.

Government employees had gathered in reluctant ranks in front of their workplaces to exercise.

"It is required for all public employees," Jean-Claude said. "Every Friday at two o'clock."

Mandatory office calisthenics: it was very much comparable to what one sees in Japan or South Korea. I could almost hear the familiar *"Ichi, ni, san!"* as we passed.

Office workers, women in constricting skirts and soft-middled men in neckties, trying desperately to touch their toes. It was an endearing sight.

Beyond the exercising bureaucrats, we passed a newly painted mosque, followed in quick succession by a Pentecostal Revival Hall and a large Seventh-Day Adventist compound, with several other churches and chapels in between. Muslim men in embroidered caps and flowing white robes poured past as a fluster of nuns hurried the other way. A Catholic priest stopped in a doorway to mop his brow with a handful of handkerchief.

Other sanctuaries were on tap as well: taverns and pubs with inviting names like Rest Stop Tranquile and Calm Yourself Bar. They offered pockets of quiet among the crowded, traffic-choked streets of the city. Theirs was a promise of oasis, of transient salvation. Throughout our trip, whenever Jean-Claude stopped to stretch, I would wander off to find a tavern. I liked Rwandan pubs, even if their patrons weren't overly gregarious, were often reserved. This, of course, was undoubtedly due to my presence; to be a muzungu in Africa is to exist in an observer-affected universe, and the dynamic of any place shifted when I walked in. Still, I found the taverns welcoming, if a little wary, sort of like strolling into one of the many clenched pubs in Northern Ireland.

Rwandan taverns were always much larger than they looked on the outside. The front, usually just a slab of adobe, opened up onto a warren of smaller rooms arranged around a central, packed-earth courtyard. The reaction when I entered was always entertaining: the bartender's perfectly executed double take, the surreptitious glances exchanged between customers, the silence pregnant with unasked questions. "Hello, everybody!" I'd say cheerfully, and they would nod, mumble *"Bonjour."*

The toilets in these taverns were usually of the squat and strain variety: a simple hole in the floor with a bucket beside to sluice it with. (One brought one's own squashed roll of pocketed toilet paper. Handy travel tip #1.) I was fine with this. Only problem was, every now and then, at the more "upscale" taverns, they would employ a young woman to sweep and clean and, yes, sluice the toilets for guests after they'd used them. I really, *really* didn't want to take advantage of this service. "No, honest, I'll sluice my own toilet, just point me in the direction of the bucket and I'll— No, really! Don't go in there!" I would say, trying to block the young woman's entry. This would rouse the perplexed curiosity of other people in the bar, who would crane their heads to peer down the hallway and see what all the commotion was about. *Muzungus were weird, no doubt about it.*

Sadly, as much as I appreciated their clay-cooled interiors and oversized, underchilled bottles of beer, as the trip went on I found myself visiting these taverns less and less. Being of chatty Oirish stock, I don't enjoy drinking alone, and I could never inveigle Jean-Claude into joining me for a lukewarm pint of Primus.

"You go ahead," he'd say. "We'll meet back here later."

As we drove past the beckoning bars of Gitarama City, which looked sleek and urbane, and almost certainly featured luxurious indoor plumbing rather than a sluice bucket, I made yet another sally, asking Jean-Claude for the umpteenth time, "Are you *sure* you don't drink? And more to the point, are you sure you don't want to start?"

He laughed on the mistaken assumption that I was joking. "You know, Will, I have never had even a single drink of alcohol in my life, ever."

"So how do you know you don't like it? Maybe if you gave it a try …"

"Oh, I don't think Christine"—his wife and fellow teetotaller—"would be very happy."

"Who's going to tell her?" I asked, taking on the role of the prover-bial devil-on-one's-shoulder. To no avail, alas. I even tried countering with an appeal to Proverbs 31:6, one of the few Biblical passages my father ever quoted— *"Give beer to those who are perishing, wine to those in need"* (or Boodles Gin in my dad's case)—again, to no effect.

I really have to work on my "corrupting the souls of others" technique.

# 18

SOUTH OF GITARAMA CITY, on a palm-lined avenue, we came to Kabgayi Cathedral, seat of the country's first Catholic bishop and still a fulcrum of faith in Rwanda.

Kabgayi is referred to as the "Vatican of Rwanda," and its cathe-dral is an understated yet stately affair, rising up cleanly from the open grounds around it, red bricks and a raised metal roof, with a seminary, a hospital, and a convent attached—as well as a small, half-forgotten museum in behind the main building that was chock-ablock with eclectic pre-colonial relics, each labelled in French with fountain-pen ink under dust as thick as dryer lint. This museum alone was reason enough to stop. The buffet was just a bonus.

A word or two about Rwandan buffets: before we left Kigali, we'd stopped in at the RDB office to pick up the park permits and paper-work for our trip. The head of Tourism and Conservation was an engaging young woman named Rica Rwigamba.

"We see Rwanda as a *boutique* tourist destination" is how she put it. The RDB wasn't looking for free-wheeling budget travellers or youth hostel layabouts. No rat-tailed backpackers, no low-end bus tours. Instead, Rwanda was positioning itself as a higher-end, lower-impact, eco-friendly travel destination with fewer guests staying longer—and spending more money. "Quality not quantity" was the rule of thumb in attracting visitors. They wanted to become a Botswana rather than a Kenya. A Costa Rica rather than a Mexico.

"We'd rather get $1,000 from a single visitor than $100 from ten different people" was how one tour company operator explained it.

Rica agreed. "We're a small country and our main attractions revolve around conservation. There is a limit to the number of people we can bring in."

The biggest challenge?

"Building a service-based economy," she said with a weary sigh.

Rwanda's hotels and restaurants were notorious for their slow, almost languid service. A two-hour wait for a meal wasn't uncommon. The rest of the country was crackling with energy, but the service sectors hadn't caught up, even though tourism revenue had grown exponentially over the last five years.

Across the hall from Rica's office was that of Vivian Kayitesi, yet another smart, educated, engaging young woman. Vivian was the RDB's head of Investment Promotion and Implementation, and she concurred with Rica. "Oh, it's a challenge," she said, with the same sort of sigh Rica had given.

Changing a country's core cultural perceptions about the value of prompt and attentive service was a difficult undertaking. "But an important one," she stressed. "Not only for tourists, but for Rwandans also. In the public sector, too. In government departments, we should be able to expect certain standards of service."

Much is made of Rwanda's high population density, as though the country were a ticking demographic time bomb. But Rwanda's population density is less than that of South Korea and roughly on par with that of Holland, and no one is fretting about the Dutch homeland being "full." The Rwandan diaspora continues to return; opportunities abound, and no one is turned away. More than three million

people have repatriated since 1994. They come from France and
Germany, from Belgium and Switzerland, from neighbouring
African countries, and from Canada, the U.S., and the U.K., and
they bring with them a new energy, new ideas, and much-needed
skill sets. They often find work in banking and hospitality, in IT
and education. Today, Rwanda has one of the most international
populations in Africa, at least in the larger cities like Kigali and
Gitarama. And members of this diaspora, coming home in some
cases after generations abroad in North America or Europe, have
rankled at the often lackadaisical approach that's greeted them when
they arrive. It was the members of this diaspora, impatient and
pushing for better customer service, who had been spearheading the
move to establish higher standards—even if it was something as
simple as showing up for an event on time.

The goal is to transform Rwanda into not only a knowledge-based
economy but a middle-income, service-based economy as well. It's
been a long, uphill slog from the sounds of it. Rica and Vivian were
both members of the diaspora, exiles returned, determined to help
rebuild and reshape their country, yet frustrated at times in their
efforts. Which brings us back to the Rwandan talent for buffets. (You
thought I'd forgotten the topic at hand.)·

With the economy and country on the move, the average Rwandan
can no longer afford to take the entire afternoon off to eat lunch. The
solution? A sharp increase in the number of buffets. Rwandan cui-
sine, with its simmering pots of *matoke* plantain, its slow-roasted
goat brochettes and beef stews served on shovelfuls of rice, its skew-
ered tilapia and the belly-ballast of ugali dumplings, lent itself well to
buffet-style eateries.

Simple ingredients in rich sauces, cauldrons of spiced soups and
savoury stews: Rwandan fare was simple, yet still hearty—with one
notable exception. I speak here of the ongoing travesty that is
Rwandan chicken. How to describe the experience of ordering
"chicken" in Rwanda? Imagine something that is not so much fried
as *dried,* a sort of chicken jerky, stringy and sinewy, more bone than

meat and with a skin the thickness—and taste—of broiled bark, though with less nutritional value. Faced with such an offering, one tries in vain to tear off a few measly orts from the withered drumsticks, only to end up gnawing on the bones, which are actually more edible than the rest of the bird.

These were birds that spent their lives dodging traffic on swift, scrawny legs. "Rwandan chickens are marathon runners," Jean-Claude liked to joke.

So when he and I discovered that Kabgayi Cathedral ran a guest house *and* a lunch buffet, we astutely avoided the chicken … while lunging into everything else. I made several trips, trying a bit of this, a bit of that.

The staff who topped up the heat trays and ran the till and cleared the tables took an abiding interest in what I was putting on my plate every time I went up. I ascribed their fascination to cultural curiosity—I was, after all, the only pink face in the crowd.

Jean-Claude, meanwhile, had noticed the sheer amount of food his fellow Rwandans were piling onto their plates. He found it mildly embarrassing.

"Look how much they are putting on," he said, under his breath. "Even dessert at the same time!" Pastry and pineapple heaped onto the same dish as the stewed meat and fried vegetables, with everything on top of everything. He shook his head at the gaucheness of it.

Jean-Claude and I were more genteel, taking modest portions over several forays. The fruit trays were especially inviting. Jean-Claude kept going back for more passion fruit.

"These are so hard to find in Canada! And when you do, they are very expensive and are not tasty," he said, scooping out the jelly-like seedy pulp of *just one more*. (By the end of the trip, I'd begun to suspect that the real name for passion fruit was "just one more.")

I, meanwhile, was captivated by the cantaloupes, a fruit I don't even like—at least, not in the woody, fibrous, fruit-cocktail-filler version I was used to back home. Here, the melons were mouth-meltingly good; it was like eating slices of summer.

Filled to the brim with mangoes and passion fruit, to say nothing of the stewed plantain and kebabs, we finally decided to see the actual cathedral.

An airy interior. Cool and muggy at the same time. The stained-glass light that streamed in formed coloured shafts on the cathedral's Stations of the Cross, which lined the walls in mosaic-work arrangements. The power of the mob, the suffering of the innocent. A carpenter from Galilee, forced to carry the instrument of his own impending death, whipped by cords, mocked by the crowds. Here, he stumbles. Here, he rises. Here, he falters amid small acts of mercy: a drink of water, a shoulder to share the burden. It might well have been the Stations of Rwanda.

During the genocide, tens of thousands of people packed themselves into the ecclesiastical grounds and cavernous interior of Kabgayi Cathedral, asking for mercy. But as at Sainte Famille in Kigali, where Jean-Claude's brother and sister had sought refuge, Kabgayi instead became a concentration camp. Soldiers came in daily to drag away victims—some identified on lists, others at random—or to choose a frightened woman from the crowd to sate other appetites. As the days turned to weeks, starvation and disease took its toll. Skeletal thin, the bodies began to pile up.

Church and state have always been intimately linked in Rwanda. After the conversion of the Tutsi king in 1943, the entire population followed suit, making it one of the quickest and most thorough mass conversions ever recorded, described by missionaries as a "tornado." Almost overnight, Rwanda had become a Christian kingdom in the heart of Africa.

President Kayibanda of Hutu Manifesto notoriety was a devout Catholic and former seminarian, and following Rwanda's independence the Catholic Church became the de facto state religion, intricately tied to the Hutu government. Juvénal Habyarimana, the man who overthrew Kayibanda, was a devout Catholic as well, and he strengthened these ties even more. Under two successive dictatorships, the Catholic Church became the most powerful organization in Rwanda (after the government itself). The archbishop sat on the central committee of the ruling party, and the Church had a lock on education. It supported ethnic ID cards and racial quotas and actively encouraged the insidious Hamitic myth that had entrenched these divisions. High-ranking bishops were often outspoken in their support of the genocidal regime, arguing that Tutsis were irredeemably "bad" by nature, a form of original sin, a mark of Cain.

"Regrettably, the Church took the side of the political regime," Rwandan human rights commissioner Tom Ndahiro writes. "It did not denounce political and social injustices, nor did it condemn the first killings, nor those which followed."

Indeed, many who took part thought they were doing the will of the Church. Rwandan theologian Laurien Ntezimana explained it thusly: "Rwandese know how to obey but they do not know how to dialogue.... The church has always exalted the virtue of obedience, and if you talk to ordinary people they will tell you that many of the massacres happened because they blindly obeyed the authorities."

Many individual priests and pastors, nuns and deacons, risked their lives to protect Tutsis and denounce the violence. But they did so without the official sanction or support of the Church, and they paid the price. More than 200 nuns and priests were killed during the genocide, a quarter of the country's clergy, and many of them died in a state of grace. But the sad fact is that many high-ranking priests, bishops, and even nuns took part in the killings, encouraging the gangs, providing information, and even picking up a club themselves when needed. Prominent Catholic, Anglican, and Seventh-Day Adventist clergy have all been implicated. Several have been arrested and convicted. Many more are still on the lam, fugitives from the truth.

By the time the genocide began, Rwanda was the most Christianized country in Africa. Fully 90 percent identified themselves as Christian, and of these, 65 percent belonged to the Catholic Church. Hutus and Tutsis went to the same Sunday services, sat on the same pews, sang from the same hymnals. In previous genocidal campaigns, Tutsis had run to the churches and been safe there. But this time, there would be no shelter. The places where victims should have received sanctuary—hospitals, schools, and especially churches—became prime killing fields. During the genocide, more people were killed in churches and on church grounds than anywhere else.

Under crowded and filthy conditions, without water or food, the ragged people inside Kabgayi Cathedral prayed and prayed for a salvation that never came.

On the complicity of the churches in Rwanda, Christian philosopher David P. Gushee came to a crushing conclusion: "Long study of the Holocaust, and now fresh study of the Rwandan genocide, has led me to the heartbroken realization that the presence of Churches in a country guarantees exactly *nothing*. The self-identification of people with the Christian faith guarantees exactly *nothing*. All of the clerical garb and regalia, all of the structures of religious accountability … guarantee exactly *nothing*."

Those few who managed to survive the Dachau of Kabgayi were rescued not by UN troops but by the RPF. Under the directives of Paul Kagame, the RPF's main force had continued its advance, sweeping around Kigali while the battle for the capital still raged, and then pushing forward, driving a wave of refugees in front of them. Hundreds of thousands of Hutu civilians, fearful that the RPF was intent on exterminating them in the same way they had tried to exterminate the Tutsis, had fled, emptying villages and leaving the landscape eerily quiet. There would be no "revenge genocide," but those who had taken part in the killings had reason to fear the RPF's arrival. RPF soldiers often dealt harshly with alleged perpetrators. At one point, Kagame had to issue a direct order to his troops to stop these summary executions. Even then, revenge killings and massacres continued as the advancing RPF forces came across the charred bodies of family and friends. Imagine a Jewish army invading Germany in 1944 only to discover the gas chambers and mass graves, the emaciated prisoners in Nazi concentration camps. Now imagine telling them to show restraint.

As the RPF closed in, the interahamwe militia and government troops at Kabgayi went on a final killing frenzy before they retreated, leaving mountains of dead bodies behind. The RPF soldiers took possession not of a cathedral but a slaughterhouse. More than 30,000 people lay dead in the region around Kabgayi. Later estimates put it as high as 64,000—and yes, you read those numbers right.

The Catholic Archbishop of Kigali was there to greet the RPF. A former collaborator with the Habyarimana regime, the archbishop was now very ingratiating, very obsequious to the new rulers. He was shot and killed, along with three other bishops and ten priests, by the RPF soldiers assigned to guard them—something that outraged the Catholic Church much more than the murder of women and children that had just occurred in the same area. (Try as I may, I've never understood why the life of a priest is worth more than that of a child.) The four soldiers responsible—teenagers, according to the RPF, who had lost their families in the genocide and blamed the Church—were duly arrested, with one killed trying to escape. Or so it is claimed. The outcome of their courts martial remains murky and difficult to determine.

As Jean-Claude and I left Kabgayi Cathedral, a site of mass murder and madness, I thought again about the meaning of buffets and the understandable yet profoundly unfair demands being made by Rwandan returnees on those who survived the horrors of 1994.

Members of the diaspora have been pivotal to the country's remarkable turnaround: they've injected capital and technological know-how into a Rwandan society cauterized by violence, and the results have been electric, like the jolt of a defibrillator to a dying heart. These returnees are building hotels and running banks and launching enterprises with an undeniable vigour. But lost amid the noise and excitement, the breathless sense of opportunity that is everywhere in evidence, is the fact that this is still a traumatized country. To ask a people who have suffered through something as unspeakable as a genocide to now perk up and join the boosterism of a new and improved Rwanda may be asking too much.

"There are tensions, for sure," Jean-Claude said, "between the people that were here in the genocide and those people who grew up outside. It is like a kind of wall. The people on the other side have trouble imagining what it was like."

Many survivors of the genocide are barely getting by. They move through life feeling numb, tormented by memories, often mired in poverty and pain. For them to watch as Rwandan exiles from other countries come swooping in, enjoying a material success untroubled by bad dreams and waking nightmares, well, it can rankle.

I now saw Rwandan buffets for what they were: an attempted solution to a deep social divide. Not between Tutsi and Hutu, not even between expat expectations and embedded cultural habits, but between the newly arrived and those still reeling, between the lucky and the wounded.

Jean-Claude was no longer with the Catholic Church, but still considered himself a Christian. It remained a big part of who he was. Being a typical, vaguely non-religious North American, I was puzzled by his ongoing commitment.

As we drove through the beautiful hills of Rwanda, I asked him, "How do you do it? How do you keep your faith after something like that?"

"It can be difficult," he admitted. "We have a saying in Rwanda, kind of like a proverb. *'Imana yilirwa ahandi igataha i Rwanda.'* It means, in the daytime God travels far away, but at night he returns to Rwanda. Every night he comes home to these hills. God sleeps in Rwanda."

# 19

LUCK COMES IN MANY GUISES.

"When my brother Elisé was ten years old he was kidnapped by Somali truck drivers," Jean-Claude said. "It was his good fortune. And mine."

We were sitting in a small café taking respite from the road, Jean-Claude with his inevitable bottled water, me with my equally inevitable Primus beer.

"I was maybe six years old when he was snatched," Jean-Claude explained. "This was after my mother died. What happened was, near my auntie's house, there was a motor park for international trucking companies with these big trucks, and the drivers they were from Kenya, Tanzania, Congo, Somalia. Lots of people everywhere. Somalians were known for long-distance driving, and me and my brother, we looked like we were Somalian. Our hair was very soft, our features were narrow, we were thinner. Even today, if I walk down a street in Calgary and a Somali sees me, he tries to speak to me in the Somalian language."

The truck drivers were convinced that Jean-Claude and his brother were the offspring of a Somali man and a local woman, probably forgotten, possibly abandoned.

"They thought maybe a truck driver had been with a girl and then he just ran away, or maybe didn't even know that he has children here, or maybe he did, but went away, had an accident, and has died and never came back. They thought *something* must have happened. For them it was like, *These children, they are our children.* They asked me and my brother if we wanted a ride in their truck. They said we could, but only if we really were Somalian. My brother Elisé, he wanted a ride in one of these big trucks, so he said, 'Yeah, we're from Somalia.' He got in. And we lost him. For me, I didn't talk with the Somalis because I was little and my auntie always said, 'Stay away from those truck drivers!' But my brother, he wasn't shy like that."

When Jean-Claude's father found out what had happened, he was distraught.

"He knew Somalians took my brother, so a search went out. But they couldn't find the trail. They even sent a message to Uganda because the main highway was going there, was passing through. But the Uganda police, they asked, 'Okay, which truck? Which driver? What's the licence plate?' We didn't know."

"That must have been horrible."

"Oh, it was devastating. For the whole family. Especially, I missed him. We used to play together, we used to fight, we used to laugh. If anyone was being a bully to me, I would call Elisé. He was my big brother. Losing him was very tough."

"What became of him?"

"We didn't know, not for many years. But what we found out was, this truck driver and his wife adopted him as their son. He was raised as a Muslim. They changed his name to Saïd. Hussein Saïd Abdi. A completely Somalian name. He learned to speak Somalian fluently. He grew up in that environment."

"Was he treated well?"

"Oh, very well. They loved him too much. And when the family moved to Kenya, my brother went too. He was working with his Somali dad, driving trucks."

Eight years after he first disappeared, Elisé returned. Or rather, *Saïd* returned.

"He just showed up at our house. It was a shock. He had driven a truck to Kigali, so he came to see us. We were very surprised, because here he was almost a man now, eighteen years, no longer a child."

"Did he stay?"

"He was planning to, yes. But after three months, he said 'I'm going home.' He didn't fit in here anymore, so he went back to Kenya. He was a truck driver and his work and business was there, so he left."

"Your dad must have been heartbroken."

"I think more he was thankful just to know what happened to his son, to know that nothing bad had befallen him."

And so, once again, Jean-Claude's brother drove away.

"That could just as easily have been you," I said. "Had you gotten into that truck when you were six."

Jean-Claude nodded. "Would have been a very different life," he said. "Very different."

Later on, his brother Saïd sent a letter to their dad, along with a photograph of himself in Nairobi. No address, just a photo. But in the background was a clue, and it was this clue that Jean-Claude would eventually pursue across eastern Africa.

When Jean-Claude crossed the bridge at Rusumo Falls, it was this brother he was searching for, and it was this brother who would give him shelter during the genocide. Somali kidnappers had inadvertently saved Jean-Claude's life—and Saïd's.

# 20

FROM THE CATHEDRAL, we drove south on a spool of asphalt that curled across the hills like a loosely unrolled ribbon. We were heading for the royal court of Nyanza, historical seat of the Rwandan monarchy.

By lining up royal genealogies and historical events with specific solar eclipses, the founding of the Kingdom of Rwanda can be dated between 1312 and 1532. According to legend, it originated even earlier, with the rule of the semi-mythical Mwami Gihanga, whose father was descended from Heaven. Gihanga's kingdom began as a small fiefdom on Gasabo Hill but quickly spread, bringing neighbouring communes under its control.

Thus began a cycle of warrior kings and pastoralists, conquerors and consolidators, of rulers known as "Bwimba the Great" and "Ndoli the Restorer," as well as the less fortunately monikered "Yuhi the Senile," poet king.

What started as a loose affiliation of warring clans became an expanding hegemony, one that would extend northward into what is now Uganda and westward to the rainforests of the Congo, having reached—quite tangibly—the end of the world. (According to Rwandan cosmology, Rwanda sat in the centre of the universe, and the dense forests of the Congo, which held up the sky, marked the outer edge of the inhabited world. Beyond that lay only endless jungle, deeper and deeper, into darkness.)

Rwandans were the Romans of central Africa, holding back invasions from Burundi and other adversarial kingdoms while building an impenetrable line of forts along the frontiers, which gave rise to the proverb *"U Rwanda ruratera ntiruterwa."* ("Rwanda is never attacked, but always attacks.") Every citizen was considered *ingabo,* a "defender of Rwanda," and the symbol of royal authority was the Kalinga drum, which was adorned, not too subtly, with the testicles of the king's defeated enemies.

The royal intrigues of Rwanda's ruling families would rival those of Shakespeare. Its inner court was home to oracles and soothsayers, tax collectors and clan leaders, chieftains and courtiers, musicians and magicians, fortune tellers and wine stewards, with dynastic poets ever present, singing praises of the king in verse.

It was to the site of this royal court that Jean-Claude and I were now heading.

Getting to Nyanza proved tricky, however, if only because—at the exact moment I said, "Y'know, the road's not as congested out here, maybe I should drive"—we got caught in a duel of the minibuses.

"Uh-oh," said Jean-Claude, which, given the unruffled nature of his temperament, was tantamount to a primal scream.

A pair of competing buses were battling for control of the road, careening wildly as they jockeyed for position, speeding up, slowing down, slamming on their brakes and cutting each other off as they raced to pluck up passengers before their competition could reach them. We were caught in the middle like townspeople at a gunfight as first one minibus then the next zoomed by—only to cut in and fall back. All of this on roads that Evel Knievel would balk at, on corners that skirted the sides of dead-drop slopes. The villages below were very small.

I swallowed my earlier offer and never suggested I take the wheel again. It was all I could do to pry my fingers from the dashboard. *Uh-oh,* indeed. I wish I could say this was the only minibus duel we saw during our trip, but no, it became so common an occurrence that I rarely shit myself more than, oh, once or twice a day.

The road was lined with eucalyptus trees. This was not, I realized now, for reasons of aesthetics or erosion control, but of safety. These trees acted like guardrails, something that became evident when we passed the wreck of a car propped up by splintered trees above the sudden-death fields far below.

And then we entered the silent green tunnel of a bamboo forest, and all was good again. Bamboo has that effect. It soothes the heart, blots up sunlight, softens sounds.

Coming out of this bamboo tunnel, the views opened up. It was breathtaking. Sculpted hills stood muted in the mist. Patchwork fields and contoured heights. It again brought to mind images of Asia. Even the cries of *"Muzungu!"* that greeted us whenever we got out to stretch or buy a bottle of Fanta might easily have been the schoolboy gasp of *"Gaijin!"* that still greets travellers in rural Japan.

The similarities were fleeting, though, and this was decidedly Africa, decidedly Rwanda. Banana leaves shredded by the wind. Dust and diesel. Women in beautiful patterns. Small children with bundled twigs and jerry cans of water balanced on their heads. Overloaded bicycles. Water-pump gatherings. African smiles, and everyone impeccably dressed. These images were repeated on every turn, and were equally captivating every time: variations on a larger theme.

Each hill revealed another valley, every valley another town. As we drove past roadside markets and crossroad crowds, truck drivers en route to the Burundian border barrelled through, scattering goats and chickens with their air-horn blasts.

And then—into Nyanza.

Once an ancient court, Nyanza today is a newly anointed district capital. A flurry of billboard exhortations greeted us on our arrival: "REPORT FAMILY VIOLENCE!" "TEST FOR HIV!" "PROTECT OUR CHILDREN." "WORK TOGETHER. STAY UNITED." "UNLEASH YOUR POTENTIAL."

Nyanza had once had a Wild West reputation, but new hotels and office towers were now springing up, polished glass reflecting the surrounding hills. The streets bustled with activity, as though the entire town was late for a meeting.

The royal compound at Nyanza, just outside of town, is a much reduced reconstruction, though still striking in its pre-colonial, wholly non-Western layout: a series of conical, beehive-shaped structures constructed from tightly woven straw, arranged inside a high wooden palisade. The buildings resembled the traditional coil-woven *agaseke* baskets of Rwandan women. (The newly built Convention Centre in Kigali, a conical, highly stylized modernist structure, was inspired by these same agaseke baskets, a national emblem so important they've been given a place of pride on Rwanda's coat of arms.)

Behind the royal residence was a pair of smaller but equally elegant outbuildings: a milk hut and a beer hut, in which would have dwelled, respectively, a milk maid and the royal brewmaster, milk being the iconic drink of the Tutsi royalty and banana beer being a Rwandan delicacy. The man and woman responsible for the beer and milk were, by order of royal decree, virgins who were never allowed to marry. (Though you have to wonder, with the two huts being in such close proximity, whether the milk maid and the beer boy ever met up late at night to relieve certain urges.)

Inside the main royal residence, Jean-Claude and I met a group of young Scottish women who were touring Rwanda. They were the ones who told us about the virginal prerequisites of said milky lass and her beery counterpart, as had been explained to them by the Rwandan guide inside.

A pair of virgins? "Couldn't do that in Glasgow," one of them snorted.

"Aye, not enough candidates like," the others laughed.

They were dressed in loose cotton, damp from the heat, with faces even pinker than mine. University students working as volunteers with a local NGO, they had nothing but good things to say about Rwanda. "My dad, he used to work in Liberia," one of them said, "and he was right worried when I signed up. Gave me all this advice on safety precautions and security and the like. Didn't need any of it. Feels safer here than back home in Dundee."

Like the typical Rwandan tavern, the interior of the royal residence was much roomier than it appeared from the outside, both coolly shaded and unusually aromatic. Enormous wooden beams provided the framework for the straw-woven exterior. (It was akin to stepping inside a geodesic dome.) And the aroma that permeated the walls? A spiced combination of incense and wet earth, it was actually the odour of dried cow-dung braziers. "They feed the cattle herbs and flowers to create a nice smell," the guide explained.

As our eyes adjusted to the smoky dark, details emerged: Twa pottery, woven mats, hanging partitions, the lowered entrance and raised sleeping quarters of the king.

The tour guide, a lanky young man with commendable English, was enlivened by the presence of all these young women and steered his talk accordingly. The sexual predilections of the king's matrimonial bed were covered in great detail (and to the keen interest of his audience, it should be noted). Rwanda's more virile mwamis, he explained, were able to juggle multiple wives and several courtesans over a single night, bringing them in discreetly, one by one, through the side door and then up onto the royal bed—a round, voluptuously cushioned platform that needed only a mirrored ceiling and some Barry White to complete its *boom-chika-bow-wow* vibe. The girls were egging the lad on, asking all sorts of leading questions and being generally saucy in a way that only Scotswomen can. By my estimation, the topics covered by the tour guide were: the geopolitical foundations of Rwanda's pre-colonial political system: 2 percent; the amorous inner workings of the royal bedchambers: 98 percent. And even then, I may have been overly generous in my estimate of the former.

With the sad wisdom that comes from age, I wanted to pull this young man aside and say, "You do realize nothing's going to happen, right? These young women are on a schedule, so even if they were up for it there's no way you'd be able to arrange a tryst, let alone a succession of them, let alone convince them to queue up outside your bedroom. The logistics alone would make it all but impossible."

Still, a boy's gotta dream, I suppose. Maybe it was the soft light or the delicate scent of dried cow dung that brought out the romantic in me, but I decided not to intervene. Instead, Jean-Claude and I went back outside, leaving our young guide to his bevy of admirers (a.k.a. band of snorting lassies).

Ankole cattle were grazing in a meadow behind the royal compound. These cows, graceful, almost feline, are known as Watusi in North America, after "Tutsi." They are renowned for their beauty: long thin hooves, delicate deer-like features with soft dewlaps—and prominent humps on the males. But what truly sets Ankole cattle apart are their horns. Although originally for defence and body cooling, selective aesthetic breeding over hundreds of years has produced not so much horns as *tusks*. They can reach a staggering two metres in length (surpassing the tusks of many elephants, in fact), and some are so curved they almost meet at the top, forming elongated ovals and heart-shaped outlines. Others form lyres. All are impressive.

Among the pastoralist Tutsis, the Ankole cattle were symbols of status, a form of "walking wealth" prized more for the envy they engendered than for their milk. (The small-uddered Ankole cattle actually produce very little.) They are rarely slaughtered; killing a fertile cow would be like burning money. It's only when they have reached their elder years, or have been injured beyond recovery, that they are reluctantly taken away, their soft leather used for drums, their horns converted into flute-like musical instruments.

These were the cows that Jean-Claude had referred to as the "Cattle of Kings," and certainly the golden Ankole grazing in the meadow behind Nyanza Courts seemed exceptionally regal to me. Elegant and gentle, sociable and highly intelligent (they are easily trained to recognize their names when their herders sing them), they were a far cry from the lunk-headed, lumbering Holsteins I knew back home—even if said Holsteins do provide more milk and better meat. The cows I'd seen sparring with that mutt back in Kigali were of the square-chested Holstein variety. I don't imagine the cur would have tried the same antics with a more nimble-footed, long-horned Ankole.

As noted earlier, Ankole cattle lay at the cultural heart of the Tutsi social class, which is precisely why they were targeted by Hutu Power militias. During the genocide, a wholesale slaughter took place, with the animals butchered for prime cuts of meat and the rest left to rot in the fields. Twenty years on, the population of the Ankole is only now recovering.

The last great king of Rwanda was Kigeri IV Rwabugiri.[10] A severe and unforgiving man, Rwabugiri, having ascended to the throne in 1853, launched a series of military and political campaigns that would extend his authority over a region twice as large as present-day Rwanda, reaching deep into the Congo and as far north as Lake Edward in present-day Uganda. King Rwabugiri spearheaded more than fourteen different military expeditions, forcing neighbouring kingdoms to bow down and pay tribute. His reign would be the high-water mark of the Tutsi ascendency. He crushed rebellions in the northwest and established the complex system of governance, from province to district to hill, that is still in existence today. A warrior in his own right, Rwabugiri was also, in a sense, the Bureaucratic

---

10. This is the anglicized spelling of his name, commonly used. A more correct rendering would be "Kigeli." The rules for when to change *r* to *l* in Kinyarwanda were explained to me several times by Jean-Claude, none of which I retained.

King—albeit one given to public executions over minor perceived slights. Rwabugiri would rule for more than forty years and was still in power, elderly but able, when the first German explorers arrived.

Our band of young Scotswomen had now joined us in the meadow, to the wistful regret of the guide inside the king's chambers, I was sure. We walked up the hill together to a very different royal residence.

Although the Belgian-built colonial manor house is only fifty steps or so from the older royal court, it might have been a world away, which I suppose it was. Built in 1932 for a now-acquiescent King of Rwanda, it is thoroughly Western in style, right down to its incongruous—and undersized—bathtub. (The final Tutsi monarch stood almost seven feet tall; how he managed to fold himself into that boxy little tub is a mystery for the ages.) Long and low, the building's doorways and windows opened to views of the hills across from it. A melancholy place, caught in a calming crosswind, it marks the end of many things. The last kings of Rwanda lived here.

Rwabugiri died in 1895, soon after the Germans arrived. His death created a dangerous power vacuum, which Germany took advantage of, moving in from Tanzania (or Tanganyika, as it was then known) and claiming the nearby Tutsi kingdom of Burundi as well.

The hapless son who succeeded Rwabugiri got caught up in a War of the Roses–style struggle between monarchists and rival clans, complete with pretenders to the throne and would-be usurpers. He was ousted in a palace coup and forced to commit ritualistic suicide. This prolonged civil war among the inner circles of the royal court sapped the strength of the monarchy at the very moment the Europeans were making their move. It was a time of cabals and cults, of prophetesses and messianic leaders. One of Rwabugiri's widows fled northward into the mountains with a band of loyal retainers, proclaiming herself Queen of Ndorwa and vowing to expel all encroaching Europeans from Rwanda.

In the end, an ambitious but distant heir named Musinga wrested power from a competing clan to claim the throne. Musinga allied

himself with the Germans to defeat his rivals; he even sent men to
fight for Germany against the Belgians in East Africa during World
War I. But he had backed the wrong horse, and with Germany's
defeat, Rwanda was handed over to Musinga's former foes.

Belgium's relationship with the monarch was tetchy at best. A
Belgian commander complained early on that Musinga was "scorn-
ing the orders we give him." Clearly appalled at the sovereign's
impudence, the commander noted that the king "intends to play the
leading part in politics of his country and to relegate the European
authorities to the background." That would not do! The Belgians
arrested Musinga at gunpoint and threw him in jail, releasing him
only in the face of a public revolt. But the damage had been done.
The aura of divine power surrounding the king was gone forever.
Muzungus were now calling the shots, and when this same king, the
last "pagan monarch" of Rwanda, refused to be baptized, he was
deposed in 1931 and replaced by one of his more compliant sons,
Charles Pierre, who had already adopted Western clothes and customs. It was Charles's public embrace of Christianity that sparked the
mass conversion of Rwanda. And when King Mutara III Rudahigwa,
as Charles was now known, proved troublesome, he too would be
removed from the equation.

Charles had become increasingly disillusioned. He chafed under
Belgian control and openly questioned the ethnic ID cards Belgium
had imposed, insisting, "There are no objective criteria whereby one
can distinguish Hutu from Tutsi." While travelling in Burundi,
Charles Rudahigwa was invited to dinner by the Belgian authorities
to discuss these matters. He took a few bites of his meal and became
violently ill. A Belgian doctor was called in; King Rudahigwa was
given an injection and died soon after. Another version of these
events begins with the king complaining of a migraine but ends in
the same manner: a visit from a Belgian doctor, a mysterious injection, sudden death. Was it simply an accident? An allergic reaction,
perhaps? Or a cerebral hemorrhage? Possibly. But his death did pave
the way for the 1959 Hutu Social Revolution, which abolished the

monarchy and proclaimed Rwanda a republic under Belgium's new policy of "majority rule." With Rudahigwa's death, many observers suspected Belgium was simply clearing the deck chairs before handing over power to the Hutu.[11]

Nyanza Hill is where the Rwanda of old came to an end, and for all the fusty feudalism of the ancient regime, it is worth noting that prior to 1959, over the course of 600 years of meticulously maintained oral history, there was not a single case of systematic violence between Hutus and Tutsis. Most violence was between competing clans, not "ethnic" groups. And most of that was regional as well. The north and southwest were never fully subjugated, and rebellions often flared up. As the French scholar Gérard Prunier noted, "It was a centre versus periphery affair and not one of Tutsi versus Hutu." Rwandan kings could be cruel and capricious; they were not genocidal. That fatal cleave occurred under colonial rule, aided and abetted by European notions of race and racial superiority.

It was Rwandans who planned the 1994 genocide and Rwandans who carried it out. Ultimate responsibility lies squarely with them. As the respected Hutu journalist and Catholic priest André Sibomana put it, "Men are products but not prisoners of their history. They decide themselves what to do." But it's also important to be aware of both the colonial context and the role Western nations played in making the genocide possible. At Nyanza Hill, two very different royal manors and two very different traditions are in evidence.

As Jean-Claude and I walked back down through grassy fields, past feline cattle and the woven palaces of a lost Rwanda, I heard a sharp *kii* and looked up to see a bird of prey turning lazy, lethal circles in the sky. Somewhere in the distance, I could hear the laughter of Scottish women growing fainter and fainter.

---

11. His successor and younger brother, Kigeli V, last king of Rwanda, was deposed by the Hutu Social Revolution and now lives in the United States, where he still refers to himself as His Majesty. He has his own website and everything.

# 21

SPEAKING OF THE SCOTS, here is the story of how I became world famous in Butare City for forty-seven minutes. That was the length of time needed for my rise to fame and fall from grace to run its course.

Butare (now known as Huye) is a university town, and when we stopped at a grocery store on the outskirts of the city, I was pleased to find a small selection of academic books for sale in among the soft drinks and snacks. While Jean-Claude ran to the bank, I poked about the dusty shelves and discovered a military history of pre-colonial Rwanda, including its many kings. Delighted at my find, I took the book up to the counter along with a raisin bun and a bottle of conveniently pre-warmed Fanta.

I am, supposedly, a professional writer. Which means—according to my reading of Revenue Canada regulations, anyway—that every scrap of reading material I ever purchase, up to and including the placemats at my local Chinese restaurant ("You are born under the sign of the Dragon. You are compatible with Horse, Rat, and Rooster"), counts as research and is, therefore, gloriously tax deductible.

So when I made my purchase, I asked for a receipt.

Rwandans, I would discover, are terrifically talented when it comes to writing up a bill of sale. They almost seem to enjoy the challenge, asking themselves, *"All righty then. Let's see just how elaborate and labour-intensive we can make this."* Shopkeepers will often have a large carbon-copy pad from 1942 for exactly this purpose, in which they painstakingly write out such crucial details as your name, nationality, address (while in Rwanda), address (in home country), phone number, age, height, weight, blood type, shoe size, date of birth, mother's maiden name, favourite singer, pet peeves, hobbies (if applicable), date of birth (again, just to be safe), preferred use of a salad fork, etc. When asking for a receipt in Rwanda, it's a good idea to allot the bulk of one's afternoon to complete the transaction.

I should also remind readers of a seemingly unrelated but important point made earlier: Rwandans *love* English Premier League soccer. They're crazy for it. In Kigali, when I went to buy a Rwanda National Soccer jersey as a souvenir for my son, the shop owner attempted to talk me out of it, saying, "The Amavubi are having a terrible season. Why don't you buy a Chelsea jersey instead? Or maybe Tottenham? They're doing well this year. Or how about a nice Arsenal jersey?" They were all the same price, so it's not as if he was attempting to upsell me. I tried to explain to him that I hadn't come all the way to Africa to buy a Chelsea FC soccer jersey, but he couldn't see my point and remained perplexed even as he rang up the sale.

So—when I gave the shopkeeper in Butare my surname for the receipt he was filling in, he looked up and said, "Ferguson? Like Alex Ferguson?"

Now, for those of you (i.e., North Americans) who may not know who Alex Ferguson is, that Rwandan shopkeeper was referring to the legendary manager of Manchester United, a towering figure in the world of soccer who has been knighted by the Queen, no less. Having grown up in a soccer-free zone (i.e., northern Alberta in the 1970s), I'd never heard of *Sir* Alex Ferguson until my wife and I happened to name our oldest son Alex. It was sheer coincidence, you understand, but soon enough, British friends were saying, "Alex Ferguson! That's fantastic! You must be a real football fan!" (as the rest of the world mistakenly calls soccer). They were baffled by my lack of enthusiasm. It was, I learned, like meeting someone whose last name is Gretzky and who had named his son "Wayne," only to look at you blankly when you said, "Like the hockey player!" *The hockey who?*

In Rwanda, Alex Ferguson is a highly respected figure. You catch him in sports magazines and on BBC TV, an older, good-looking fellow often seen yelling at his players. The clerk at that shop didn't think I *was* Alex Ferguson; that would have been ridiculous.

"No," I said with a laugh. "No relation."

"No?"

"But the funny thing is, my son is named Alex."

"Son?"

"That's right. *He's* Alex Ferguson. Just a fluke, of course. Who knew my kid had a famous name? I sure as heck didn't."

And I left, thinking the matter was done.

Jean-Claude and I stopped for lunch at a nearby café, and then headed back to where our vehicle was parked. What we didn't realize was that word had spread, anticipation was mounting.

As we approached the Land Cruiser, our pace slowed. We could see the shopkeeper standing there, beaming, pen and paper in hand. He asked, somewhat breathlessly, if I might sign my name for him. More and more people appeared, the entire street it seemed, all smiling at me with the same enthusiasm. Several of them had their phones out, camera mode ready, making "Can I take one?" gestures.

We were flummoxed. Jean-Claude had a long and, from the sounds of it, highly convoluted conversation with the shopkeeper in Kinyarwanda. He then pulled me to one side and asked in a hushed and—it must be said—slightly accusatory tone, "Will, did you tell these people you are Alex Ferguson's son?"

"What? God, no."

"But that's what they think. They are asking if they can take their picture with you, get your autograph."

I was probably the most famous person ever to stop by that little shop, even if it was under false pretenses.

"What should I do?" I whispered to Jean-Claude.

"I don't know."

Jean-Claude and I seriously considered having me shake a few hands, slap a few backs, pose for a few selfies, scribble a few signatures that looked vaguely like *"Alex Ferguson's son, Esq."* and then leave with a munificent wave of the hand. One hated to pop their bubble. But then I thought, What if word spreads? What if, God forbid, it ends up in the papers? *Alex Ferguson's son tours Rwanda!*

And so, against my better instincts, we fessed up to my true (non) identity. Even then, it took some doing for Jean-Claude to convince the group that I was *not* Alex Ferguson's offspring. When he finally did, their expressions soured. They seemed to think I'd been trying to pull a fast one on them (to what end?), and as they grumpily dispersed, several of them shot *highly* disapproving glares our way. (I say "our" because Jean-Claude was fully implicated by this point.)

Sigh.

"Maybe I should have just signed some autographs," I said as we limped away in our 4x4, chests deflated.

Jean-Claude agreed. "I think that would have been better. They were a little bit angry at being tricked."

*Tricked?* But, but—oh, never mind.

Even worse, my Icarus-like arc had reaped no benefits, no rewards, not a single beer cadged or meal on the house proffered. Next time.

# 22

RWANDA, "LAND OF A THOUSAND HILLS," is also renowned as an Empire of Primates, and the first ones I saw were not in the forest but on the road. As we drove into Butare, a monkey scampered across, baby bouncing on its back like a rodeo clown atop a runaway steer. I shouted for Jean-Claude to stop the vehicle as I scrambled to unsheath my camera—a reaction, I soon learned, that was like squealing with delight at the sight of a squirrel in Canada.

When we pulled over, a welcoming committee of white-throated L'Hoest's monkeys greeted us. I burst out of the 4x4 like a primate paparazzo, unleashing a salvo of shots in rapid-fire bursts. More and more monkeys appeared, some of them looking awfully shifty, like potential pickpockets—and appropriately so, as it turned out, because Butare, Jean-Claude informed me, used to be where the majority of pickpockets in Rwanda came from. The citizens of Butare, hailing as they do from a university town, considered themselves smarter than average as well, a lethal combination. "People in Butare are born with a high school education, it's what we say," Jean-Claude explained. "But keep your hand on your wallet."

I filled up half a memory card with near-identical photos, and we set off again, leaving our white-bearded, fleet-footed friends behind. As the roads grew more congested, the traffic, counter-intuitively, grew quicker. A battered hatchback from the Better Driving School lurched out in front of us, a nervous young woman clutching the steering wheel with a terrified grasp. Her instructor was teaching her to drive by having her plunge right in, the way our grandparents supposedly learned to swim—anecdotally anyway. *"Rowed us out to the middle of the lake and tossed us over, said 'See you at the shore.'"*

"Did I tell you how I learned to drive?" Jean-Claude asked.

"Blindfolded on a tightrope, I'm guessing."

But no.

"Was at a soccer field in Kigali. It was packed dirt, red clay, where we used to play. This guy, he owned a Volkswagen—I don't know how it was still running, everything inside had been replaced with wood: the floor, the handles, even the gas pedal, it all was wood. This car had nothing. No insurance, no registration. It was manual trans-mission, too, so maybe even the gears were made from wood! For fifty francs he would let you drive it once around the field, and it didn't matter how old you were. If you could reach the gas pedal, you could drive. And if you couldn't reach the gas pedal, you could sit on someone's lap. Also, there was someone had a motorcycle. Was cheaper. You could drive it around the soccer field for twenty francs."

"You didn't need a learner's licence?"

"We weren't driving on the street."

"But—weren't kids playing soccer in the middle of the field?"

"Oh yes, but we were careful. We went around the edge." He said this as though it were the most reasonable statement one could make about letting children drive a motorcycle and patchwork Volkswagen around a field filled with other children chasing a ball.

Jean-Claude saved up any scraps of money he could get—"If my father gave me a few francs to see a soccer game, I would save the money and sneak into the stadium instead, or I would deliver notes between teenage boys and the girls they liked and they would pay me. City kids always know how to find a little cash here, there"—and he'd use this money to drive the motorcycle on the soccer field, going round and round and round and round. He was twelve or thirteen at the time.

"I wanted to drive the car, but this was expensive. So I came to be friends with the owner. He liked to take a nap, listening to the kids driving his car. Even sleeping, he was counting. He knew how many rounds. But also he had to collect the money, or send someone with a five-litres jug to bring back gas for the car, so I said to him, 'I will take care of the business. Just give me a free round.' It became my responsibility. He could sleep and I could learn how to drive."

With that, Jean-Claude steered us into the heart of Butare, the city leaning in from all sides, full of life.

When the genocide began, Butare had been an island of sanity amid a welter of madness. The prefecture was the only province in Rwanda with a Tutsi governor, and he refused to issue the order to clean out the "cockroaches," calling instead for level heads and reason to prevail. This insanity would soon pass, he assured the populace.

Given hope, Tutsis flooded into the region from all over, believing they would be protected. Butare, after all, was a centre of higher learning, known for its tolerance, its inclusiveness, and its sizable Tutsi population, a city where the Hutus and Tutsis got along. Among the southern Hutu of Butare, a burgeoning grassroots movement was even calling for full equality. Surely the killings would not reach Butare.

The calm lasted two weeks. Outraged at the governor's refusal to follow orders, Rwanda's Hutu Power interim government sent in the Presidential Guard to have him arrested. He was executed, along with his family. As a more obedient governor was being sworn in, trucks rolled up. Youth militias and French-trained soldiers climbed out. They had work to do.

One of the first to die was the eighty-year-old widow of Charles Mutara III Rudahigwa, the Queen Dowager Rosalie Gicanda. Known as a "people's queen," Rosalie was a much-loved figure, and her execution sent a signal to the entire Tutsi population: no one was safe. The killings in Butare—especially on the campuses—were notably brutal, as Hutu students tortured Tutsi classmates, as professors betrayed their fellow teachers, as moderate journalists and intellectuals were rounded up. Hutu professors who had proven unpopular or students who were too successful and thus resented by their peers—or who simply lived on campus alongside Tutsis— were also purged. Entire villages in the outlying areas were laid to waste, the homes looted, possessions plundered. Genocide can be lucrative.

The zealous enthusiasm the professors and their students showed for killing people provides a secular parallel to David Gushee's lament: *The presence of universities in a community, the self-identification of people as scholars in the pursuit of knowledge, of understanding, guarantees exactly* nothing ...

# 23

RWANDAN GOATS ARE SURPRISINGLY AGILE.

"Did you notice?" Jean-Claude asked. "They look both ways before they cross the street."

He was right, though I imagine goats that didn't look both ways would have been weeded out rather quickly. The road we were on rose higher and higher as we left Butare. The air was thinner, as was the asphalt; potholes in the pavement revealed pockets of soft red earth underneath.

Motorcycle taxis gave way to scooters. Scooters gave way to bicycles-for-hire, pulling goods and passengers over never-ending humps of hill. And finally, even the bicycles disappeared, replaced by bare feet and head-balanced burdens.

We were entering the country's remote western region, the Ozarks of Rwanda in a sense. Pedestrians still crowded the roads, but the traffic consisted almost entirely of us. We passed the occasional public bus, riding low and packed with people, but for long stretches we were the only vehicle in sight. A nice change from the PRAISE GOD! trucks that had bullied past us on the main routes, but it actually made driving more dangerous. Having fewer vehicles on the road made people oblivious to our approach. And they weren't as adept at dodging oncoming traffic as pedestrians elsewhere were. Several times children ran alongside us, perilously close, daring each other to touch our truck as we rumbled past. When this happened, Jean-Claude would come to a stop and scold them until they withdrew, looking downcast.

"It's a dangerous game," Jean-Claude said.

It was also evidence of how rare traffic was in the villages we were rolling through. By the time we reached Karambi, the dust on our truck was mottled with fingerprints. We had planned to stop there for some food-stall victuals, but a rural pig auction was underway in the town's main square, and the odour was so overpowering that we rolled up our windows, tried not to inhale, and pushed on.

The road wound through fields terraced in ascending curves, lush and green all the way up. In the flooded rice paddies below, water reflected the sky like panes of glass. We were now deep into La Zone Turquoise and the tragic history that this region entailed.

As the old regime collapsed, the RPF had continued its advance across the killing grounds of Rwanda, scattering the interahamwe and government armed forces. With the end of the genocide in sight, France decided to intervene. They announced they would be sending a fully equipped, heavily armed "humanitarian" mission into western Rwanda to secure a safe zone to protect—who, exactly? Although Opération Turquoise was ostensibly about saving lives, in reality it was about stopping the RPF and, failing that, providing cover for France's retreating Hutu Power allies: political leaders and high-ranking military officers, government functionaries, and members of the militia and their families, together with a wealth of weaponry and Rwanda's entire reserve of hard currency. The explicit aim was to counterattack later and reclaim the country.

As journalist Philip Gourevitch notes, "From the moment they arrived, and wherever they went, the French forces supported and preserved the same local political leaders who had presided over the genocide."

The creation of La Zone Turquoise, as the area under French control was known, effectively allowed the organizers of the genocide to escape. They moved en masse into eastern Zaire (as the Congo was then known), where they were given unconditional support by that country's notorious dictator, President Mobutu, another loyal French ally.

Human Rights Watch had tracked at least five shipments of weapons and heavy armour delivered by France to the Hutu Power regime at the height of the killings. The French did not arrest a single génocidaire or war criminal and even aided many of them in their getaway. General Dallaire was convinced that the real goal of

Opération Turquoise was to split Rwanda in two, like Cyprus, with France's Hutu Power allies ensconced on one side and the English-speaking Ugandan Tutsis of the RPF on the other. Certainly, when French troops did arrive, the interahamwe militias—many still covered in blood—took to the streets dancing and singing. "Our French brothers have arrived! They are coming to save us!" Flags were all aflutter. WELCOME FRENCH HUTUS! read the banners.

"You Hutu girls, wash yourselves and put on your best dresses to welcome our French allies," the announcers on Radio RTLM crowed. "The Tutsi girls are all dead, so now you have your chance!"

One of the French soldiers would later complain that he was fed up with being "cheered along by murderers."

French troops did indeed set up refugee camps and are credited with having protected perhaps 10,000 Tutsis, maybe more. But their presence cost more lives than it saved. Some of the most complete ethnic cleansings in Rwanda occurred inside the French "safe" zone. Unhindered by UN witnesses or RPF incursions, and emboldened by what they took to be France's tacit support, the killers within La Zone Turquoise were able to complete their work with a thoroughness not possible elsewhere. Entire populations of Tutsis were wiped out.

"What was achieved by Opération Turquoise," Linda Melvern writes in *Conspiracy to Murder,* "was in fact nothing less than a resurgence in the genocide.... It provided a sanctuary for the killers."[12]

François Mitterrand, president of France and the man behind many of the African policies implemented at that time, brushed it off: with a perfectly executed Gallic shrug, I imagine. "In countries such as these," he said, "genocide is not so important."

As we drove in to Murambi, a goat looked right, then left, and then scampered across the road.

---

12. For an in-depth look at France's role in the Rwandan genocide, see *Silent Accomplice* by Andrew Wallis.

# 24

EVEN IN THIS LAND OF PANORAMAS, the rounded summit of the Murambi Technical School stands out. A beautiful symmetry is at play: grassy meadows slope away, giving the school a full 360-degree view of the seven hills surrounding it.

This very beauty would be the cause of Murambi's infamy. There was no escaping from this hilltop, no secret route, no thick forests or papyrus swamps to flee to: just a wide-open emptiness exposed on all sides. Tidy rows of blond-brick buildings are lined up on top: classrooms and dormitories, would-be lecture halls.

The school was brand new and had not yet opened when the killings began. Local administrators encouraged Tutsis in the area to seek refuge there. As would become clear, this was done not out of concern for their safety but to better round up the targeted populace in one convenient, central location. More than 50,000 people crowded in on Murambi Hill. Only a dozen survived.

They fought back as best they could. Armed with rocks and sticks, the men formed a circle around the women and children, held the militias at bay. But then the soldiers came. They surrounded the school, cut off water and food, began handing out grenades to the intera-hamwe. The attacks lasted for days at a time. Victims of the Murambi massacre were eventually bulldozed into open pits and then buried under packed soil. Many of them were still alive when this happened. Later, French forces would set up camp at Murambi and turn this newly flattened surface into a sports field, would play volleyball on top of these mass graves.

After the genocide ended, the burial pits at Murambi were exhumed, and a disconcerting discovery was made: having been packed together so tightly, the remains had mummified under the heat and compression. Contorted in their death throes, the bodies were packed into each other, leather-skinned and macabre.

Thousands of these ghostly white figures, preserved in lime, are now laid out, row after row, on wooden platforms inside the classrooms of the Murambi Technical School. As you move silently from one building to the next, a chalky smell clings to you. The heat is stultifying. You don't want to look, but at the same time, you can't avoid it. Your eye is drawn to these endless tableaux. Elongated, etiolated figures, reverse silhouettes with tufts of hair sticking to the skulls. Severed tendons, broken femurs. Many of the bodies are torqued and twisted, with mouths open, arms raised as though fending off a blow. These are the ones who were buried alive, and the terror of their final moments lives on. Several are caught in midscream, like real-life renderings of Edvard Munch. Others, already dead when buried, lie like stacks of firewood.

In *We Wish to Inform You That Tomorrow We Will Be Killed with Our Families,* Philip Gourevitch describes the dead of Rwanda as aesthetically attractive, which for him only added to the affront of these sites. "There was no getting around it," he notes. "The skeleton is a beautiful thing." But I must confess, as I moved from room to room, feeling fogbound and forlorn, the beauty eluded me. These weren't statues at Murambi, these were people—people whose lives had been cut short in the ugliest manner possible. There was no beauty here, only a crushing sense of loss.

The hardest to enter was the Children's Room, where the bodies of infants and toddlers, some found still clinging to their mothers, were laid out on the tables like small offerings. Of the thousands of bodies I saw at Murambi that day, the one that haunts me most was that of a child, maybe two or three, with his tiny hands held over his face. As a father, I knew this posture, knew it with a stomach-blow of recognition. When you're little, you believe that if you can't see something bad, it can't see you either. The child had died with his eyes tightly shut, hands covering his face. It's the desperate strategy of children confronting monsters, but it only works when the monsters are imaginary.

Jean-Claude and I were the only two visitors at Murambi that afternoon. Blue skies, clear views. Hills on all sides. Surrounded.

The thin, angular young man who walked us through the quiet carnage had escaped a similar massacre by, in his words, "running." He was just twelve when the genocide began, he told us, and when the killings started, he ran. He ran and he ran and they did not catch him. He ran and he ran, and he is running still. His head bobbed when he talked, he spoke in dull monotones, could not make eye contact. He recited his story and that of Murambi's as if repeating a redemptive mantra. I imagine it's as much compulsive as it is therapeutic, the need to tell these stories, to tell them again and again.

And again.

A sign near one of the open excavation pits reads, with pointed understatement, FRENCH SOLDIERS PLAYED VOLLEY ON THIS SPOT. The museum at Murambi included photographs of French soldiers training interahamwe death squads.

It was time to leave. The sun was lying low across the grassy fields, and as our guide walked us down to the front gate to let us out, a blond, sun-tousled young man with a rucksack showed up, asking if he could sneak in. He was from Sweden, was down from Kigali for the day, and he wanted to see the bodies. "Just five minutes. I will be quick. I promise." No, he was told. It was closing time. He would have to return during regular hours. But he had travelled all this way, he said, and wouldn't be able to come back. He was leaving Rwanda tomorrow. The young man coaxed and pleaded, tried to charm his way in—and was clearly expecting to be admitted. But the hours of operation at the Murambi Genocide Memorial were clearly posted, and it was time to close up.

Jean-Claude and I gave the young Swedish man a ride to the nearest bus centre. He had been travelling around East Africa, was based out of Uganda. "Too many rules in Rwanda," he said with a breezy smile.

I asked him if, in Sweden, people who showed up at a museum or national memorial after hours would be admitted. Well, no, he said. So why should Rwanda be any different?

He seemed like an affable enough chap, admirably unflustered and travelling light, but I couldn't shake the feeling he had expected to be allowed in solely because he was white. That might have worked elsewhere in Africa. Perhaps. But not here. Not in Rwanda. And for good reason. Figuratively, historically, politically, the West has been playing volley on top of Rwanda's graves for many years.

At Murambi, the lime had turned the dead the one colour that might have saved them.

# 25

WE FOLLOWED A NARROW ROAD into Gikongoro (now known as Nyamagabe), and along the way passed workers in a field who were dressed in what appeared to be pyjamas.

"Pink is for the long-term prisoners," Jean-Claude explained. "Orange is for the ones who are going to be released soon."

"So any génocidaires among them would be in pink?"

He nodded. "And both colours are easy to see against the green, if they try to run."

Pyjamaed prisoners chopping at the earth, churning the rust-coloured soil.

At Gikongoro Town, three sharp ridges converge, high above the valleys below. A topographical high-wire act, it's an improbable place to build a community, let alone one with a cantilevered hotel hanging over one side and a market spilling out on the other. Being the town drunk in Gikongoro must be a perilous undertaking; one wobbly false step and you would be somersaulting downward a long while.

We'd come to Gikongoro to find childhood friends of Jean-Claude, friends he hadn't seen in twenty years. Several confused phone calls, false turns, and head-scratching dead ends finally got us onto a rutted road outside of town, where we pulled into a yard and were met by beaming, floodlight smiles. Clementine, who was a few years younger than Jean-Claude, her brother Eric, nicknamed Petite, and their mother, Immaculée, had come out to greet us.

"We thought you were dead!" the mother exclaimed. And in Rwanda, this is no mere turn of phrase.

They were thrilled to see him. Several times the mother, in mid-laughter, reached out and touched his arm, softly, almost as if to reassure herself that he was indeed real.

They'd known Jean-Claude as a boy who often dropped by their neighbourhood in Kigali. "He was like a little bird" is how their mother put it. But while Jean-Claude's ethnic identity card was marked TUTSI, theirs had been marked HUTU. And that would make all the difference.

Clementine had lost her father and seen her country destroyed and rebuilt. She divided her time between an apartment in Kigali and this modest home in Gikongoro, where her mother and brother now lived. She held a bachelor's degree in economics, was working toward her master's, had been employed at the Ministry of Infrastructure and later at the Ministry of Finance, in economics, and was now the administrative assistant at a nearby United Nations refugee camp housing Congolese who had fled the violence next door.

The back of our Land Cruiser was weighted down by several duffle bags stuffed with gear: uniforms, goalie gloves and jerseys, deflated soccer balls, and more, all brand new and donated by the Calgary Foothills Soccer Club. Jean-Claude had lugged these bags all the way from Canada, intending to donate them to schools in Rwanda. On hearing that thousands of Congolese children were playing without proper equipment at the refugee camp where Clementine worked, he decided to split his inventory, bringing half here.

Through Clementine, Jean-Claude and I had contacted the UN Head of Camp, and he had invited us to visit, to deliver the soccer equipment in person and speak with the kids directly.

But before we headed to the regional UN office in Gikongoro, I thought I'd get some inside dirt on Jean-Claude. While he and Clementine's mother were talking, I sidled up beside Clementine.

"You remember Jean-Claude?"

"Yes, of course. I only had ten years when he left, but I remember him so much."

"What was he like? Any secrets you can share? Troubles he got into. That sort of thing. I promise I won't tell."

"Secrets?"

"Bad things he did as a kid."

"Oh no! He was very kind, I remember. Very kind and social. Kind, intelligent, social. Very friendly. And very calm."

"So he hasn't changed."

She looked over at him and smiled. "He hasn't changed."

# 26

BEFORE THE EUROPEANS ARRIVED and began parcelling off sections of it to neighbouring colonies, the Kingdom of Rwanda included broad swaths of what is now eastern Congo. The entire Lake Kivu district, which is now divided between the two countries, was once Rwandan territory, and more than 400,000 Rwandese descendants—the Banyamulenge, as they are known—still live in eastern Congo today, where they are often targeted, attacked, scapegoated, and killed.

Where tiny Rwanda is one of the most culturally homogeneous countries in Africa, the vast republic of Congo is among its most heterogeneous. Apart from being a geographical description, it's hard to define what "Congolese" even means. As a palimpsest of overlapping claims and cultures, Congo is less a nation than a border drawn on a map. It encompasses one of the world's greatest rainforest basins and is ruled by a distant capital. The city of Kinshasa sits on the other side of Congo, some 1,500 kilometres away from the

Lake Kivu district, with an endless jungle dividing them. The capital is more overlord than caretaker. Eastern Congo is, in a very real sense, a colony of Kinshasa.

It's important to remember that the Hutu Power extremists who launched the genocide were not destroyed so much as routed. They have regrouped in the Lake Kivu district of eastern Congo under the Orwellian-named "Democratic Forces for the Liberation of Rwanda" (usually given with its French acronym, FDLR), and they have continued their campaign to destabilize Rwanda.[13]

The ominous presence of the FDLR in eastern Congo has been countered by the appearance of the M23 rebels, a group of Tutsi Congolese soldiers who mutinied against the Congolese army and are named for a March 23, 2009, peace accord they signed, which they say has yet to be implemented.

The M23 have a ruthless reputation, and the Congolese government has accused Rwanda of supplying arms to the rebels, something the Rwandan government has denied with a wide-eyed innocence that isn't fooling anyone. Rwanda, just as pointedly, has asked why the UN and the Democratic Republic of Congo haven't been pursuing the genocidal ideologues of the FDLR with the same enthusiasm they've shown for fighting the M23. The Congolese government, meanwhile, has been giving aid and ammunition to the FDLR to help "guard their eastern door." To complicate matters further, there were at least ten other separate, distinct rebel groups operating in Congo's North Kivu province alone, a mishmash of competing acronyms too difficult to sort out here.

Amid this sabre-rattling brinkmanship, the people in the Lake Kivu region of Congo have been caught, literally at times, in the crossfire. The conflict is about more than protecting minorities or defeating the remnants of a genocidal regime; it is fuelled by the

---

13. To put that into context, imagine for a moment that the Nazi party hadn't been eradicated, but instead had retreated and regrouped *just across the border* from Germany.

region's diamond, gold, and coltan reserves, the latter being a rare mineral used in cell phones and video game consoles. Which is to say, to blood diamonds and blood oil, we can now add the consumer demand for faster cell phones and better PlayStation controls. South Africa, Uganda, Tanzania, and other countries have also elbowed their way into Congo's Lake Kivu region, making it a free-for-all at times. This is a Gordian knot of the first order.

Hundreds of thousands of refugees have fled the ongoing violence, and more than 35,000 of them have ended up in Rwanda. The UN has set up several camps to house them, including one in the small town of Kigeme, just west of Gikorongo.

And so, with our Land Cruiser loaded down with soccer gear, Jean-Claude, Clementine, and I drove to the UN headquarters nearby, a tidy gated home with pleasant views across the hills, where we were met by Urooj Saifi, the Canadian Head of Camp.

Originally from Pakistan, now of Oakville, Ontario, Urooj had been with the United Nations High Commission for Refugees (UNHCR) for twenty-two years, starting in Iraq just after the first Gulf War. But nothing prepared him for the Kigeme refugee camp.

He had arrived earlier in the year to confront a full crush of humanity. "It was a shock," he admits. "The camp was designed to hold a maximum of fifteen thousand, and we were already over that. There was very little space, with everyone living on top of each other. It was … a challenge."

I liked Urooj. He spoke quietly, thoughtfully. "Come," he said. "I'll introduce you to Deo, my Rwandan counterpart. He's the camp manager."

Deo Ntirenganya was more serious and slightly guarded. We shook hands with a quick clench. Jean-Claude had presented me to Deo, misguidedly perhaps, as "an important journalist" here to investigate "the situation in Rwanda."

True, *Canadian Geographic* magazine had asked me to write an article about my trip, and I'd printed up a lavish stack of business cards, which I'd been dealing out with a generous hand and on the slightest provocation. (The cards stated that I was "on assignment.") Unfortunately, as I've learned, nothing clenches administrative jaws—or handshakes—quicker than meeting a journalist.

Urooj introduced us to his wife, who was elegant and gracious, as well as their daughter, who was visiting with some of her schoolmates from university in Edinburgh. Urooj's wife also seemed wary about my intentions, but happily Urooj was not.

"You can talk to anyone you like, ask whatever you wish," he said as we changed vehicles, loading the duffle bags and ourselves into the back of a UN jeep for the short but bumpy ride upward to Kigeme Camp. (Hard to imagine, but Kigeme was even higher in the hills than the already ear-popping Gikongoro.) The road grew steeper and steeper, sides flanking away. We were above the clouds now, and the sun opened up like a fan.

"Kigeme Camp is something unique," Urooj said, turning around to talk to me. "It's a new way of thinking about refugees."

The crowds along the roadside grew thicker, leaving barely a lane's worth of space for our vehicle to squeeze through at times. I leaned up as the truck inched its way along. "So these people, they're all …"

Urooj nodded. "From the camp."

On one of the few flat patches of dirt available, a hundred or more raggedy children, barefoot and shouting, were playing with a soccer ball cobbled together from scraps of foam mattress wrapped in twine. They were calling for passes and sending sprawling shots between bamboo-rigged goalposts. Hundreds of feet kicking up clouds of red dust. We could taste the peppery earth as we passed.

"It's very congested," Urooj said, voice rising to be heard. "Most other places with refugee camps have more space, a lot of open land. Not Rwanda."

The driver pulled over and we climbed out. The UN site was divided between two hilltop summits, with rows of clay-walled huts and the blue tents of the UN scaling the hills on both sides. We walked uphill, through further crowds of people.

Kigeme Camp sits on the edge of a rainforest, deep in the humid heart of Africa. But we were there in the dry season and the sun had baked the gumbo roads into a hardened terra-cotta clay.

"Rainy season is very tough," Urooj said, answering the question I was about to ask.

Kigeme Camp was crowded, but not in despair.

"This camp is meant to be a showcase," Urooj explained. A template for Rwanda, and potentially the world. "The goal," he said, "is integration, not isolation."

Refugees at Kigeme Camp are given full legal protection under the same constitution that governs Rwandans. Any children born in the camp, regardless of ethnic background, are given Rwandan citizenship and birth certificates.

"This camp, and the others in Rwanda, are joint ventures," said Urooj. "The UN," he reminded me, "has to be invited in. We are guests. We have to remember that."

The problems facing the Congolese refugees at Kigeme Camp were daunting, and Deo ticked them off for me as we walked: nutrition, medical attention, child safety, education, employment, overcrowding. Daunting, but again, not insurmountable.

In refugee zones elsewhere in the world, schooling and medical care are typically provided inside the confines of the camp, with residents limited in their ability to travel outside it or to seek employment beyond. At Kigeme, they can come and go as they wish—"They are not prisoners," as Deo put it—and are actively encouraged to look for outside employment. They are also allowed to sell or barter whatever supplies they accumulate. Indeed, a small market economy had already taken root; on the walk in, we passed stalls set up by some of the more enterprising residents to sell extra soap, candy, packets of laundry powder. Urooj stopped to buy some sweets, and the price immediately jumped 400 percent. He laughed, haggled the seller down to a mere 300 percent. A small victory, for both sides.

Children jostled in, smiling, laughing, running away when I said,

*"Bonjour, comment ça va?"* (Thereby using up my entire stock of high school French in one throw.)

"These kids attend school outside the camp as part of the Rwandan school system, following the regular curriculum," Urooj said. This included lessons in English.

I pulled out a notepad and pen. If I was going to present myself as a journalist, I might as well do it properly. "And how are the local schools coping with this huge influx of children?" I asked.

"Very well. We expanded the existing schools in this area," he explained. "There are five thousand refugee children from Kigeme Camp in school, and we built sixty-two new classrooms to accommodate them. We provide them with school uniforms and shoes as well, and we helped pay salaries to hire the extra teachers."

And medical care?

"We have a small clinic inside the camp for basic health issues: malnutrition, pregnancy care, vaccinations. For anything else, we refer them to the local Rwandan health centre at the district hospital."

The UNHCR had helped recruit and train extra health workers as well.

"The hospital itself is very close," Urooj said. "Walking distance from the camp."

In many ways, the camp was now part of the community. And rather than seeing the refugees as a drain, the people here, in one of the poorest regions of Rwanda, were seeing tangible benefits in hosting the Congolese: extra classrooms, extra teachers, better medical access.

"It's working very well," Urooj said. "But employment remains a big challenge."

Deo agreed. "There are people with master's degrees in the camps who can't find work. We are talking to the local business community to see how these educated people can use their training and abilities, instead of wasting their talents. If one person in the camps gets a job, five families benefit."

The initial emergency had stabilized, and Urooj and Deo were now looking at quality of life, as opposed to basic survival needs. "Skill development, handicap needs, trades. Some of the women are now employed by the camp to sew school uniforms instead of having us buy them from a supply company. It saves the camp a bit of money and provides some income for the women. Many of their husbands were killed, so this income is important."

On the day we arrived, a group of women were attending classes on how to use a new fuel-efficient stove that would be distributed throughout the camp. These stoves, manufactured by a German NGO, had a parabolic design that retained 80 percent of their wood-burning heat. With charcoal in short supply, this increased efficiency was crucial. The women, sent as delegates, listened intently to the instructions so that they in turn could teach their neighbours.

In addition to thousands of widows, there were thousands of orphans in the camp. Restless children who needed guidance, who needed team building, who needed a sense of belonging. In a word: soccer.

The camp had organized its own league, all ages, with boys' and girls' teams that regularly challenged neighbouring villages to matches. The sport was well-organized, with volunteer coaches and referees from the camp, regular practices, games ... and an utter lack of equipment. Many of the balls they played with were made from inflated condoms, pilfered from the camp's medical kits and bound with strips of scrap taken from UN gunnysacks. The balls were inflated, ingeniously I thought, with medical syringes. They had a nice bounce to them, but were still a far cry from the real thing.

As the day cooled, Jean-Claude lugged out the duffle bags: roughly 200 soccer uniforms in total, along with goalie gear, deflated balls, and a proper pump. Kids crowded in as the coaches handed out uniforms, noting which numbers went to which kids. The players pulled on their new jerseys and assembled, grinning, looking like the teams they were. Jean-Claude was asked to say a few words.

"Have fun. Play fair. And remember, being a refugee is not a crime," he said. "Having less doesn't make you a lesser person.

Remember, you are the lucky ones. You have the chance to go to school and make something of yourself. Working hard will give you power and a voice. Who knows, there could be a future president among you! Or a future Messi!"

His reference to the Argentine soccer star drew a loud cheer from the kids, and afterward I was invited to interview some of the players. Their coach, a Congolese refugee like the others, recommended I speak with a sixteen-year-old striker named Steven Nshizirungu and a goalkeeper named Eric Iradukunda, also sixteen. Stephen and Eric were exemplary players, I was told, dedicated, well-behaved, helpful with the younger children.

"You can ask them their story," Jean-Claude suggested. "Why they came to this camp." But I couldn't. I just couldn't.

It would have ruined the alchemy of that moment, would have soured the giddy and simple joy of kids suiting up. Of looking *like a real team*. Of having *real soccer balls*. It would have been gauche to confront them with a journalist's horrible and inevitable questions: So tell me, are both your parents dead? How did they die? Did you watch them die? Who killed them, do you know?

No. None of that. Instead, I decided that these would be *sports* interviews. This would not be about geopolitical forces beyond their control, but about something very much under their auspices: the handling of a soccer ball, the clarity of a crossover, the sudden strike, the blocked shot, the floating perfection of a chipped-in goal. After all, if they were going to become soccer stars, they had better get used to dealing with the media.

When I asked the crowd of kids who their best player was on the girls' team, the response was immediate. A solid-looking sixteen-year-old player named Appoline Nyiramugisha was pushed to the front, looking equal parts embarrassed and proud.

Appoline was a striker and by all accounts formidable.

"Could you score on Eric?" I asked. "On a penalty kick?"

She looked him over, slowly, delivered a withering one-word assessment. "Certainly."

This brought cheers from the girls and loud protests from the boys. But when I asked Appoline who her soccer role model was, which women's player she looked up to, she didn't understand the question. She was puzzled by it, in fact.

Appoline Nyiramugisha didn't know there was such a thing as professional women's soccer players. When I told her there most certainly was, and that, if she kept at it, she might make a living at soccer when she got older, her smile looked as though it were lit from within. (If in the future, a Congolese player named Appoline is tearing up the women's pro-soccer pitch, you will know where she got her start.)

I told her: "The best women's soccer player in the world is a Canadian. Her name is Christine Sinclair, and she's a striker like you. So when people ask you, Who do you play like? you tell them *I play like Christine Sinclair.*"

She practised the name, said it aloud several times. Smiled.

And so passed the rest of the afternoon, not in talk of war or hardships or pain, but of something much more important: soccer.

As the sun softened and evening settled on the hills, as the smell of cooking fires drifted across, Jean-Claude and I said our goodbyes to the kids and met up with Urooj and the others for the steep descent back to the jeep.

The younger children in the camp had grown bolder, with the more brazen among them risking a hurried burst of English; they'd figured out quickly enough that I didn't speak French. Their greetings were thrown my way like an unexploded water balloon— *"Good morning teacher how are you I am fine!"*—as the kids in question ran back to squeals of congratulations from their friends. That they were using the exact phrasing the kids in Kigali did was a testament to the fact that they were now part of the Rwandan school curriculum.

Urooj stopped, looked back at the hills above us. He said, "Good things are happening here."

But Kigeme was still a camp, and these were still refugees.

"The real solution," Deo said back at the UN office, "is political." The turmoil in Congo needed to be resolved.

"Remember," he said, "these refugees are civilians. They are innocent of any crimes. They had homes, farms, shops. They had full lives. They were established. What do they need, more than anything? What do they want, more than anything? They want to go home."

# 27

A SMALL SIGN, caught in the fleeting headlights of dusk, it might have flitted past unnoticed, save for the weight of its message: RIVER CONGO–RIVER NILE DIVIDE: STREAMS FLOWING WEST OF THESE HILLS FLOW INTO THE RIVER CONGO, WHILE THOSE TOWARD THE EAST FLOW INTO THE RIVER NILE.

We were travelling along Africa's central watershed. The farthest capillaries of the continent's two major arteries came within metres of touching—here, on this remote forest ridge. The great rivers of Africa, sorting themselves out. On one side of the road, rain and runoff were channelled west, through a vast rainforest and a labyrinthine delta, into the warm currents of the equatorial Atlantic; water on the other side ran east and then north, through deserts and swamps, over waterfalls and past pyramids, before emptying at last into the Mediterranean.

Jean-Claude and I had been following this watershed without realizing it, along a thin strip of asphalt, the forest pressing in from both sides. Seeing the sign for the Congo–Nile divide, we pulled over to mug for photographs. Tripod and self-timer. Flash frames in the jungle. We considered a shot of Jean-Claude peeing on one side of the road and me on the other, but decided it might not convey the dignity of the moment properly.

All around us, the forest seemed to be breathing. Cold mist. A mossy smell, part soil, part soggy rot. The taste of mulch and wet leaves. I could hear something whuffling about in the underbrush.

It was a shame I'd come to Rwanda in the dry season. This is what everyone kept telling me. They bemoaned my timing, arriving in the red-dust days of the dry. "You should have come in March or November, or in June, right after the rainy season has ended when everything is green." I would say, "It looks green now." But they would say, "No. You haven't seen green. After the rains, *that*—that is green."

But Rwanda seemed plenty green to me, even in the dry season. Nyungwe Forest in particular seemed to defy the notion of seasons.

"There is no dry season in Nyungwe," I'd been told. "Even when it's dry, it's wet."

Nyungwe is where the moist air of the Congo River pushes up against the cooler alpine heights of Rwanda's western mountains. These peaks catch the heavy underbelly of these clouds, splitting them open. Much of the country's groundwater starts here, in these forests, these mountains. In Nyungwe, the annual rainfall is measured in *metres*.

Soon after the sign marking the Congo–Nile divide, we came upon sheaves of broad leaves that had been laid across the road; Jean-Claude quickly geared down as we drove over them. It looked like a clumsy attempt at a highwayman-style ambush, but in actuality was a warning.

"It's for safety," Jean-Claude explained. "When there's an accident, it is required by law. You must put out leaves to tell the other drivers." We slowed up, came around a corner, and there it was: a single-vehicle accident. A transport truck had jackknifed on a sharp turn. No injuries, thankfully, but a great deal of collateral damage. In Jungle vs. Truck Driver, round one had clearly gone to the jungle. The transport truck had slammed sideways into the trees and was now impaled on broken branches.

The driver, on muddy hands and knees, was trying to wrap the truck's front-winch cable around the axle. He'd already looped the same cable around a large tree trunk and back again, and was clearly planning to hoist the vehicle out under its own steam. It seemed sort of like trying to fly by grabbing hold of one's belt loops and pulling upward, but then again, physics never was my long suit.

We slowed to a crawl, passing a long-distance bus that was idling on the other side. We had just enough space to squeeze through on the road, but the bus did not. Several passengers had disembarked and were watching the proceedings with frowny-faced interest, poised to leap in with helpful advice at a moment's notice. These passengers were, it goes without saying, of the male persuasion. The women were tending to young children, juggling bundles, preparing food, adjusting shoulder slings. It's a failing of their sex, but they didn't seem to appreciate the art of unsolicited advice. (Men. We're sort of philanthropists that way.)

We were deep in the protected realm of a national park, and the road, although paved, was exceedingly narrow at certain points. There were times it felt as though we were being swallowed whole by a python, our Land Cruiser a lump moving through a serpentine intestinal tract.

"Nyungwe has a reputation," Jean-Claude said. "For being scary. A lot of legends. Ghosts and creatures that can flip over cars. For Rwandans, it's like a haunted forest."

Ha ha, I laughed. Ha ha.

Neither of us said anything for a long while. *Maybe that's what had thrown that transport truck off the road earlier. It had seemed odd, a vehicle suddenly tossing itself into the jungle like that.*

The air became cooler the higher we went. Bits of mist were caught in the forest canopy, like cotton batting. In the rear-view mirror, the jungle closed behind us. Smatterings of flowers, mad dabs of purple and red among the feathered ferns and tangled vines, flickered past. Scents swirled through the open window, some sweet, some skunky. The silvery leaves of the eucalyptus tree had their own distinct aroma: partly pine, mainly menthol. A medicinal scent. It gave the air a tiger-balm tinge.

There was one smell, though, that Jean-Claude racked his memory trying to identify. "Did you catch that?" he would ask. "Just now. *There*. Again. Is some kind of plant. Smells like roasted peanuts. I know that smell." He never was able to identify it, though. Perhaps it was more a presence than a scent, the echo of something long gone.

"It's not there anymore," he said. "But I know it. I know that smell."

The road folded in on itself, twisting and turning, almost meeting on the way back. Dizzying views. Stomach-sloshing corners. A low rumble of thunder as the sky cleared its throat. Flashes of light behind the clouds. The road ahead of us was drenched, potholes filled with splash-pockets of water. We were driving into the aftermath of a thunder shower, and tattered debris, blown by wind, was freshly scattered across the road. At every bend we expected to come upon a storm in progress, but we never did. It was like following the path of an advancing army. With each slash of lightning, the thunderclap that followed was farther and farther away. Rwanda was one of the lightning capitals of the world, a place of frequent and sudden strikes. *Forget car-flipping phantasms*, I thought. *Let's hope the tires on our 4x4 are insulation enough if we get hit.*

As we wound our way back down into the lower forest, away from potential lightning strikes and car-tossing gremlins, a carpet of bright green appeared: tea plantations, carved out of the jungle. We drove between these tightly rounded hedges, and they seemed to glow in the half-light.

The road branched off and a gate appeared. Jean-Claude brought the Land Cruiser to a halt as a night watchman, rifle slung loosely over his shoulder, ambled out to check our names against a list. He nodded, shunted the barrier aside, and gave us a sleepy raised-palm wave as we passed. We drove deeper into tea, splitting a sea of green with the prow of our truck.

Things you don't expect to find in the middle of a rainforest: valet parking.

There is no place in Rwanda quite like Nyungwe Forest Lodge. Clean, modernist lines with African decor, an infinity pool, and a dining-room veranda offering sublime views. Five-star elegance with a low-impact design: the lodge has received environmental accreditation for its low carbon footprint. When Jean-Claude and I pulled up, we were greeted with hot face towels, pineapple juice served in chilled glasses, and a valet to park our vehicle.

"Here's to roughing it in Africa," we said, clinking glasses.

I hadn't come to Nyungwe Forest Lodge merely to soak up the good life, though. No sir. I was on assignment, remember. Jean-Claude and I were here to carry out a socioeconomic investigation of strategic marketing paradigms. (Whatever that meant.) If this required our own private elevated cabins with full bath and cumulus pillows, so be it.

On the restaurant's veranda we further toasted our good fortune: me with a light Riesling, Jean-Claude with his infernal alcohol-free mineral water. We stretched out our legs under linen tablecloths, dined on the views (and the filet of beef, that too), then retired to our respective cabins, following a path through a sea of tea. A German family pushed past us, impatient to start relaxing. A silver-coin moon hung in the air, and above the lights of the lodge, the Nyungwe mountains formed layered horizons, overlapping in gradations of torn blue. A mood so splendid not even the Germans could ruin it, and that's saying a lot.[14]

---

14. Kidding! Germans are lovely people.

# 28

I WOKE TO THE CHIRPLE AND TRILL of tropical birds, the scamper of monkeys across tiled rooftops, the wry chuckle of primates in the trees. My cabin, sitting on stilts, looked out at a wall of forest. The jungle began two feet from my balcony.

I went for an early-morning walk, met the same German family tromping purposefully toward the lodge, circled back, and ate breakfast as far from them as possible. Jean-Claude showed up soon after, looking spry and surprisingly refreshed. "I dreamed I was driving," he said.

"Oh. Would you like me to ..." I offered half-heartedly.

"Are you kidding? I'm enjoying this."

Nyungwe Forest Lodge has won international awards for hotel design, and the person overseeing the operation was another one of those smart, educated young women Rwanda seemed to specialize in. I stopped by to see her after breakfast.

Alice Kampire had been with the lodge for three years, since it first opened. She was originally the financial supervisor, but had been moved to assistant manager, in charge of customer service. The hardest part, she told me, was keeping staff. Having been trained at the highest level, employees often jumped ship to work at other hotels or to launch businesses of their own. Hoteliers, chefs, and niche-market tour company ventures have all sprung from Nyungwe Forest Lodge.

"We are like a training ground," Alice said with a half-sigh. "But," she shrugged, "it's good for them to grow. And other people are always joining. Many want to work here, so we can pick the best."

I'd seen this firsthand over breakfast. When I asked the waiter if they had multi-grain toast, I was told that sadly, no, they had only white or brown. When the meal arrived—slices of fresh fruit, soft-poached eggs with sausage, and caramelized slices of plantain—the toast that accompanied it was exactly what we would call "multi-grain." When I mentioned this to the waiter, he pulled out a pencil and recorded the information for future reference. "And whole wheat?" he asked. "What is that? Sometimes American tourists ask for whole wheat."

He was planning to open a café on the shores of Lake Kivu, he confided, one that would cater to international guests. "You will come? When it's open?" It wasn't really a question, the way he said it. Of course I would. Why wouldn't I? His place would have multi-grain *and* whole wheat.

I thought it best not to mention to Alice that she was about to lose yet another staff member. I did, however, consider canvassing her opinion about the socioeconomic importance of strategic marketing paradigms, but, given that I didn't understand the question myself, decided against it.

"Ready for the monkeys?" she asked.

"I am," I said, then added knowingly, "and for the *chimpanzees,* too." I'd already learned, childhood readings of *Curious George* to the contrary, that chimpanzees are not technically "monkeys." They are apes, a fact I liked to drop into conversations whenever possible.

Jean-Claude and I had booked two nights at the lodge, with primate treks lined up on both days. We'd be starting with the monkeys. The apes would come later.

Thirteen distinct species of primate make their home in the forested hills of Rwanda, and Nyungwe Forest contains almost every species save gorillas, a remarkable concentration.

After putting together our day packs, we drove—note the ongoing use of the royal "we"; Jean-Claude drove, I jotted down insights and observations—to the park's main office to meet up with a trio of guides, two of whom were disquietingly armed. Rebels were operating in Congo, I'd been told, but Congo wasn't that close, surely.

"The rifles are in case of animals," one of the guides explained.

"What kinds of animals?"

"Oh, all kinds."

As the other armed guide passed by, he whispered cryptically, "Not for animals."

The pursuit of monkeys is a strange undertaking. You go crashing through the underbrush like the clumsy, ground-bound primate you are, engaged in a dogged steeplechase. To what end? Primarily for the amusement of our nimbler airborne cousins, I suspect.

At the lodge I'd seen fleeting tufts of fur bounding from rooftop to rooftop and into the forest, but those were more heard than seen: the sound of monkeys being monkeys. Out here, on trails so faint they seemed to exist mainly in the imagination of our guides, we were tracking a troop of acrobatic colobus as they leapt from branch to branch far overhead, their white-tipped tails flipping us the bird. We were, apparently, playing an extended game of monkey tag, which is as exhausting as it sounds. Whenever we stopped, hands on knees, panting, they would stop as well, waiting for us to catch our breath before starting the game anew.

At one point, we came upon a scruffy band of mangabeys hanging out in the lower branches. These monkeys were smaller but scrappier than other species, our guide told us, and the rest of the forest tended to leave them alone. Unlike the gentle-eyed vervets, which everybody else picked on, no one messed with the mangabeys. (I noted how the high-flying colobus monkeys gave the mangabeys a wide berth when they passed them in the forest. *"That's right, pal, keep movin'."*)

"If one mangabey gets hurt, the others will fight off anyone who comes near," our guide said. "They are tough little monkeys."

The mangabeys watched us pass with a jaundiced eye. Jaundiced in every sense of the word; their gaze seemed yellow and liquid, as though raw from late-night poker marathons and cigarette smoke. I half-expected to see roll-your-own cheroots dangling from their lips. If monkeys could get tattoos, the mangabeys would be first in line.

Personally, I was hoping to spot the aptly named owl-faced monkey, if only because they look so sadly comical with their morose eyes and long white stripe down the middle of their noses, but none appeared. Damn rude of them not to show up. Didn't they know we were on a schedule?

The monkeys that we did see were of the taunting variety. There was something about the sight of a telephoto lens that inspired them. They'd be sitting on a branch in perfect profile, dramatically backlit by a shaft of sun, peering at the far horizon with a look of ancient monkey wisdom, only to bolt the moment I raised my viewfinder. I have an entire catalogue of monkey-butt photographs. Blurred tails. A bunch of leaves where a monkey just was. That sort of thing.

The trail we were allegedly following traced a line of gummy clay through tanglements of foliage, the air redolent with the smell of growth and decay, of rot and rebirth feeding off each other.

"Path must be slick in the rainy season," I gasped, unsnagging myself again from the grasp of Rwanda's prehensile vines.

"Yes. Very muddy. But more greener," said our lead guide, waving a disappointed hand at the towering stands of beauty surrounding us. "You should have come after the rains. It's much nicer. More green."

The fluted trunks of strombosia trees rose like cathedral columns under the ceiling of sunshade canopy. *Were these the trees that inspired Rwandan legends about the forests of the Congo holding up the sky?* Monkeys fed on the nutlike fruit of the strombosia, gnawing off the outside and tossing away the pits. The trails were scattered with them.

A white-bearded L'Hoest's monkey, looking every bit the wizened old hermit, watched us as we came out onto a rutted road. The colobus assembled in the leaves above us, waiting for us to come back and play. When we didn't, they gave a collective shrug and went off to look for some vervets to beat up.

As we stood on the road chugging water, a band of Twa villagers appeared, walking uphill at a slow, steady pace, bundles on heads, dressed in loose cloth, shoulders bare. They lived in these forests, in remote communities barely linked to the outside world. I was fairly sure one of our own guides was Twa himself (he barely came up to my chest and moved through the forest with an ease the other guides must have envied), but there was no way to ask him without causing all sorts of awkwardness. As the villagers approached, our guide raised his hand in greeting. He spoke with them softly for a moment, nodding when they pointed down the road. More monkeys that way. He thanked them, and we strode off with renewed vigour.

Several hours and an enlightening conversation about leopards later—*"Yes, there are leopards in these forests, but rarely seen, we'd be 'lucky' if we actually met one, and no the rifles are not for leopards, they are for ... other things"*—we arrived back at the main road. Our Land Cruiser was waiting right where we'd left it.

On the assumption that leopards strike from behind, picking off the laggards, I'd pushed my way to the middle of the line, leaving Jean-Claude to pull up the rear. We ended our day with a canopy walk, where a series of ropelike bridges was strung between the treetops like a laundry line.

Bird calls and the chirr of insects. Vertigo views. The sudden bombastic shake of a tree as a monkey leapt through the leaves below. *Finally, we have the high ground on the little buggers.* One monkey, on hearing our heavy footsteps above, looked up with an expression of abject befuddlement—*"What on earth are you doing way up there?"*—before scurrying away.

The canopy below seemed soft and fluffy, as though, if you took a swan dive over the edge, you might bounce on its quilt-like softness. I stood awhile, gently swinging, looking down. We could hear the whoop of monkeys in the distance and, nearer at hand, the panicked cries of a heavy-hipped woman being coaxed onto the cat's cradle of the canopy walk by her barrel-bellied husband.

I'd chatted with them earlier. They ran a boarding school in Kigali, were here on holiday, and as such represented the growing number of Rwandans travelling within their own country: domestic tourists, a sure sign of a nascent middle class. Though, given the woman's shrieks and deathlike grip on the swaying cables, I don't imagine she had quite as positive a take on the matter.

"What was she saying?" I asked Jean-Claude afterward. "In Kinyarwanda."

"Oh," he said. "Many bad things. Mainly about her husband."

"This is where the rest of my life began." Jean-Claude on the bridge over Rusumo Falls.

A fateful bottleneck in the Akagera River.

Bullet holes at Camp Kigali where the Belgian peacekeepers were killed.

Aftermath of an attack: the communal kitchen at Ntarama.

Putting faces to statistics at the Kigali Genocide Memorial Centre.

The clothing of victims piled in front of the bullet-scarred tabernacle at Nyamata Church.

Coffins on the pews at Ntarama. The clothing of victims hangs from the rafters.

"I ran and I ran and they could not catch me." Survivor on Murambi Hill.

Two very different palaces. Belgian-built residence of the last kings of Rwanda.

The mwami's residence in the Royal Courts of Nyanza.

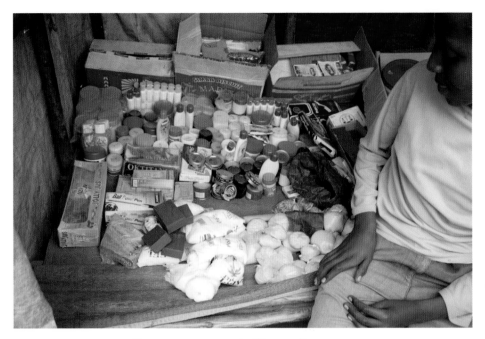

Young entrepreneur at the Kigeme refugee camp.

"They are not prisoners." A community takes shape at Kigeme Camp.

Jean-Claude with some of the newly suited future soccer stars of Kigeme refugee camp.

Our 4×4 at the end of the known world. The rainforests of the Congo were once thought to hold up the sky.

Trail guide in the Rwandan rainforest. A paint-by-numbers where every colour is green.

If monkeys could get tattoos, mangabeys would be first in line.

"Many bad things. Mainly about her husband." Canopy walk at Nyungwe.

View from the entranceway of Nyungwe Forest Lodge.

The art of hitchhiking: Betty, Grace, and Anuarite, the three students we gave a ride to.

Dust in the jungle. Our 4×4 marked with fingerprints.

# 29

THE CHIMPANZEES PROVED MORE MANAGEABLE. Now there's a sentence you don't often read!

We gathered in the early hours the next morning, an assortment of travellers, all yawns and neck cricks, awaiting instruction. Destinations were confirmed, with some groups bound for waterfalls, others for a summit, still others setting off in search of chimps. A second vehicle would be joining Jean-Claude and me on our trek, an equally dusty 4x4 carrying a psychiatrist from Toronto named Lorne and his indomitable daughter Adriana. Lorne and Adriana had been travelling across East Africa after Adriana's tour of duty as a volunteer in Tanzania ended. She was fifteen and dauntless. Also prone to carsickness, which made their ongoing road trip tough at times. She spent much of it bobble-headed in the backseat.

Over the course of their father-daughter expedition, they'd observed some interesting contrasts between the countries they visited. "When we crossed into Rwanda," Lorne noted, with a nod to their driver, "everything changed. It was suddenly very clean. The quality of the roads immediately improved, and the police checkpoints simply … stopped."

Travellers in Africa so often get used to the mild but constant harassment of police officers and border officials wheedling people for bribes that the sudden absence of this in Rwanda is almost unnerving.

"Rwanda has a very different vibe," Lorne said.

Adriana was more ambivalent about it. Echoing the tousle-haired Swede we'd met earlier, she said, with a sigh, "There are too many rules in Rwanda."

Lorne and I exchanged looks. *Ah, youth. When you get older, you won't find messy inefficiency quite so charming.*

We headed south just before dawn, driving through the tunnel of our own headlights. The road curved sleepily through one village, then the next.

It would take more than an hour to get to the trailhead in Cyamudongo, where a band of twenty-five chimps was living in a protected enclave of montane, "cloud," forest. It was Sunday, and as if on cue, hundreds of women appeared, dressed in proud patterns, dragging their husbands in ill-fitting suits behind them. Off to church.

With a jar, the pavement ended.

Our two-vehicle convoy had left the main road and turned onto rougher routes. As we rattled across corduroy surfaces, the father-daughter vehicle in front of us disappeared into a kickback of powdered clay. Our wipers smeared a slurry of mud across the glass, opening up a narrow view. Steep sides dropped away on either side. We were ridge running, half-blind.

"Don't worry," said Jean-Claude, referring to the rows of trees along the side. "We have guardrails."

The road crested, and we were soon deep in forest again. The vehicle ahead rolled to a stop and we pulled up alongside. When I opened my door, clay fountained off. *Dust in the jungle.* A strange combination.

A pair of trail guides were waiting for us, trim young men dressed in the dark-green uniforms of Rwanda's National Park Service.

"Welcome to Cyamudongo. From here," they said, "we will walk. This could take an hour, maybe more, maybe less. Probably more."

Another vehicle appeared, and four more people climbed out, Spanish students touring the region. This brought our tally to eight, which was the cap for these treks. The motto, as always, was small numbers, low impact.

The path was wide and easy to follow. It ran flat for a while and then headed down a steep incline, where the thick roots of trees formed natural steps. When we came upon a pile of monkey poop, we got very excited.

"Not monkey poop," the guide corrected us. "*Chimpanzee* poop." Not that it mattered. *Click-whirr, click-whirr, click.* Said poop was immortalized in a flurry of photographs from numerous angles while our guides stood to one side, trying not to shake their heads in wonderment. Like the Twa villagers we'd met in the jungle the day before, they must have thought we were more than a bit batty.

*Forget the primates,* I thought. *You could tour their poop.* I made a mental note to get rich on this later.

By now, I had the feeling that our guides—fully trained in forest conservation—were also a wee bit hungover. They were besieged with yawns and bleary of eye. When a bird of prey similar to the one I'd seen at the royal court *kii*ed above us, swooping low and then arcing up and away, I said, "I've seen that bird before. Is that a hawk or an eagle?"

The guide I was walking beside mumbled "Yes."

Um.

"So … is it a hawk? Or is it an eagle?" (I don't know why I needed to know; I'm not a birdwatcher or anything.)

"It's uh—it's a hawk-eagle," the guide said.

Really? "A hawk-eagle?"

"That's right."

Mental note: *Check to see if there really is such a thing as a hawk-eagle.*[15]

"Sometimes hawk-eagles catch baby monkeys," he added helpfully. "They take them right from the trees."

"You mean, they take baby *chimpanzees*," I said.

He shrugged. *Tomayto, tomahto.*

We came upon more poop, fresher than the last batch, and with anticipation mounting on every step, we stumble-walked through the forest, eyes everywhere except on the trail, ready to catch sight of these mysterious forest denizens.

We needn't have worried. When you come across chimps, you know it. They are, as Jean-Claude put it, "the teenagers of the forest." Noisy, gratuitously destructive, endlessly argumentative, fully obsessed

---

15. Turns out, yes. There is. *Aquila spilogaster*, the African hawk-eagle.

with bodily functions, and constantly laughing at their own antics. You hear them long before you see them: that reverberating hooting pant, the *ooo-ooo-ooo-ah-ah-ah*, from the soundtrack of every Tarzan movie. It's a sound that tingles the spine when you hear it, gets louder, more pitched as you draw nearer. And then suddenly, right in front of you, is a tree full of chimps. I don't know if you remember the classic children's book *Go, Dog. Go!*, but it ends with a dog party! A big dog party! on top of an enormous umbrella-like tree. That's what it was like. A chimp party! A big chimp party! Thirty or so primates with party hats and cake and noisemakers had congregated on a single massive tree.

We spent an hour watching them as they scrambled from branch to branch, fighting, hooting, mating (eww), grooming, feeding, picking at their anuses. The whole gamut of the chimpanzee lifestyle was on proud display that day.

They seemed able-footed, but the guides assured us that chimps did fall from trees now and then. "Sometimes, when they try to jump, they miss. And if they are too high up, they can be killed by the fall."

Jean-Claude figured that must be the single most embarrassing way to die if you're a monkey: falling from a tree.

"If the neighbours ask," Jean-Claude whispered, "I will bet the chimpanzee's family will say to them 'He died fighting a leopard,' or had a heart attack."

Anything but falling from a tree.

I don't know why we were whispering. It's not as if we were at a chimp funeral; the entire tree was in a ruckus. We were standing on a spongy mat of moss and mulch, and when I climbed over a fallen tree trunk to get a closer look, I didn't notice that I was now standing on top of—

The guide tapped my shoulder and said, at the exact moment I felt the first burning stings on my ankles, "Fire ants. You should maybe move."

Though, of course, by that point I was already running in circles, mid-air, swatting at my ankles. I may have said something as well. Something along the lines of *"Gettim off me! Gettim off me!"*

Jean-Claude told me later that several chimps had stopped to watch. "They were very entertained," he said.

Shortly before it was time to go, I spotted a solitary chimp sitting on a low branch, lips pursed in a pensive manner as he looked into the middle distance, one long arm hanging down. As I drew closer, the guide again tapped my shoulder. "Maybe not too close," he said. He gestured to the chimp's dangling hand and what was cupped inside it: a moist lump of poop, ready for the flinging. And there he was, looking oh-so-innocent, hoping I would come ... just ... a little ... bit ... closer.

"Was he really going to?" I asked.

"Probably."

Chimpanzees have thirty kinds of sounds to communicate with, from breathy pants to sudden screeches to low growls. They organize hunting parties against colobus monkeys, the guide said as we tromped back toward the trailhead.

"There are wars going on in these forests?"

He nodded. "All the time."

# 30

OUR JOURNEY TO SEE THE CHIMPS had taken us to the edge of the Burundian border. At one point, when I asked the guide which way Burundi lay, he pointed to the next mountain and said, "Other side."

Burundi and Rwanda existed as separate—but mirrored—Tutsi–Hutu kingdoms for centuries prior to European arrival. The Germans lumped them together into a single administrative unit known as "Ruanda-Urundi." Belgium continued this policy, but when the two countries gained independence, their destinies diverged—dramatically.

In many ways, Burundi and Rwanda are distorted reflections of each other. Much like Rwanda, Burundi was a centralized, semi-feudalistic society with two main social classes: Tutsi herders and Hutu farmers, with the ruling kings drawn from the Tutsi class. But whereas in Rwanda the Hutu majority took control after independence, in Burundi the Tutsi minority dug in. Drawing lessons from the 1959 massacre of Tutsis in neighbouring Rwanda, the ruling elite in Burundi tightened their grip, slaughtering Hutu civilians on any pretext, with every failed rebellion or attempt at raising a political opposition.

Multi-party rule in Burundi eventually signalled the end of Tutsi hegemony, but the Tutsi elite would not go down without a fight. In the same month that the Arusha Accords were signed, ending Rwanda's civil war, Burundi elected its first Hutu president. It boded well for democracy in the region. But just four months after he was elected, the new president was assassinated by Tutsi army officers. When the Hutu population rose up, the government responded with a further slaughter of Hutu citizens under a series of scorched-earth pogroms. Hundreds of thousands fled into Rwanda, bringing with them warnings of Tutsi Power. The message was clear: *"Do not trust the Tutsis!"* Burundi and Rwanda were caught in an echo chamber, each one's outrages fuelling the fears and intransigence of the other, a *danse macabre* in which both sides led, both sides followed. The two countries were, in Gérard Prunier's memorable description, "opposite ends of a political seesaw."

In Calgary, I once mistakenly referred to a pastor Jean-Claude had introduced me to as being Rwandan. He wasn't. He was from Burundi. "But don't worry," the pastor laughed. "This is a very easy mistake to make. In Burundi, you see, we are always copying Rwanda. They kill *their* president, we have to kill *our* president. *They* have a genocide, we have to have one too."

Jean-Claude and the pastor from Burundi had a good chuckle over this. Gallows humour, I suppose, but true.

In Burundi, massacres followed counter-massacres in a cycle of violence that feeds itself even now. Burundi was never laid low the way Rwanda was, but it has never rebuilt itself, either. It remains mired in corruption and poverty, with political turmoil and ethnic tensions flaring up constantly.[16]

If Rwanda today has too many rules, Burundi has too few. The same surveys that routinely place Rwanda among the least corrupt nations in Africa inevitably place Burundi among the worst. Rwanda's economy is growing; Burundi's is stagnant. It remains among the poorest countries on the continent. And even today, along this border, in these remote hills and clandestine forests, secret wars are being waged.

---

16. As I write this chapter, Burundi is caught up in another failed military coup, and thousands of Burundian refugees are fleeing into Rwanda to escape the violence. It's also worth noting that while Rwanda adopted a strict "one country, one culture" model, Burundi chose instead to entrench political and ethnic quotas, giving Hutus and Tutsis mandated proportional representation in their legislature. In Burundi, the Hutu–Tutsi divide is alive and well.

# 31

JEAN-CLAUDE AND I SAID a reluctant farewell to the five-star luxury of Nyungwe Forest Lodge, knowing that every subsequent lodging would suffer by comparison. *"Glacier-chilled strawberries topped with papaya, you say? At Nyungwe Forest Lodge they had glacier-chilled strawberries topped with papaya and a selection of sliced cantaloupe arranged in festive formations, but I suppose this will have to do."*

The hotel staff had washed the Land Cruiser for us without our asking—the ol' girl gleamed—and as we wound our way through neon-green fields of tea beneath smoke-coloured mountains, an early-morning mist settled on the landscape. It felt as if we were starring in a truck commercial.

Jean-Claude told me about a dream he'd been having, in which he and I were being chased by a mob of people. "I couldn't see who they were, just that they wanted to kill us."

"Us?" I asked. "What the hell did I do?"

"Guilt by association," Jean-Claude said with a laugh. "Your skin is so light maybe they thought you were a Tutsi."

"Well, keep me out of your nightmares, okay?"

He smiled. "Oh, I can't promise that."

What must it be like to come back to this landscape, to this land, and dream of faceless people chasing you? I couldn't begin to imagine.

Having left Nyungwe National Park, we came to a T in the road, freshly paved in both directions with a new market alongside. Women bustled about, setting up shop for the day.

"Buhinga," said Jean-Claude. "That's the name of this place."

It wasn't even on the map. Formerly a huddle of clay huts, today it is a crossroads town teeming with trade.

"I was out here once, many years ago," Jean-Claude said. "It's changed."

"For the better?"

He looked at me as if I were mad. "Of course."

They used to hunt Tutsis along the muddy trails outside of Buhinga. Now they were shopping at a new, purpose-built market on freshly paved roads, a reminder that in Rwanda the past was never something to feel nostalgic about. There were no "good old days" to pine for.

Jean-Claude turned onto wider roads, pointed us north.

Beyond the red-clay escarpments of Buhinga, we got our first clear views of Lake Kivu in the distance. Then, as quickly as it appeared, Kivu was gone, disappearing behind leafy stands of banana trees. Every yard seemed to have several of these oversized plants out front, surrounding and at times obscuring the homes behind them. The tightly bunched bananas formed rubbery green chandeliers.

"Out here, if you have an extra foot of land, you plant a banana tree."

It felt as though someone had overturned a giant bowl of lettuce on us. The leaves hung down, slapping the sides of the Land Cruiser as we passed. And with every break in the greenery, every gap in the hills, a backdrop of blue.

Less a lake than an inland sea, Kivu divides the Democratic Republic of Congo from that of Rwanda, and as the road grew steeper, we found ourselves looking over across the dramatic headlands of Ijwi Island. The island sits on the Congo side of the great divide, and with the mist that had pooled on the lake, Ijwi seemed to be floating on a fog bank. Other islands hovered above the water as well, but as the sun climbed higher, the mist on Lake Kivu melted away and the Congo emerged, full force, on the far side of the lake. *The end of the known world.*

Beginning a slow descent into the next valley, we passed through the town of Kagano where a new church was taking shape: jerry-rigged scaffolding and red-brick walls the same colour as the soil. Faith, under construction. Like the crossroads community of Buhinga, Kagano sported a brand-new market as well, with freshly painted shops in earthen reds and tawny yellows. (The brighter phone-company-sponsored colours hadn't yet reached this remote region.) A quarry works was taking bloodless bites from the side of a hill as men in sweat-stained undershirts shovelled gravel into wooden containers. A young girl stepped back to watch us pass.

The road seemed to fall out from under us; we came down so fast I could feel the drop in my stomach. On a marshy plain, the Kamiranzovu flowed into Lake Kivu in a coffee-swirl of silt. We crossed the river on a rickety bridge of dubious integrity, past hordes of small children who were cannonballing off the sides.

"Morning bath time," said Jean-Claude. "Really just a chance to play."

Banyan trees lined the banks of the Kamiranzovu. They looked like plants that, triffid-like, had somehow learned to walk, ambulatory trees struggling to free themselves from reechy waters. We drove alongside Lake Kivu, a polished plane with islands embedded, before starting our ascent anew.

This would set the pattern for the rest of the day, as we cut across the rise-and-fall fjords of Lake Kivu, climbing over high ridges then slaloming back down the other side, crossing the mouth of a marshy river or stream that emptied into the lake and then climbing back up again over the next row of serrated hills.

At the RDB tourism office back in Kigali, Rica Rwigamba had confided in me, with a slightly abashed laugh, that the bureau was planning to package this route as the "Rwanda Riviera." It seemed a bit of harmless hubris at the time, but having travelled it, I concur. The scenery along Lake Kivu stands with the best of the Mediterranean.

However, as we soon discovered, the road itself wasn't ready for tourists.

It started off well enough. We'd been driving over asphalt that unfurled as smoothly as silk, an image that was particularly apt because we were, as Jean-Claude noted, travelling on a "Chinese highway."

China's all-in move into Africa is one of the least-known stories on the continent. Across sub-Saharan Africa, hundreds of thousands of

Chinese workers are pouring in, building bridges and dams and massive infrastructure projects: all part of China's long-term strategy to supplant the West as Africa's main trade partner while gaining access to the continent's vast resources. China needs fuel, minerals, raw materials. Africa needs roads, infrastructure, and, to judge by the number of Chinese-made trinkets that have swamped the area, cheap manufactured goods as well. More and more local markets in Africa have come to resemble dollar stores. Africa is not just a source of resources for China but a source of consumers as well.

In stark contrast to the stance the West takes, at least *pretending* to make human rights a precondition for favoured trade status, China makes no such demands. (Given their own track record, how could they?) China will happily work with anyone, anywhere, from dictators to struggling democracies, no strings attached.[17] But Rwanda's cooperation comes with stringent conditions, the most important of which is that large-scale projects hire and train a local workforce.

As we rolled toward what would turn out to be the End of Asphalt, we passed Rwandan surveyors and work crews widening the road base, grading the surfaces, pushing the blacktop ever forward. Chinese supervisors in hard hats and putty-grey uniforms worked alongside, and an open field rumbled with cumbersome trucks and massive earthmovers, looking not unlike a gathering of brontosauri. A few of the younger Rwandan drivers-in-training looked slightly terrified behind the controls, even with a Chinese instructor beside them hanging off the door, but most were thundering about with gusto, shifting gears and communicating—how exactly?

"The Chinese learn to speak Kinyarwanda," Jean-Claude explained. "They take lessons before they come."

In Africa, the Chinese have circumvented English as the default mode of trade and are communicating with workers in their own language, a feat the West never mastered. From the first German

---

17. For a look at the scope and impact of the Chinese presence in Africa, see *China's Second Continent* by Howard W. French.

colonizers, through Belgium and France, to Rwanda's current membership in the English-speaking Commonwealth of Nations, the language of business has always depended on what the current political alignment happened to be. As Jean-Claude put it, "My grandfather learned German, my father learned French, I learned English."[18]

Europeans had always expected Africans to learn their language; the Chinese were the first to meet them halfway. They have made it reciprocal as well, opening "Confucius Centres" in several African countries, including Rwanda, where students can learn Chinese culture and language for free.

On the road north, we passed Chinese dormitories, simple structures with high walls and carefully cultivated rice paddies out front. Behind those doors there would be chopsticks and rice wine, Chinese DVDs and photos of sweethearts back in Shanghai. These were cultural outposts we were passing, where Asia and Africa met, and this stretch of road was the only one where, on seeing my sweaty pink face in the window, children ran alongside shouting *"Nihau! Nihau!"* rather than the usual *"Goo'moaning'teacha!"*

That's right. Out here on Lake Kivu, in the remote would-be Rwanda Riviera of central Africa, I was assumed to be Chinese. It made sense: what else could I be? The only muzungus these kids ever saw were Chinese work crews. I clearly wasn't Rwandese, *ipso facto* ... Personally, I loved it. I took to shouting *"Nihau!"* back at them with what I presumed was a fluent Mandarin accent. I even toyed with the idea of getting out and really messing with their heads by introducing myself as Alex Ferguson's son. *"Alex Ferguson is Chinese?"*

Coming upon one construction site, I caught the eye of a weary-looking Chinese worker. He was taking a break, squatting beside the asphalt, elbow resting on his knees as he smoked the stub of a cigarette, and he gave me a nod as we drove by. Just a pair of muzungus passing on the road.

---

18. Jean-Claude also speaks Kinyarwanda, Swahili, and French. Four languages in all.

The highway was pushing prosperity ahead of it. You could see this in both the number and the quality of new rooftops: sheets of metal, catching the light above crumbling clay walls. And in many cases, not clay but cement, freshly painted. The Rwandans who drove the work trucks were well-paid, and they in turn were injecting income back into the local economy. New homes employed local builders, and builders required supplies. More cash meant more cafés. More cafés meant more refrigerators, more Fanta to stock, more food to sell. And as we drove north along this Chinese highway, motorcycles began to appear, shiny and new, dipping and weaving with an undeniable élan.

Financial institutions with tinted glass had popped up amid every clutch of homes, it seemed, offering business loans and compound savings accounts with the latest interest rates posted out front, while girls in traditional head wraps herded goats past the front doors. I realize that at this point one is expected to wax elegiac about the woeful effect of wealth on traditional cultures and the "loss of innocence" that comes with it. But I've never subscribed to the notion that poverty is quaint or that isolation is somehow ennobling. And anyway, this is Rwanda. There is very little innocence left to lose.

# 32

SOMETHING ELSE WAS GOING ON, just below the surface. The Rwanda Riviera was about to become a conduit for information technology as well.

The government was taking advantage of highway construction to run fibre-optic and electrical cables up the length of Lake Kivu. A narrow trench had been cut beside the asphalt, and as the road pushed through, braided cables were being unspooled into the earth alongside it. Jean-Claude and I would follow these cables for hundreds of miles. It was a remarkable undertaking for such a rugged and remote region. The goal, of course, was to bring the world to Rwanda, with full internet access for the entire nation, even in the dusty boondocks—especially in the dusty boondocks.

This embrace of the wider world is also reflected in the country's open-door visa policies. Rwanda is a key member of the East African Community (EAC), which hopes to create a NAFTA-style free-trade zone encompassing Rwanda, Burundi, Uganda, Tanzania, and Kenya. The aim is to lower tariffs and increase cross-border trade throughout the region. This would include shared visas and, potentially, a shared currency as well. Rwanda wants to take things even further, and has been calling on all African states to eliminate barriers to trade, study, and travel in order to encourage the open exchange of goods, people, and ideas. Rwanda has led by example, with an open-door visa policy for *all* Africans, not just members of the EAC.

Rwanda today is one of the only countries in the world that issues automatic visas to all African nationals at point of entry. When asked why he'd brought in such sweeping changes, President Kagame answered, "Common sense and enlightened self-interest."

Enlightened self-interest, the notion that what's in the public's best interest is also in the individual's, motivates much of what Rwanda does. This is seen not simply as a way to claim a better future, but to avoid sinking back into a darker past. The strategy—socially, economically, politically—is predicated on a single overriding obsession: to prevent another genocide from occurring. If everyone is invested in the success of the country, if everyone has a stake in its prosperity, they won't be tempted to tear it down.

Even the laws mandating the percentage of women in parliament and on the Supreme Court are based on this notion. The belief is that if women had had a greater say in government policy, there would never have been a genocide in the first place. And much as I hate to pander to preconceptions about gender, and knowing full well that many women *were* involved, taunting the victims, urging their husbands onward, taking an active role in the lootings, even operating as genocidal militia leaders, the killings themselves were almost exclusively a male undertaking—from the top all the way down. It's hard to imagine a parliament with 64 percent women approving the wholesale slaughter of children.

This is also the reasoning behind Rwanda's full-scale investment in information technology. If the genocide was caused by ignorance and isolation, change that: connect the populace to a larger network, allow trade to move freely across borders, remove travel restrictions, encourage entrepreneurs, reward initiative. These were more than just fibre-optic cables being unspooled. This was a thin line of hope.

If you're going to dream, dream big.

Rwanda already had widespread Wi-Fi coverage in public buildings, hotels, schools, and bus centres, and it was now positioning itself to become a major IT and telecommunications hub as well. To that end, the government signed a massive public–private partnership with South Korea's KT Corporation to provide high-speed 4G internet access to 95 percent of the population by 2018. But of course, access alone isn't enough. Rwanda also aims to have the internet in 70 percent of households on the same timeline.

The fibre-optic cables Jean-Claude and I were driving alongside represented just a small part of a 3,000-kilometre network crisscrossing the country. Rwanda has signed onto the One Laptop per

Child initiative as well. More than 200,000 laptops have been distributed to hundreds of schools across the country, among the highest levels of any country involved in the program.

It's all very ambitious, considering that almost 80 percent of Rwandan homes are still not connected to a national power grid. How do you introduce the internet to villages that are without electricity? Easy. Solar-powered battery chargers. The Rwandan Board of Education, together with a U.S. aid organization, provides low-cost solar panels to schools and community centres across Rwanda so that they can charge laptops, DVD players, and even cell phones (which are used in schools for remote audio instruction programs, such as second-language learning). Many of these schools have no light bulbs, yet can access Google. Thomas Edison has yet to reach them, but Bill Gates has already arrived.

Rwanda is attempting something extraordinary: to leapfrog directly from the agricultural age into the information age, bypassing the industrial stage entirely. It may seem unrealistic, but Asian countries have done it. As one young Rwandan IT entrepreneur gushed, prematurely perhaps, "Rwanda is the Silicon Valley of Africa!" Singapore, Switzerland, and now Silicon Valley: if nothing else, Rwanda may well be the first truly postmodern country in Africa.

"*Nihau, nihau!*" the children yell as they run beside us. Nihau indeed.

# 33

AS WE CONTINUED NORTHWARD, keeping pace with the cables and drawing ever nearer to the dreaded End of Asphalt, I was reminded of something President Kagame said: "The internet today is not a luxury. It is a public utility as much as water and electricity."

Kagame is known to be something of a techno-geek himself, commanding a huge following on Twitter and championing IT at every turn. He's been dubbed "the digital president," though a more accurate nickname might be the one the business community gave him. They refer to him not as the president of Rwanda, but its "CEO." It's often said that Kagame runs the country like a corporation, making sure every director is accountable for their department—and to their shareholders. It's about return on investment, streamlining production, increasing market shares. I was struck when speaking to public employees and government officials by how often they referred to their constituents, and the Rwandan people in general, as "stakeholders."

As the CEO of Rwanda, Kagame is focused on what could best be described as "results-based management," though he uses an older Rwandan term to describe the process. Historically, Rwanda had a custom known as *imihigo,* wherein chiefs and village leaders would stand before their people and proclaim the goals they wished to achieve that year, and then be held responsible for meeting them. Kagame has brought back imihigo in modern form to ensure that the appointed mayors—or *bourgmestres,* as they were once known—and other local administrators and regional heads are made accountable to their constituents.

In a ceremony that's broadcast on television and radio, these leaders make public vows—involving three-year, five-year, and annual plans—and then sign an imihigo contract, which is available online for anyone to read. Their goals have to be ambitious but also measurable and attainable. They might include adding so many classrooms or planting so many trees or distributing a certain number of contraceptives under a family planning program; they might involve paving roads or relocating homes built on a flood plain. If leaders fail to meet their imihigo goals, they are reprimanded or even replaced. (The tenure of mayors in Rwanda is notoriously short.) Those who do meet their goals are feted and publicly praised.

As a member of the Ministry of Local Government put it, "People wouldn't understand if you talk about 'performance contracts,' but if you say *imihigo* they understand."

President Kagame sees his role very clearly: "People can complain, but I have a job to do, and that is to give Rwandans security, development, and opportunity."

*Note:* Not "life, liberty and the pursuit of happiness," but "security, development, and opportunity." Spoken like a true CEO.

Or are these the words of a dictator?

Open-door visa policies, full internet access, the free flow of trade and information, a zero-tolerance policy for corruption, the abolition of the death penalty—these are not the actions one normally associates with a totalitarian regime. Yet this is precisely the criticism levelled at Paul Kagame: that he is, in fact, presiding over a ruthless dictatorship. And therein lies the Great Paradox of today's Rwanda.

In 1994, this small landlocked country was, with no exaggeration, *the worst place on earth.* An open-air abattoir, a failed state, a gutted nation, Rwanda was a land left in genocidal ruin. Today, across the board—in terms of child mortality, health care, education, women's rights, poverty reduction—it's leading the way in Africa. The World Economic Forum places Rwanda among the best countries in the world when it comes to good governance, with accountability "built into the system."

But "good governance" is not the same as "democratic."

The accusation that Paul Kagame is running a dictatorship rests primarily on four pillars: freedom of the press, or lack thereof; the constraints placed on opposition parties; an intolerance for dissent;

and most disturbingly, what appears to be the targeted assassination of political opponents both at home and abroad.

Human Rights Watch, a respected non-partisan organization, may applaud Rwanda's success, but it warns that progress in the social, health care, and economic realms has not been matched in the political arena, that freedom of expression and association is still too tightly controlled. So effective is the RPF's grip on the political sphere that Amnesty International has raised the alarm that Rwanda is in danger of becoming—in tone, if not in fact—a one-party state.

These are serious charges, yet Kagame has brushed them aside, saying, "If you don't want to be criticized, say nothing, do nothing and be nothing. I have no desire of doing nothing."

Love him or hate him, no one is neutral when it comes to Paul Kagame. His exiled former head of the military has denounced President Kagame as being "worse than Gaddafi." A former economic adviser, also in exile, describes the president as "no better than Stalin"—which seems a bit much, considering that Joseph Stalin was responsible for the death of 20 million people, while Paul Kagame led an army that ended a genocide. Even Human Rights Watch credits him with that. If nothing else, Kagame is an equal-opportunity intimidator: prominent Hutus and Tutsis alike have fallen out of favour with him and paid the price. The two men mentioned above? Both are Tutsi, both former RPF insiders.

On paper, Rwanda has very liberal legislation regarding the media. The country has passed an access to information law, and the media operates under a self-regulated body. But the same constitution that guarantees freedom of speech also forbids propagating "divisionism," which can include merely reporting on issues that involve ethnic, racial, or regional conflict. This "shoot-the-messenger" mentality can often inhibit the free discussion of ideas.

The government cites the murderous hate propaganda of the Hutu Power media as a cautionary tale about allowing unbridled free speech, but critics say that this is simply a smokescreen aimed at stifling honest debate. Human rights organizations warn that government accusations of "stirring up ethnic divisions" or propagating a genocidal ideology are being used like a bludgeon to silence opponents.

Certainly, the media in Rwanda *seems* lively enough. There is a proliferation of private radio (thirty-three stations at last count, while during the genocide the country had only two: a government-run station and the infamous RTLM, both of which promoted ethnic violence). Rwanda has several new television stations, and a wide range of newspapers, both domestic and from across East Africa, are readily available—to say nothing of online access. This isn't exactly North Korea we're talking about. Or Cuba, for that matter.

One of the news stories I was following while I was in Rwanda was about a knuckle-rapping the government had received. As reported in the papers, the woman heading the Office of the Ombudsman, Aloysie Cyanzayire, was seeking to recover public funds from anti-corruption cases the government had brought forward and lost. Legal experts in the judiciary scolded the government for wasting public money by rushing to prosecute without gathering sufficient evidence first. A fairly mundane story, but its significance shouldn't be overlooked: the government of Rwanda had been going through the courts, not acting by fiat or decree, but through proper judicial process—and had been *losing*. The government was reprimanded for this and, most importantly perhaps, the press had been reporting it. Can you imagine any of that occurring in a country like Putin's Russia? Or Castro's Cuba?

One article I read while perusing the local papers criticized the government for providing too much public funding to the agricultural sector, arguing that these subsidies were undermining private initiatives. (Imagine a newspaper in Cuba running that story!) Another item, on the front page no less—slow news day, I'm guessing—listed complaints by regional administrators about the amount of money the national government allotted for them to complete their projects, arguing that it wasn't enough. DISTRICTS BLAME MISSED TARGETS ON ALLOCATION GAPS screamed the headline. Sleepy yet? My point, for those of you still awake, is that none of these news stories are unduly remarkable, yet all challenge the notion that Rwanda is some sort of Stalinist state.

When I was in Rwanda, President Kagame got in hot water for remarks he'd made at a local youth association when he suggested that the children of génocidaires should ask for forgiveness on behalf of their community (meaning "on behalf of all Hutus"). This elicited sharp rebukes in the media and from survivors' groups as well, who pointed out that the Rwandan constitution is very explicit: criminal responsibility is *individual* and cannot be transferred or extended to other parties—certainly not to an entire group. "We have children who are below nineteen," one newspaper editorial read. "They were not even born when the genocide was being committed by their relatives, so one cannot ask them to apologize for crimes that they never committed." The same newspaper presented the other side as well, quoting a lawyer who argued that in Rwandan culture, "When people commit mistakes in your name, your ethnicity, you have a duty to apologize on behalf of your people." Such an apology would aid reconciliation, he said. The debate was aired in public, in the press.

So, on the surface anyway, Rwanda's media seems robust. But journalists on the ground tell a different story, one of threats (veiled and not-so-veiled), of political interference and harassment, with a resulting tendency toward "self-censorship" when faced with a story that might be damaging to the ruling RPF. Democracy Watch and the advocacy organization Reporters Without Borders both rank Rwanda very low in their freedom of the press index—162 out of 180 countries, at last count. The Committee to Protect Journalists has been equally outspoken, accusing the Rwandan government of imprisoning and even killing journalists it considered troublesome. In the past, the government has closed down newspapers, once during an election campaign while its editors faced a variety of trumped-up charges.

But it's also worth remembering that at the height of the genocide, the United States refused to take out the broadcast tower, or even jam the signals, of hate-radio RTLM, which was openly calling for the mass murder of Tutsis, even though the American military was the only presence in the region with the capability to block them. The Clinton administration cited "freedom of speech." So now, when the West calls for an unfettered press in Rwanda, it is perhaps not surprising that this is received with stony silence. This doesn't excuse the constraints put on reporters, or attacks on individuals—of course it doesn't—but it does go a long way toward explaining them. Like the clergy, journalists played an active role in promulgating the genocide. It is a distrust born of history.

# 34

HUMAN RIGHTS ORGANIZATIONS have also accused the Rwandan government of suppressing political opposition, of quashing attempts to launch new parties, and of co-opting those few that do exist. The government often clamps down on the opposition in the lead-up to elections, usually on the pretext of preventing ethnic division.

One opposition leader, Victoire Ingabire of the UDF-Inkingi Party, met with one of the leaders of the outlawed FDLR (the Hutu Power rebels in eastern Congo, a group classified by the UN as a terrorist organization) and later complained that the Hutus who died in the genocide had not been commemorated properly. (She made her comments while standing in front of the genocide museum in Kigali, which explicitly states that many Hutus also died.) She was arrested and eventually sentenced to eight years in prison on charges of mobilizing ethnic divisions, promoting a "genocide ideology," and collaborating with the FDLR. When she appealed, her sentence was extended to fifteen years.

The notion that opposition parties are a healthy and needed aspect of political life has never really taken root in Rwanda, where criticism of the government is often considered tantamount to treason. Kagame has purged his own party as well, so often in fact that one begins to suspect that having government ministers arrested is his version of a Cabinet shuffle. When Kagame's former chief of intelligence, a fellow Tutsi, was implicated in a movement to over-throw the government (something the man's supporters adamantly deny), he fled the country, only to turn up dead in a South African hotel room, strangled.

Asked point-blank if he had ordered the hit on his former spy chief, President Kagame replied with typical bluntness, "No. But I wish we had. I really wish it," later adding—at a Sunday prayer meeting, no less—"You cannot betray Rwanda and get away with it. There are consequences." Not a warm and fuzzy guy, our Paul.

Make no mistake. There is a war going on in the shadows, and dozens of government opponents have been forcibly "disappeared." A former prosecutor, a human rights investigator, the vice-president of one of the main opposition parties, and a journalist investigating the attempted assassination of one of Kagame's opponents have all been killed. Anyone with even a passing connection to the FDLR is immediately suspect, and in much the same way that Israel can shut down criticism of its policies by slapping an "anti-Semite" label on it, in Rwanda opponents of the ruling party are routinely denounced as "genocide deniers" and carted away. And the parallel goes even further than that. Although presented as the "Singapore of Africa," Rwanda is seen by some as an African Israel. "A country," in the words of journalist Geoffrey York, "that rose from the ashes of a holocaust to become militarily the strongest in its region, often in conflict with its neighbours and unafraid to pursue its enemies abroad."

The dilemma inherent in the West's relationship with Kagame is often posed as a question: *"Paul Kagame: Rwanda's saviour or strong-man?"* as though the two were mutually exclusive. Or, as the *Washington Post* put it: "Does Rwanda's economic prosperity justify President Kagame's political repression?"

Once again, we may be looking through the wrong end of the telescope. We should perhaps be turning our attention east instead, to countries where these contradictory traits are all too common. If you wish to critique the autocratic nature of Rwanda, you probably need to look to Asia to find the proper parallel: to Japan historically, South Korea recently, and Singapore inevitably. Rather than being just another second-rate, tinpot despot in the tradition of a Mugabe or a Mobutu, an Obote or an Emperor Bokassa, Paul Kagame is closer to being the Rwandan Lee Kuan Yew. Lee was the father of modern Singapore, who took his country from poverty-riven backwater to first-world economic powerhouse in a single generation, a man who famously believed in democracy but not too much democracy.

*New York Times* columnist David Brooks summed up the reality of today's Rwanda by reminding readers that Kagame has "publicly embraced the Singaporean style of autocracy, which has produced tangible economic progress," while still noting that "those of us who champion democracy might hope that freedom, pluralism and democracy can replace chaos. But the best hope may be along South Korean lines, an authoritarian government that softens over time."

Joseph Sebarenzi, a thoughtful and articulate genocide escapee from the Lake Kivu district, was Speaker of the Rwandan Parliament for three years in the post-genocide era. During that time, he strove to assert the parliament's autonomy and legal supremacy over the office of the presidency. "A real government of checks and balances," as he put it. Sebarenzi failed, and having failed, ran afoul of Kagame. Forced to flee Rwanda, he later wrote a memoir about his childhood, the genocide, and his protracted political struggles with President Kagame, titled *God Sleeps in Rwanda*.[19] Sebarenzi describes Rwanda as "a nation of wounded souls," and warns that "Rwanda moved from a single-party system under President Habyarimana to a cosmetic multi-party system under President Kagame. Before war broke out in 1990, Habyarimana's regime was hailed as a model of development

---

19. For Kagame's own journey, from a refugee camp in Uganda to leader of the RPF and president of Rwanda, see Stephen Kinzer's biography *A Thousand Hills: Rwanda's Rebirth and the Man Who Dreamed It.*

and stability in Africa. But that was an illusion.... Similarly, today Kagame's regime is hailed by the international community as a model of stability and economic development."

This is a chilling passage, if it were true. But I'm not sure it is. It strikes me as an example of false equivalence. Rwanda under Habyarimana was indeed a darling of foreign aid, but that's where the comparison ends. Habyarimana and his cronies filled their own pockets and emptied the nation's coffers while fomenting ethnic divisions and allowing the cancer of corruption to flourish. There are valid criticisms to be made of today's Rwanda, but denouncing Kagame as a dictator on par with Habyarimana—or Stalin or Gaddafi, for that matter—is neither helpful nor accurate.

In Rwanda's most recent parliamentary election, the RPF garnered 76 percent of the vote. But in the presidential election, held separately, Kagame won with a whopping 93 percent, which raised eyebrows to say the least. It was the sort of result usually claimed by leaders in the former Communist bloc.[20] But here's the weird part—an independent Gallup poll came back with some surprising results: 77 percent of Rwandans felt they enjoyed a high degree of freedom of expression, association, and personal autonomy, and 94 percent—fourth highest in the world— expressed confidence in their national government. So perhaps Kagame's election results were not as off-kilter as we might think. (Jean-Claude comments, "If you knew what the country was like before, compared to how it is now, you wouldn't be surprised by those results, Will.") But the poll's most significant finding was in measuring *hope*. A full 93 percent of Rwandans believe that hard work will allow you to get ahead. This is a staggering wellspring of optimism, and it hardly suggests, as one dissident claimed, a gulag state filled with "11 million prisoners."

---

20. Habyarimana managed similar electoral feats. In the 1988 presidential election, he received 99.98 percent of the vote. Not a full 100 percent? No. Because that would have been suspicious.

What worries me is not that Rwanda is a Stalinist state whose people are paralyzed with fear—it's not, and those who claim it is are indulging in hyperbole—but that so much of its tightly controlled, Asian-style recovery is centred on the will of one man. *Après Kagame, le déluge?*

If there even is an après Kagame.

Rwanda's constitution limits the presidential mandate to two terms of seven years each. Having served as vice-president and minister of defence, Paul Kagame was elected president in 2003 and then again in 2010, which means his second and final term will end in 2017. (If you're reading this in the future, you know better than I how it turned out.) But there are already growing calls, carefully orchestrated and presented as "popular demand," for parliament to rewrite the constitution and allow Kagame to rule indefinitely—or at least long enough to see his Vision 2020 blueprint through to completion. Kagame himself has rejected this offer. Repeatedly. But rumours are rife that he will allow himself to be "talked into" staying by the so-called will of the people.

Whatever happens, the presidential election of 2017 will be a watershed moment in Rwandan democracy. Will the office change hands peacefully—or will the rules be rewritten to allow Kagame a third term? And if a third, what about a fourth? Or a fifth? This is a Pandora's box waiting to be opened. If you can rewrite your country's foundational rules to suit one leader, what's to stop the next leader from doing the same, or the next? What's to stop a future president from reneging on legal restraints entirely in order to bring back ethnic quotas, to start classifying the populace once again as Hutu or Tutsi? These are the dangers of having an Etch-a-Sketch constitution. Canada is a peaceful and prosperous nation not because of the quality of our leaders (snort) but on the strength of our institutions, and Rwanda will truly be secure only when it can survive lesser leaders, when it doesn't need to rely on having a President Kagame at the helm. If the institutions of state are well-entrenched and unassailable, you can survive less-inspired leaders in the future; you can even survive incompetence. You should be able to put the most inept, stumblebum person you like in power without bringing down the entire structure. Africa is littered with once prosperous states ruined by initially successful men who changed the rules to suit themselves. Here's hoping Rwanda doesn't join their ranks.

Something else I worry about. At the refugee camp we'd visited earlier, a pair of formal portraits greet you when you enter the main office: one of António Guterres, head of the UNHCR, and the other of President Paul Kagame. The photographs hang side by side on the wall, and yet there is something slightly off about this pair of framed photographs, something askew. Then I spotted it: President Kagame's portrait was set *slightly higher* than that of Guterres. Maybe an inch or two, but still noticeable.

I'd said to Urooj, the UN Head of Camp, "I see you put President Kagame's portrait above that of the UN's."

I thought I was joking, but no.

"We had to," Urooj admitted. "When we open a new office, we always put up a portrait of the head of UNHCR. It's standard practice. But in Rwanda we were told we had to put up President Kagame's portrait as well. And when we did, we were then told we had to move the president's picture *up,* so it would sit above the other one. And so, we did."

It wasn't a big deal to Urooj. Raising a presidential portrait by a couple of inches seemed a simple enough gesture to make, an easy point of protocol to concede. But it gave me a shiver nonetheless. As with other countries in Africa, portraits of His Excellency the President of Rwanda stare down at the populace from the walls of government offices and private businesses. You see him in hotels and coffee shops. In bakeries and banks. That's fine, but Rwanda isn't supposed to be like other countries. This is supposed to be a country that's reinventing itself as a progressive, modern nation—not a regressive realm prone to the cult of personality. When government functionaries are using measuring tapes to see whose portrait is hanging higher than whose, it doesn't bode well. It hints at something unsettling bubbling just below the surface.

# 35

WE WERE HIGH ABOVE LAKE KIVU when the asphalt ended, suddenly and without fanfare, as we left the blacktop and slammed onto rougher roads.

The unspooling of fibre-optic and electrical cables continued, running in anticipation alongside the unpaved route, but the earth-movers and Chinese engineers were gone; we had outstripped them.

Other than a single bus coming at us downhill, straining in low gear, there was no other traffic. Children were chasing rusted bicycle rims, kept rolling with the deft flick of a stick. They stopped to stare as we passed, letting the rims wobble and fall, too dumbstruck to wave back. The welcoming cry of *"Nihau!"* was gone, as we juddered and jounced across roads rutted and ruined.

Washboard striations and molar-loosening thumps. At times the road threw us forward, then slammed us back, doing its best to buck us off, it seemed. The lake below was a distant haze of blue. *We miss a corner up here, and we'll be a long time falling ...*

"Is a good thing we're driving a 4x4!" Jean-Claude shouted, and I agreed, one hand on the ceiling, the other on the dash.

Around the next bend we saw the toll these roads could take. A local bus had hit a rut, hard, and had broken down. The driver's turn boy was ambling downhill with a sheaf of leaves cradled in his arms. When he saw our vehicle, he was so startled that he flung the requisite warning leaves down in front of us like a scene from Palm Sunday, and then waved frantically for us to slow down, in case we hadn't spotted the enormous vehicle stranded in the middle of the road.

The passengers had filed off the bus, and were watching as the driver grappled with a chain. One of the front tires had been wrenched upward at a violent tilt.

"The axle is broken," Jean-Claude said. "That's not good."

We pulled over to talk to the bus driver, but he wasn't in the mood for any help. Someone had been sent by bicycle to rouse the nearest repairman, and the driver waved us through impatiently.

Over the next hump of hill, we came upon a crowd of people waiting for the very bus that had broken down.

"It's going to be a long wait," Jean-Claude said to me with a sympathetic shake of his head.

As we slowed down, a high school student in a neatly ironed blouse stepped from the crowd and thrust her hand out at our passing vehicle, wagging her fingers into her upturned palm almost in a "come here" gesture. She smiled, dazzlingly bold, as her friends stood back, laughing.

I was puzzled. It looked like she was asking for money. "Is she asking for money?"

"Not money, a ride. It's how we hitchhike in Rwanda, not with our thumb. We do like that." On impulse, he pulled over. "Let's give her a ride. We're going that way anyway."

As soon as the crowd realized we were offering a lift, a mob scene erupted. You'd have thought we were the last helicopter out of Vietnam. One pushy fellow elbowed past women and children, forcing his way to the front, where he grabbed hold of my side mirror and refused to let go. On the mistaken assumption that, being a muzungu, I was somehow in charge, he began wheedling me directly, imploring all the angels and Saints in Heaven in carefully enunciated French (we were in the former Zone Turquoise, after all), pleading for a ride.

"Hey, don't ask me," I said. "Talk to my friend. He's the one driving."

Jean-Claude was adamant. The student was the one who had asked for a ride, so she could choose who was coming. With our own luggage and duffle bags of soccer gear weighing us down, we had space for only three people in the back. There were at least half a dozen girls in her group, so they had a quick huddle, decided who would go with us and who would stay behind. They were heading home from boarding school and had their beds with them: foam mattresses rolled up and tied with twine. The three young women who climbed into the backseat had agreed to take the other girls' mattresses with them, which were then shoved in through our rear window, filling what little space we had left.

Wedged in, with three well-mannered students in tow, we headed for the other side of the mountain.

The students were named Betty, Grace, and Anuarite. They were Congolese refugees from a camp similar to the one we'd visited at Kigeme, and though there was a school nearer to them, they attended class out here because it was more academically suitable. One of them was studying accounting, another business. The third wanted to go into engineering. And not just any sort of engineering; she wanted to be a *civil* engineer, "but not for the bridge." If I followed her heavily accented English, she wanted to be "an engineer for the chemical surface." "Like paint?" I asked. No, not for the paint, for the business. So, industrial? Exactly! So, like, industrial paints? No, no, for the chemicals. So … chemical engineering? No, not chemical engineering, engineering *for* the chemical. And so on. I'll spare you the details. I eventually gave up, much to my relief and hers too, I'm sure. They were speaking to me in their third language, after all—French and their local Congolese dialect taking precedence—while I was speaking in a language I'd long since forgotten (high school chemistry).

Jean-Claude chatted with them in French via the rear-view mirror. They told him about the term that had just ended, the teachers they liked, the teachers they didn't, the subjects they found easiest, the ones they found hardest, and about life in the camp. They lived in canvas tents that got very cold at night. They were missing parts of their families. Parents. Siblings. They had made new friends in the camp. Had left old ones behind. They found it tiring travelling back and forth between the refugee camp and the boarding school on buses that often broke down, but all three agreed it was worth it.

We were still following the braided IT cables, though by now the road itself was little more than a sandy trail. At times the Land Cruiser sank into it, with our wheels barely churning us through.

The pedestrians we encountered agreed: this was a walking path, not a road. It was as though we were driving a truck down a private hallway, and those who stepped aside did so with marked resentment. The adults, that is; the children once again ran beside us, daring each other to touch our vehicle. Jean-Claude pulled over several times to scold them.

We followed this road to the heights of Hanika, an improbable town balanced between sheer inclines. No guardrails, of course. *Maybe they should have put those in before they started with the fibre optics,* I thought. If nothing else, were we to plunge over the side, we would have had a beautiful view on the way down.

The lake grew larger. Fingers of land reaching out, fingers of water reaching back.

Down, down, down we went, into the sand-bedevilled town of Kibingo. We were still high in the hills above Lake Kivu, yet the road itself was so sandy it had dunes. It was a remarkable juxtaposition, akin to finding a tropical beach suspended in the mountains. A surfer's town, Kibingo; just mind that first drop.

The roads were so soft it felt as though we were driving over flour. Eucalyptus trees and the wind-shredded leaves of banana plants were completely dusted in it, prematurely grey. And the clustered homes we passed, small as dovecotes, were whitewashed with the stuff, painted pale intentionally.

"Mixed with water, it makes good paint," Jean-Claude said.

A final plunge, of the non-fatal variety, took us back to water's edge. We rattled across another river—little more than a trickle in the dry season, brackish green and murky—over a jerry-rigged bridge that was lashed together primarily with old rope and good intentions. Out on the lake, a three-man pirogue drifted across the surface. The cast of a net. The turn of a road. And they were gone, and so were we.

At the next saddleback of hill we came to a rural intersection. One of the girls leaned up, tapped Jean-Claude on the shoulder.

We pulled over to say our goodbyes. From here the girls would hike uphill to the refugee camp, a two-and-a-half-hour trek along a narrow footpath. Before they could load up on mattresses and school bags, I asked if I could take their picture.

They said "Sure!"—and instantly struck a pose, arms draped over shoulders with a sudden confidence. They asked to see the photo. I scrolled back, showed them. They frowned, asked for another take, adjusted their poses accordingly. On the third try, I finally got it right. "Yes!" they said. "That's the one." Then: "Can you send us a copy?"

Let's pause here a moment to consider my advanced age (pushing fifty at the time) and the clutch of assumptions surrounding the terms "refugee" and "refugee camps." Given these factors, it is perhaps understandable that I would have a certain notion about how this would play out. I would return to my home, sadder but wiser, would think of these young women, so full of hope, so full of promise. I would print three copies of the photograph I took, wrap them carefully in wax paper and seal them in an envelope, would send it "to Betty and her two friends" c/o the United Nations. A supply plane would airdrop it in, along with foodstuffs and medicines, wherein the children at the camp would crowd around to watch as this treasure was slowly unwrapped. The wonderment in Betty's eyes would be felt an ocean away where, as I puttered about in my garden shed, I would suddenly stop, feel the flutter of wings, and know, in my heart, *The photos have arrived.* The girls' spirits would be lifted, as would mine. Perhaps a single tear would form in the corner of my eye, but, gruff fellow that I am, I would rub it away brusquely with the heel of my hand, allowing myself only a small but satisfied smile. *The photos have arrived.*

Here's what actually happened:

Me, speaking slowly and carefully so that the portentous nature of what I was saying would not be lost: "Yes. I can send you copies of the photograph."

Girls: "Great."

Me: "And how shall I mail it? Shall I send it to the camp? Or maybe to your boarding school?"

Girls: "Can you email it to us instead? That would be easier."

Yes, in the world we live in, Congolese refugees in the western rain-forests of Rwanda have email addresses. *Of course* they have email addresses. They're students at a high school. The school has a computer. And the kids there all have hotmail accounts. Or Yahoo. Or Gmail.

I transferred the photo they'd selected onto Jean-Claude's smartphone, and he then sent it as an attachment to one of the girls' accounts. Done.

"Thanks!" they said and then headed off, mattresses stacked on their heads, bouncing with every step, into a future I couldn't even begin to predict.

# 36

INKLINGS OF PROSPERITY, in the form of sheet-metal rooftops, returned as we neared the lakeside city of Kibuye (now known as Karongi). The evening sun was coming in low across the fields, limning the trees and hilltops with gold.

Driving through a small valley, we came upon a catchment of older homes that stood hollowed out amid tall grass, with scorched walls and fanned stains of charcoal rising above each darkened window. The rooftops were missing, the yards overgrown.

Tutsi homes.

Jean-Claude stopped so we could investigate the ruins. A goat was ripping up grass inside one of the shells. Small birds flitted through. These were haunted homes, left abandoned, with owners long gone and with few surviving relatives to reclaim them.

We drove on, into silence.

More and more shops began to appear. The outskirts of Kibuye clustered closer. Storefront facades once again proclaimed their cell phone company allegiances: that familiar green, red, yellow, blue. We were back on blacktop, and the sudden smoothness provided much-needed succour to my bruised tailbone and saucer-stacked spinal column.

"That was a fun road to drive," Jean-Claude said. "But I'm glad we are through it."

Traffic circles sent us into the centre of town, past several new office buildings perched on hillocks of land scarcely wider than they were. In the cooling breeze of evening, everybody in Kibuye seemed to be out for a stroll. Long considered a getaway for Rwanda's mon-eyed set, the city had a faded charm about it: patio lights bobbing on the wind, late-night taverns and French cafés, but no sense of urgency. It was busy, but in a languid sort of way, as resort towns often are.

On the way in, we had passed Gatwaro Stadium. "I lost a friend there, in that stadium," Jean-Claude said.

The friend's name was Jean-Népomscène, but everyone called him Nepo.

"I met him in Kenya. He was a student. He was preparing for university, and we became good friends. He used to take me to Wimpy's. Do you know Wimpy's? It's like a British fast food, very popular in Nairobi at that time. Of all the people who died, Nepo makes me the saddest, because he didn't have to be here. He came back for his uncle's funeral. It was dangerous, and he didn't want to go, but his family pressured him. They told him, 'The UN is here, don't worry. It's safe.' So he went back and that was that. Two days later the president's plane was shot down."

Twenty thousand people died in Gatwaro Stadium. Among them, a kind-hearted student named Nepo.

Kibuye had been a Tutsi town deep inside the French "humanitar-ian" zone, which meant the killings here were even more thorough than usual. Indeed, the eradication of Tutsis in Kibuye and its out-lying regions came very close to reaching a "final solution."

None of this was reflected in the beauty of the town, though, which was situated among the palm trees and corrugated coves of Lake Kivu. Jean-Claude and I checked in at the Moriah Hill Resort, an older but comfortable hotel built on a bay that was dotted with islands. When we dropped in at the hotel's large, and largely empty, restaurant, we came upon two of our cohorts from the chimpanzee trek: the psychiatrist from Toronto, Lorne, with his daughter Adriana.

They'd been enjoying a leisurely two-hour wait for dinner. Thus warned away, Jean-Claude and I went to a nearby church-run lodge, the Bethany, where we dined on *isombe,* stewed cassava leaves and eggplant. No beer though, as alcohol was not served at Bethany due to the Presbyterian dictates of its hosts. The service proved much speedier here; we waited only an hour for our bowl of stewed leaves. We headed back to our hotel only to find Lorne still waiting for his supper, elbows on table, jaw resting on open palms, a Job-like resignation in his eyes. There were no other guests in the restaurant by that point, Adriana having given up and gone back to her room, so why on earth it was taking that long remained a mystery. Perhaps they were waiting for the eggs to hatch so that they could raise the chickens to put on the skewers. Jean-Claude pulled a chair up to join Lorne while I went for a walk along the lake. I wanted to say, *"Use some reverse psychology on 'em, Lorne ol' boy! I mean, that's your field, right? Maybe say in a loud voice, 'I sure don't want any supper tonight. No sir! And nobody better bring me any!'"* But given that he'd already wasted three hours waiting for whatever it was he'd ordered, I feared he might not appreciate my finely tuned japery.

I followed my feet to Lake Kivu instead. Cat tongues of waves, lapping at the shore. A wind, stirring the trees. Lights and laughter across the water. The moon was like a searchlight, sweeping the waves for a wreck that had long since vanished.

How do you reconcile the barbarity and beauty of such a place? Could you? *Should* you?

A small boat puttered by, more shadow than real, leaving a swirl of light in its wake. I tossed a stone, heard it plunk. Took off my shoes, rolled up my pant legs, and waded out into shallow waves. I stood awhile in Lake Kivu, toes gripping and releasing sand. On other hotel patios on other inlets, Rwandan families were relaxing. I could hear their strangely disembodied voices, muffled but still boisterous.

Families had drowned themselves in this lake. Families drowned themselves rather than be raped or hunted or chopped down piece by piece to the mocking jeers of their neighbours. Families drowned themselves. *In this lake.*

I thought of the students who'd hitched a ride with us earlier and of the killings and deprivations that were occurring in Congo even now. I thought of people forced to flee. Those three young women would contribute to Rwanda's success, would work in business, accounting, computers, and—well, some sort of chemical engineering. Their arrival was Rwanda's gain, Congo's loss. Suddenly Rwanda's open-door policies made perfect sense. These people were not a burden, they were an asset. This was *value added.* This was Rwanda.

# 37

JUST ABOUT MY ONLY CLAIM to fame is that I am a descendant of Scottish explorer David Livingstone. A paltry example of pride by proxy, to be sure, and one that would be more impressive had Livingstone not died scurvy-ridden and half-mad, dressed in tattered rags with teeth rotting and an arm crimped from a lion attack years earlier. There was no lucrative Livingstone estate, no snooty inheritance for me and my siblings to squabble over. More's the pity. David Livingstone was but a humble missionary, and a damn poor one at that; the records indicate that over the course of twenty-eight years in Africa, he converted a grand total of 1 (one) person.

During his extended treks across central Africa, the saintly Livingstone would sire—then promptly abandon—several illegitimate children with African women, in between praying for their eternal souls, of course. A contradictory character to say the least. Missionary? Hardly. He was an explorer, first and foremost: a driven, obsessive

Scotsman with a streak of masochism who was determined to unlock one of the greatest, most pointless quests of his day, the source of the River Nile—or die trying. He never did unlock the secrets of the Nile, but he did succeed handsomely in the latter, dying a tragically avoidable and painfully drawn-out death.

The Nile is the longest river in the world, flowing more than 6,700 kilometres out of the heart of Africa, through nine different countries. It replenishes the flood plains of Egypt, making it a wellspring of civilization. Its source was one of the world's enduring mysteries. The ancient Greeks tried to find it. Roman emperors sent expeditions inland and failed. As did the Egyptians, the Persians, and others. But it was the English who really picked up the flag and ran with it. The search for the Source of the Nile would become a fixation in Victorian England.

The greatest explorer of his era, Richard Burton, set out to solve the riddle once and for all. He was accompanied by a thoroughly unlikeable fellow named John Hanning Speke, an early proponent of the Hamitic hypothesis who often wrote about the racial inferiority of the African "Negroid."

Burton was convinced that the source of the Nile lay near Lake Tanganyika. Speke remained unconvinced, and when Burton was laid low with malarial fever, he pushed on without him, heading north instead to become the first European to set eyes upon the vast reaches of Lake Victoria. This was in 1858. Speke hurried back to England ahead of Burton to claim his laurels and, following a second expedition to Lake Victoria, declared, "The Nile is settled!" But it wasn't.

A bitter enmity took root between Burton's camp and Speke's, with each man seeking to ruin the other's reputation and destroy his claim. So intense was their rivalry that the Royal Geographical Society decided to hold a Great Debate on the matter in 1864. But on the day of the main event, only hours before it was to begin, Speke had gone hunting and had discharged a shotgun into his own heart while crossing a stile. That was the official version, anyway. Many suspected he had taken his own life rather than face Burton on the podium.

With the matter still not resolved, the Royal Geographical Society sent respected doctor/missionary David Livingstone in to confirm or refute Burton's claim that the Nile began at Lake Tanganyika. But Livingstone was convinced the source lay even farther south, and he disappeared into the jungle. Years went by with no word from Livingstone, and as public concern grew, an American newspaper, with much fanfare, sent a Welsh-born reporter by the name of Henry Morton Stanley in to find him. Stanley tracked Livingstone down to an Arab trading post, where he greeted the malnourished and dysentery-ravaged Scotsman with what are arguably the most famous words uttered in the history of British exploration: *"Jesus, David, you look like shit."* No. The words, of course, were *"Dr. Livingstone, I presume?"*

Stanley urged Livingstone to return with him, but the doctor refused. His obsession had taken hold of him, and he pushed on, still seeking that elusive wellspring. He died eighteen months later, his quest unanswered. Stanley went on to greater fame, leading an epic cross-African trek that at one point saw him skirting the outer edges of the kingdom known as Rwanda. He'd set up camp on Lake Ihema, in what is now Akagera National Park, but when he attempted to cross over, he was met with a volley of arrows from the mwami's army and decided, what with discretion being the better part of et cetera, he would move on instead. Later, as an agent of King Léopold, Stanley would help secure the Congo for the Belgian monarch, but the Nile remained unsolved.

In 1937, a German explorer traced the headwaters to a small spring in Burundi, a site that has been commemorated ever since, but this marked only the *southernmost* point of the River Nile. Incredibly, the *farthest* reach of the Nile—the source, in other words—would remain unknown until 2006, when a British-led expedition traced the Nile in its entirety, using GPS satellites to pinpoint it to a remote mountainous hill south of Kibuye City, just inside the northern tip of Nyungwe National Park.

This would be our next destination.

# 38

I WOKE TO THE SOUND of wind searching my room. I'd left the balcony open to catch a night breeze off the lake, and I lay there awhile watching the aurora borealis movements of the curtains, feeling calmly elated.

Today, I would do my forebear proud. Today, I would reach the uppermost limits of the River Nile, for which stout-hearted men had long strived, many to perish, others to be driven mad with malnutrition and malaria, starved and crippled in body and spirit. But first I had to get some breakfast. One can't go about conquering the Mighty Nile on an empty stomach.

And so, after a hearty meal followed by coffee so buttery rich it might have come from the gods themselves, we set out, Jean-Claude having once again passed on a cuppa joe.

How was this possible? How could anyone from Rwanda not drink coffee? Rwandan coffee has won international awards. It was all very strange.

"I'm just not a coffee drinker" was how he put it.

No matter. Onward and upward.

Kibuye is a leafy town, jumbled in around the hills of Lake Kivu, and as the road wound upward in loops and lariats, we had sidelong views of the rolling landscape below.

The road alternated between a boulder-strewn obstacle course and a clay trail so loamy and soft the 4x4 struggled to get traction.

"Would hate to try this in the rainy season," Jean-Claude said, ratcheting the gears ever higher.

We were once again ascending to the top of Rwanda, but the top of Rwanda never arrived. Every time we thought we'd reached the ceiling, there was more ceiling beyond. The slopes became steeper and the terraced fields narrower, until they formed the thinnest ribbons of green possible, outlining the elevations like a life-sized contour map.

Cattle were following these contour lines with a gingerly step.

"More mountain goat than cattle," I said, and Jean-Claude agreed.

"Most of this"—he was referring to the fields below—"is coffee. With some sweet potatoes, over there. That's cabbage."

We passed a band of young men in baggy pants and broken flip-flops, grinning at the world, lugging kerosene containers on their shoulders.

"Banana beer," Jean-Claude explained. "They rinse the jugs out, use them to ferment mashed-up bananas. The containers are plastic, so they expand with the gases." We could see several that had their sides blown up like balloons.

"Moonshine!" I said. "Home brew."

"Exactly." Then, just in case I was getting any ideas, "It's better not to drink it."

As we drove through the Gisovu tea plantations, the world grew lush. Women with wicker baskets slung across their backs were moving through the topiary fields, harvesting the tea leaves by hand. Miniature pickup trucks buzzed about like bumblebees, darting from the nearby warehouses to the endless hand-sculpted hedges and back again. It was a striking arrangement: pastoral, yet busy; bucolic, but all business.

Soon after, we came to the town of Gisovu itself. Shops lined both sides of a single street, and the storefronts were painted a soft shade of blue, giving the place a melancholy feel.

We stopped for a bit of bellyfare: sticky buns and bottles of Fanta, pulled lukewarm from a fridge. (How Rwandan refrigeration is able to maintain warm drinks is a puzzle I was never able to unravel.) Not a particularly welcoming town, Gisovu. Jean-Claude and I were eyed with a curiosity that bordered on the antagonistic. Even the roadside barbers paused, clippers in mid-air, waiting for me to do something interesting. Oh, if only I could juggle. *"Alex Ferguson's son juggles?"*

Beyond Gisovu, the fields gave way to forest. Pine and eucalyptus. Dark-green needles and the silvery-blue shimmer of leaves. We had reached Nyungwe National Park from the other side.

A rough road took us to a clearing where a hiking trail disappeared into the trees. The signpost—in English only, appropriately, given the overwhelmingly British nature of the obsession—identified the Source of the Nile as that-a-way.

I don't know why Livingstone had such trouble finding it. I mean, there was a sign and everything.

It was still a national park, though, and we needed to check in first. This involved a long bumpy drive to a park office, returning with a pair of park rangers, Joseph and Antoine, who would accompany us on our quest. Nice enough blokes, even if their main task involved leading us down the only marked path in the forest. But this too was appropriate. After all, any such undertaking traditionally required a contingent of Gunga Din–type porters to cut a path through the jungle for pith-helmeted Englishmen adorned with well-waxed handlebar moustaches and long-bore rifles who would later lounge about the campfire, swishing brandy whilst making snide comments about the natives, regaling all and sundry about their time amongst the Zulu and how it wasn't half so bad as this. One couldn't set off without one's entourage.

Furthermore, given my own claim to Nile fame, I thought it apropos to present the account of my Death-Defying Exploration and Subsequent Discoverie Most Fortunate of the Mysterious Source of the River Nyle, Whence So Many a Valiant Standard-Bearer of Empire Has Perished in Quests Thereof with Perils Unparalleled and Dangers Most Foul, in the proper style.

THE DISCOVERY OF THE SOURCE OF THE NILE, BY ME. AND ONLY ME.

### Tuesday, July 23rd: Heading Out

I feel it prudent to tally the many torments of which I have been forced to endure if only so that my example may act as a deterrent to anyone who might be tempted to follow, foolishly, in my footsteps.

I woke this day feeling somewhat queasy, both from trepidation at what lies ahead and from the malaria pills I have been taking, an ordeal which—it should be noted—Mr. Livingstone never had to face, for there was no such thing as malaria pills in his day. He simply got malaria and never had to worry about forgetting to take his pills or having a slightly upset stomach afterward. Lucky, lucky chap. Even then, stricken as I was with an almost crippling nausea, did my faithful guides offer to carry me? They did not.

**10:19 a.m.:** We gather our day packs and strike out, single file, into the deepest heart of Africa.

**10:20 a.m.:** We stop at a park bench to adjust our boot laces, poorly tied boot laces being one of the leading causes of death among explorers. That and lions.

**10:21 a.m.:** Forced to step over cow dung on the trail. Is this but a foreshadow of the travails we have yet to face? (Note the etymological relationship between "travail" and "travel.")

**10:23 a.m.:** We pass a line of electrical towers running through the forest. This would suggest that someone may have been here before us. Dastardly Arab traders no doubt, attempting to undermine the prerogatives of the British Empire, hup hup.

**10:24 a.m.:** Entering a forest of pine and eucalyptus. Fragrant and foreboding. One of the guides falls in beside me (our single-file discipline is already starting to collapse!) and points out a drum tree. *Umuvumu.* "They can be hollowed out, to make music," he tells me. "Royal drums?" I ask. "Yes, for intore dancers." These would be the same drums that Rwandan kings used to adorn *with the testicles of their enemies!* I fear an ambush and do not wish to see my fear-shrunken testes adorning any percussive instrument, royal or otherwise.

**10:38 a.m.:** The trail begins to slope downward under trellises of vine. The path beneath our feet is layered with pine needles, which might seem rustic were it not for the fact that tree roots are lurking beneath this seemingly innocent blanket. I nearly trip several times. (Difficult to walk whilst clutching both hands pre-emptively over one's testicles.)

**10:39 a.m.:** The sound of water! Oh joy! Have we reached the Source of the Nile already? My heart leaps like a salmon in a clear Scottish stream only to be dashed upon the rocks of disappointment, for it is not the sound of water I hear, but only the wind. I'm not sure how much longer I can carry on, parched and harried by thirst as I am.

"Jean-Claude, can I have some of your water? My bottle's way at the bottom of my rucksack, sort of hard to reach."

"Sure," he says. Hands bottle over. Crisis averted.

**10:42 a.m.:** A slight incline up.

**10:43 a.m.:** A slight incline down.

**10:44 a.m.:** As the day drags on, I grow suspicious of my supposedly "loyal" companion, Jean-Claude. He seems to be pulling ahead with every stride. Determined to reach the Source of the Nile before me, perchance?

**10:46 a.m.:** Wilderness exploration is simply a matter of learning to read the signs correctly. We have come upon one such clue, a notice-board with a large arrow and the words FURTHEST SOURCE OF THE NILE THIS WAY painted on it—which, after careful study, I decipher to mean that the coveted wellspring of the Nile lies farther ahead, perhaps in the direction indicated by the arrow. (There is only the one trail, so that helps as well.) *"This way!"* I say with bold initiative. My entourage, however, has pushed on by this point, and I must scurry to catch up. Are they plotting to abandon me in the woods?

One must stay on one's toes (figuratively speaking, of course; toe-walking in the jungle is never a good idea).

**10:47 a.m.:** The trail begins a long, steep descent. Knowing that this same descent will become an *ascent* on our return only adds to the mental anguish I am under.

**10:48 a.m.:** Egads! Wildlife rooting about in the underbrush! We have come upon a bush pig, normally nocturnal, tusks down, snuffling around. Looking for truffles perhaps? (Ah, what I wouldn't give for a plate of truffles right about now. Maybe a dash of sherry.) Having not had the foresight to bring a long-bore rifle with us, we are not able to shoot said creature in a properly perfunctory manner, but must instead creep past so as "not to frighten him."

**10:50 a.m.:** Our way is barred! Oh, fie on you, cruel fates! We have reached what I fear is an insurmountable obstacle: a tree branch has fallen across our path. I am about to turn back when one of our steadfast guides strides forward and lifts said branch, tossing it to one side. "Heavy winds last night," he notes. We continue, spirits buoyed, but also burdened (buoyed *and* burdened!) with the knowledge that we shall now have to make up for lost time. The Matter of the Fallen Branch has delayed us a good twenty-eight seconds by my count. Will we ever be able to make this up? I am not confident we can, but I put on a brave face and carry on against increasingly demoralizing odds.

**10:52 a.m.:** Monkey spoor has replaced cow flops as the obstacle of choice. High in the trees above us I spot them leaping, long-tailed and lithe, treetop to treetop, mocking our slow, lugubrious progress below. Oh, for a long-bore rifle right about now!

**10:53 a.m.:** The trail begins to descend at an even steeper angle than before. True, there are stairs carved into it, but they are inconsistently sized, which only increases the ordeal. I am not sure how much longer I can continue.

**10:57 a.m.:** The dangers we face continue to multiply. Our guides point out a tall stand of stinging nettles. They also point out something they refer to as a "tomato fruit," telling us that "birds plant it, and when the fruit turns red, you can eat it." The tomato fruits here are still green, but at least now I know what I shall dine upon should we become lost or if our expedition takes too long or if I get a little peckish and find that the sandwiches the hotel packed have not provided sufficient sustenance. Always prepare for the worst! This is the first rule of exploration. The second is: when your hotel is packing you a lunch, ask for an extra sandwich.

The ground grows squelchier as we descend. Through the trees I see a wooden sign and a small pond. Could it be …?

**11:03 a.m.:** Success! Huzzahs all round!

A hand-painted notice, set in a secluded hollow of forest, informs us that THIS IS THE FURTHEST SOURCE OF NILE RIVER. Little more than a puddle, really. A mountain spring pooled amid mud and mulch, but if it is a puddle, it is a majestic puddle nonetheless, epic in its importance. The world's most sought-after puddle, as it were. Men died, legends were born, empires made, and lives ruined in search of this very puddle. We dip our hands into the cold water, scoop up the Nile, drink it from our palms. It tastes of glory. Clear, clean glory. A splendid milestone, and one—it should also be noted—which David Livingstone was never able to enjoy. I'd achieved that which my venerable forebear never did; this is, in its way, strangely poignant.

And let the record show that although *technically* Jean-Claude arrived at the Source of the Nile at 11:01 a.m., two minutes before I did, I had spotted said puddle through the trees a full four minutes prior to that. Which is to say, I was the first to *see* the Source of the Nile. Therefore, as I'm sure we can all agree, I should receive sole credit for the discovery.

Jean-Claude, unfortunately, seems to be operating under the misconception that "we"—meaning he and I equally, if you can imagine such a thing—have reached the Source of the Nile "together." (In his exact words, "We made it!" *We*.)

In the face of such unabashed effrontery, there is but one course of action available to me. I mustn't dally. I must return to civilization immediately and start a campaign to discredit Jean-Claude's claims and destroy his reputation.

"We did indeed," I say, with just the faintest sliver of a smile.

# 39

BACK AT OUR HOTEL ON LAKE KIVU, Jean-Claude started an international incident with a single posting on Facebook.

It seemed innocuous enough. He'd put up a photo with the message: "Here I am at the farthest point of the Nile. Sorry Burundi, but the Nile River actually starts in Rwanda!"

He then went to sleep not knowing he'd stirred a hornet's nest. Throughout the night angry responses began to pile up. The Rwandan and Burundian communities are intertwined—they're cultural cousins, after all—and word had spread quickly.

The retorts that set Jean-Claude's Facebook account on fire were of the exclamatory "Wrong!!! The Source of the Nile is in Burundi! Look at a map, JC!! Burundi is clearly further south than Rwanda and is therefore further away! Case closed!! No appeal!" variety.

Jean-Claude posted a reply reminding everyone that this was not conjecture on his part; a British survey team had located the exact spot using GPS. No one was placated, however. Some smelled a conspiracy. Who were these British surveyors really working for? Everyone knew that Britain favoured Rwanda over Burundi, and a series of increasingly peeved messages flew back and forth across the Atlantic, rhetoric escalating rapidly. It might well have ended in a full-blown political crisis, with ambassadors recalled, lecterns thumped, pyrrhic trade sanctions incurred, and armies massing along the borders, had Jean-Claude not played his trump card.

"Listen. I visited the geographic source of the Nile with a descendant of David Livingstone, and"—here Jean-Claude was relying on my expertise as a Fine Arts major—"he agrees." Game, set, and match.

With that, the protests slowed to a trickle. The flame war flickered and died, but not without a few final forlorn barbs from the Burundians. "You Rwandans already have everything else. Now you want the Nile too? Can't you at least give us that?"

Jean-Claude's reply? A very Canadian "Sorry. But no."

# 40

WE RETURNED TO GISOVU the next day, following a route first through valleys thick with tea and then high over exposed, raw-knuckle heights.

At times, it was not clear whether these were roads we were travelling along or simply desiccated riverbeds that had been baked into a hard red clay by the kiln heat of the dry season.

We had entered the shadowy green hills of Bisesero.

When the genocide began, any resistance was soon smothered. Unarmed people, cornered in churches or picked off at roadblocks, were up against well-trained mobs equipped with machetes, grenades, and guns. It was a one-sided slaughter, and those who did fight back—and there were many—were quickly overcome.

But up here, in the remote and mountainous Bisesero region, the people banded together, falling back to higher ground. Far behind

French lines, lost in La Zone Turquoise, the Tutsis in Bisesero were under no illusion that the UN or anyone else in the international community would rescue them. The Tutsis of Bisesero staged the longest, most resolute and sustained resistance seen in Rwanda. This was a heroic landscape. Heroic, and tragic.

At Bisesero, the Tutsis armed themselves with farming tools. They dug in, set up perimeters, kept the women and children in the middle. They laid traps of their own, ambushing their attackers, fighting them off hand to hand. But time was against them, and as the siege of Bisesero wore on, week after week, through heavy rains and cold nights, starvation and fatigue took their toll. The people's energy was sapped, and the resistance began to falter.

More than 50,000 people took refuge on that mountain. Of those, only 1,437 are known to have survived. France's role in Bisesero was particularly shameful. When French troops arrived, the survivors thought they were finally going to be rescued. They came out from hiding only to be told by the soldiers to stay put. "We'll be back in three days," the soldiers promised. And then the French ... left.

There is a photograph on display at the Bisesero memorial. It shows Hutu militias taunting a ragged crowd of starving women and children while French soldiers in a jeep look on. Moments after this photo was taken, the French withdrew. The Tutsis fled, and the Hutu militias pursued. The final massacre at Bisesero had begun. All the French had done was to inadvertently flush out targets, making it easier for the génocidaires to do their job.

You think I'm being unduly harsh? Perhaps. So I will give final word on the matter to a pair of respected French figures. Author and intellectual Bernard-Henri Lévy states, unequivocally, that "France bears political and moral responsibility for the sadly foreseeable chain of monstrous events that unfolded on its watch.... The sooner France's politicians admit to their responsibility for failures during the Rwandan genocide, the better." And the former French foreign minister, Bernard Kouchner, co-founder of Médecins Sans Frontières and in Rwanda himself during the genocide, has publicly called on France to apologize for what it did. Belgium and the United States have apologized. France never has.

The reason the resistance at Bisesero could be sustained for so long was that the terrain was so inaccessible. Muyira Hill, where most of the fighting took place, is crowded with boulders, cleaved by cliffs, tangled with forest, pocked with bogs, and interlaced with twisting trails that favoured those who knew the lay of the land. Indeed, so rugged is the terrain on Muyira Hill that the Bisesero genocide memorial had to be built on the hill beside it. Even there, the buildings are set at a steep angle.

At Bisesero, 1,400 skulls are arranged twelve rows deep on a series of elevated platforms. Walking among them, you can identify how people died. Some skulls had been crushed, others impaled. Some bore the puncture holes of nail-studded clubs, others had bullet holes in the back. Many carried the killing slash of a machete, and others were blackened with soot.

"Burned alive," Jean-Claude explained, his voice barely above a whisper.

The security guard at the Bisesero memorial was a soft-spoken man in his early thirties named Félicien Nzabamwita. He'd been born in Bisesero, had spent his entire life in these hills, and he accompanied us as we walked among the buildings.

Félicien was thirteen years old when his family heard the news that President Habyarimana was dead. "It was mayhem," he said quietly. "Mobs began burning houses and demolishing homes right away. The older people told us this was not the first time. It had happened before. We just needed to band together, and in three or four days it would stop."

But it didn't stop.

"The older men began organizing people, telling them how they'd done it in the past, where to position ourselves, how to keep the women and children behind the lines, how to fight back without putting ourselves at risk. The younger men would draw the attackers away, running past them, leading them in the opposite direction of where people were hiding."

At the beginning of May, the attacks ceased.

"It was very quiet for two weeks. But on the 13th of May, they returned. They came from all over. When you looked out you could see them everywhere, all around us. There were so many it looked like grass covering the hills. Buses brought in military men and they began shooting rockets into the mountain, killing so many people. It shattered the rocks."

The Tutsis moved their sick and wounded, along with the younger children and the elderly, into a cave to protect them. When the French arrived, the soldiers called everyone out.

"We thought, 'We are saved! We are not going to die. They have come to rescue us.' People came out from hiding everywhere. They were starving and tired, but now they had hope. But the interahamwe were watching, and now they knew how many of us there were. They could see where we had been hiding, and as soon as the French left, they attacked. They attacked and they never stopped. By the time the French came back, there were very few people left alive."

Félicien was badly wounded during the final assault, but recovered. Physically, at least.

"Today, I have a wife and two children. I try to work hard. I do what I can and forget what I can't. But when I went to get married, I could see what the genocide had done. In Rwanda, a wedding is supposed to be about bringing together families. The groom's relatives will go to meet the bride's and get their blessing, and the two families will sit beside each other at the ceremony to celebrate. But at my wedding there was no one there for me. I had no family. My mother, my father, my older brothers and my little sister, six children, they all died. I was the only one left." He looked across the green hills of Bisesero. "That was a difficult moment."

# 41

REVEREND ATHANASE SEROMBA, the Catholic priest at Nyange church, had a problem.

Following the plane crash that killed President Habyarimana, the massacre of Tutsis had spread across Rwanda like a brush fire buffeted by strong winds. In Nyange, Father Seromba sent urgent word to the Tutsis in his parish to gather at the church. They would be safe there, he promised. Those who were being sheltered by their Hutu neighbours should come out of hiding as well, to join their brethren in the House of God. More than 2,000 people crowded into the Nyange church, desperate and frightened.

The problem that presented itself to Reverend Seromba was this: How to kill these people in the most efficient manner possible? Grenades? Frontal assault? Set the interior on fire? The church was made of brick; that might work, it might turn the building into an oven. Or should he simply starve them out? The church was completely surrounded, and the streets were ringed with roadblocks, but with a few weak-willed Hutus still sneaking food into the church at night, starvation could take some time. The priest met with local authorities—the bourgmestre, an inspector with the judicial police, a judge, leaders of the local militia—to mull over their options.

The church at Nyange was a solid Gothic structure built in 1935, with a heavy tower and thick doors. Previous attacks had been repelled. Every sortie had left scores of Tutsis dead, but as a group, the Tutsis had stubbornly refused to die. Gasoline had been sprayed through a window and a banana-leaf torch thrown in, but with recent rains, and the people inside quickly smothering the flames, that had been ineffective. A waste of good fuel. Grenades created only pockets of destruction—those thrown at the door barely scorched the wood—and those few times when the church had been breached and the killers had managed to swarm in with clubs and machetes, they were beaten back. It was most annoying.

A bulldozer had been brought over from a construction site to dig a mass grave, and this presented Father Seromba with a possible solution. Why not simply pull down the church on top of their tall Tutsi heads? That should, in his words, "clean up the rubbish." So a second bulldozer was brought in, and the drivers were given their instructions: start with the main wall. Topple the tower and the roof will follow.

When the drivers balked—not out of concern for the people inside, but over desecrating a House of God—they were reassured by the priest not to worry. The chalice and Bible had already been removed, so it was no longer a church. Just a pile of bricks, waiting to be dismantled. Once the cockroaches inside had been killed, Seromba promised he would build a new church.

The attack began on April 16, 1994. The bulldozers pushed in, collapsing one side of the building, then another. The people cowering within were crushed under the weight of the debris. Some escaped into the tower and were trapped there when it fell, with a mighty groan, in a cloud of dust and mortar. Small children survived longer in the rubble; their cries could be heard even as the wreckage was being bulldozed clear. Those who tried to flee were chopped down outside with machetes and clubs, with sharpened bamboo and spike-headed spears. The broken bodies were then rolled into open pits along with wreckage from the church. Of the almost 2,000 people who fled to Nyange church, only six are known to have survived.

Father Seromba went on to have an exemplary career with the Church, relocating to Italy where he continued preaching the gospel in the Florence area. He was sheltered and protected for years by the hierarchy in Rome, before finally being arrested and extradited on charges of genocide by the International Criminal Tribunal in Arusha. In 2008, an initial sentence of fifteen years was extended on appeal to life imprisonment.

The bourgmestre who had spearheaded the attacks was captured in Congo, having eluded capture for more than fourteen years. He was caught fighting alongside the FDLR. Other perpetrators of the Nyange atrocities are still at large and, contrary to Father Seromba's promise, the church has never been rebuilt.

Today, the empty grounds form a vacant lot in the heart of the community. Nyange itself is a prosperous arrangement of tidy shops strategically located on the main road between Kibuye and Kigali, high above contoured fields. With its alpine air and pine trees, Nyange feels almost Swiss. It is a Catholic community, still. A monument to the Virgin Mary remains the town centrepiece, but of all the sermons Reverend Seromba preached, the one he never seemed to have gotten around to was that of a single man confronting a murderous mob, telling them, "Let he who is without sin cast the first stone."

There is another monument in the town of Nyange, one that honours neither emptiness nor virgin births, but something smaller. Smaller, but in some ways stronger, more astonishing. Certainly more real.

Nyange Secondary School is off the main road, not far from the church. Jean-Claude and I had to stop to let a herd of goats cross. The well-scrubbed storefronts of the main town fell away as we followed a dusty lane along a steep slope. We could see banana trees and the adobe tiles of rooftops directly below us. The Land Cruiser rolled down the lane until we reached what looked like a dead end.

A large metal gate was drawn across the road. We'd arrived unannounced, as was our habit, but were met graciously nonetheless. An elderly security guard rolled open the gate for us. He was a sun-varnished man with crooked limbs and an equally crooked smile, and he followed us in.

Nyange Secondary is a boarding school with red-brick dormitories and long, low classrooms arranged around a central courtyard. It seemed sleepy and safe. A Rwandan flag flapped on a listless wind as students milled about discussing upcoming exams with a hushed nervousness. A few were scribbling furiously in their notebooks.

The school's Master of Discipline (his translation of his job title) came out to meet us. Title aside, he was a soft-spoken younger teacher of uncertain English who invited us in for tea. We were introduced to the school's office manager, a formidably regal woman named Yvette who rose to accept us with the deportment of a queen in the presence of cap-wringing chimney sweeps.

Having made our introductions, we were taken through the grounds.

Nyange Secondary School has impeccably high standards and a solid academic reputation. More than 250 students from across Rwanda, boys and girls alike, come here to study. Here's a sample question posted, in English, outside one of the classrooms:

*S6 ACCOUNTANCY: PRACTICAL EXAM INTERVIEW TOPICS.*
*The student will be required to complete the following and discuss:*

1.  Calculate the net profit and net loss
2.  Prepare the final accounts
3.  Close and reopen the company accounts
4.  Design the documents relating to remuneration of employees
5.  Participate in the certification of accounting entries
6.  Calculate the tax due within the time limits

It's important to recall that the killings in Rwanda didn't stop when the genocide officially ended. It wasn't a clean cessation, in the manner of a book being closed. Far from it. The leaders of the defeated Hutu Power government-in-exile had fallen back to Zaire, and over the next decade they continued to launch cross-border assaults against civilians, with Hutu and Tutsi alike caught in the middle. When Tutsis were massacred, random Hutus were killed in retaliation by enraged lynch mobs, which was the whole point of the initial attacks: to stir up ethnic divides. Genocide survivors were stalked down and killed ("finishing the job," as it was known) while isolated farms were looted and public buses ambushed. This ongoing terror campaign had left western Rwanda in a state of near collapse. The entire region was in turmoil.

So on March 18, 1997, when students at Nyange Secondary, having gathered for an evening prep class, heard gunshots nearby, they assumed it was RPF soldiers and Hutu Power rebels exchanging fire. Many of them felt secure knowing they were protected by a gate. They didn't realize it was their own school that was under attack, or that they themselves had been targeted.

Nyange, you see, was a mixed school. Hutus and Tutsis were both welcome, and the two sides got on well. This infuriated the Hutu Power rebels. When you trafficked in hatred you couldn't allow that. The school was about to be taught a lesson—or at least, that was the plan. In fact, a very different lesson was about to unfold, a lesson in the strength of the human spirit.

Men armed with grenades and automatic weapons slipped through nearby Mukura Forest and fell upon Nyange Secondary School, killing the night watchman and storming a classroom, shouting for the students to segregate themselves.

"We want the Tutsis on the left, Hutus on the right!" they yelled.

The students knew what that meant.

No one said a word, so the armed men repeated their command. "Hutus on the right, Tutsis on the left!"

A Grade 12 student, Marie-Chantal Mujawamahoro, stood up. Speaking on behalf of her classmates, she replied to the gunmen with a single forceful word: "No."

*No?* Their attackers were taken aback by this. *What do you mean, no?*

"No," she said quietly. "We won't do it. There are no Hutus or Tutsis here. We are all Rwandans."

The other students agreed, murmuring the same answer. "We are all Rwandans."

So the gunmen dragged one of their classmates from the crowd, a girl named Seraphine, who by chance came from a Tutsi family. They killed Seraphine in front of her classmates and then repeated their demand, screaming now: "We know there are Tutsis among you! Divide yourselves! Hutu on the right, Tutsis on the left."

Again the students refused.

"We won't do it!" Marie-Chantal yelled back.

This time it was a boy named Sylvestre who stood up and repeated the words his classmates had spoken. *"Twese turi abanyarwanda."* We are all Rwandans.

The gunmen shot another student, a boy this time.

Flustered and livid, and not knowing who were Tutsis and who were Hutus, the men attacked indiscriminately, lobbing a grenade into the classroom from outside and then firing on the wounded through the smoke. Six students died in the attack, two boys and four girls. Several others were severely wounded, some for life. One of the students, Theodette Abayisenga, lost a leg in the attack; it was mangled so badly by the grenade she had to have it amputated. She now oversees the district's People with Disabilities program and continues to speak on behalf of reconciliation, reminding audiences that they are all Rwandans. She was one of the students who, had she betrayed her classmates, could have walked free.

Today, the room where the attack occurred is still in use, defiantly so to my mind. Students there were studying for their exams when Jean-Claude and I came by. The blast from the grenade still speckles the walls inside, and bullet holes are still visible in the sheet-metal roofing. The students in the classroom looked up at me from their notebooks.

"I just wanted to wish you luck," I said. "On your test."

They nodded. *"Murakoze."* Thank you.

Behind the school sits the grave of Marie-Chantal. Located on a knoll looking out over the valley below, it is, perhaps, the most beautiful monument in all of Rwanda. Not in size or grandeur, but in spirit.

Of the million who lost their lives we might, I feel, give name to six here. These are students who died three years *after* the genocide was supposed to have ended, who died for refusing to betray their classmates, for refusing to label themselves Hutu or Tutsi, for refusing to take part in such a rigged and evil game:

| | |
|---|---|
| Marie-Chantal Mujawamahoro | Grade 12 |
| Sylvestre Bizimana | Grade 12 |
| Béatrice Mukambaraga | Grade 12 |
| Seraphine Mukarutwaza | Grade 11 |
| Helène Benimana | Grade 11 |
| Valens Ndemeye | Grade 11 |

These students remind us that the older animosities are generational. Rwanda today is a remarkably young country; an estimated 60 percent of the population are under the age of twenty-five. They are the first generation in one hundred years to grow up without the artificial construct of a Hutu–Tutsi divide as the defining aspect of their lives. They have never known ID cards or racial quotas or hate radio or propaganda cartoons depicting one segment of their population as cockroaches. They are coming of age in a new Rwanda, a better Rwanda. Those pessimists in the West and elsewhere who insist that Rwanda's "one people, one language, one culture" policy is pure folly, doomed to fail (one gets the feeling certain commentators are almost cheering on another ethnic clash), do not realize that the world has changed. The ground has shifted beneath their feet. Sheer demographics and twenty years of growth and opportunity, of *hope,* have helped dismantle the old paradigms. The six students who died at Nyange didn't die in vain.

I think perhaps it was on that day, March 18, 1997, at 8:00 p.m., at a boarding school in western Rwanda, that the genocide finally came to a close.

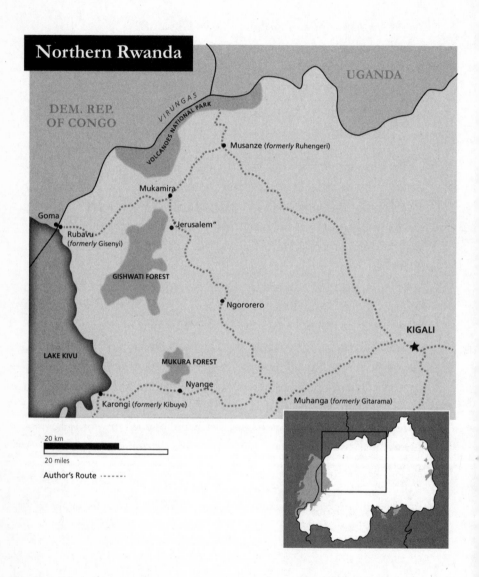

# Northern Rwanda

**UGANDA**

**DEM. REP. OF CONGO**

*VIRUNGAS*

VOLCANOES NATIONAL PARK

Musanze (*formerly* Ruhengeri)

Mukamira

Goma

Rubavu
(*formerly* Gisenyi)

"Jerusalem"

**GISHWATI FOREST**

Ngororero

**KIGALI**

**LAKE KIVU**

**MUKURA FOREST**

Nyange

Karongi (*formerly* Kibuye)

Muhanga (*formerly* Gitarama)

20 km

20 miles

Author's Route ·······

# PART THREE

## KING KONG & THE SHROUD OF TURIN

## 42

SMOKY EYES PEER THROUGH GREEN LEAVES. Furry figures appear, curious and calm, throat-catchingly near. *Gorillas in our midst.*

Our journey to see the mountain gorillas of the Virunga rainforests began in a suitably roundabout way. Leaving the grounds of Nyange Secondary School, Jean-Claude and I continued across the map in connect-the-dots fashion. But now we were carrying a passenger. Not a hitchhiker catching a lift at the end of the day, but a fully accredited driver and guide with nothing to do.

The fee for renting a vehicle in Rwanda, as in much of Africa, generally includes the cost of a driver. Making your way through the mountainous roads of a Thousand Hills is no simple task, and most visitors opt to have someone else behind the wheel. Lorne and his daughter had been travelling with the same fellow since Tanzania, I believe. But having Jean-Claude on the driver's side meant there'd been no overriding reason to avail ourselves of this service.

My role as navigator, meanwhile, had been primarily to sit with the map unfolded on my lap, looking at the scenery and checking off the towns we passed through whilst agreeing with whatever Jean-Claude said. As in: "This doesn't look right …" Me: "No, it does not." Alternatively: "Wait, I think that's the road we're supposed to take over there!" Me: "I concur." Jean-Claude: "You know, I have a hunch about this. If we turn left instead of right, we should come back to the main highway." Me: "I agree. I also have a hunch."

But faced with a long northern loop, up to Congo and then east along the Virunga Mountains, I finally convinced a reluctant Jean-Claude to let us take on a driver. This service was included in the price, so I figured we might as well take advantage.

"I can climb in the back," I said. "He can drive. You can relax."

Jean-Claude was dubious, and not without cause, it must be said. The driver the rental company sent us looked to be, oh, about twelve years old. His name was Patrice. A sweet kid, dressed in an over-starched, olive-green uniform several sizes too big—"Don't worry, you'll grow into it," I imagine the car rental company had assured him—which only accentuated his undersized presence.

The two of them would take turns, it was decided, even though Patrice had expected to drive the entire way and was a bit baffled by Jean-Claude's plan. Even then, he was at the wheel only twenty minutes—if that—before Jean-Claude announced it was time to switch. Patrice pulled over, and we all shuffled positions. Me to the front passenger seat, Patrice crawling into the back, Jean-Claude returning to where he clearly wanted to be. *Christine was right,* I thought. *He really doesn't passenger well.* I wondered if it had some-thing to do with how he had escaped as a teenager: as cargo, hidden, not in control, his life dependent on other drivers. It seemed there was an act of reclamation going on.

Marooned in the backseat, Patrice would occasionally lean up to provide an interesting tidbit about this or that. He carried a well-thumbed guide to *Birds of Rwanda* and was constantly trying to point out red-footed falcons or pink-bellied pelicans, spot-breasted ibises and scarlet-chested sunbirds and what have you, as we sped by with-out stopping, or even slowing down. He seemed disappointed when that line of conversation fizzled—at first we feigned interest, but when Jean-Claude and I were deep in conversation, we didn't even bother turning our heads to look, but just made vague *mm-hmm* sounds. Patrice did confirm the existence of the "hawk-eagle," though, which was about the extent of my interest. Gradually he lapsed into silence, and then sleep. (Later, I found out he'd been misinformed that I was "an important journalist here to write about birdwatching." He must have thought I was the least committed birdwatcher on the planet.)

No matter. On we went.

Patrice dozed, Jean-Claude drove, and all was well.

Much more problematic was that in accordance with company policy, Patrice ate separately from us whenever we stopped. This struck me as ridiculous, but no matter how often we tried to call him over to our table, he gently declined. It was an understandable rule, I suppose. The car rental office arranged for separate accommodations for their drivers and provided them with an allowance for meals, and they didn't want them importuning clients. But still.

"C'mon," I would urge. "Join us. Have a drink. The goat brochettes are excellent. Grab some. We won't tell. I promise."

Jean-Claude tried as well, cajoling Patrice in Kinyarwanda, but with no better results. I can't tell you how awkward this was, especially when we were the only customers in a place, sitting on opposite sides of the room. We would send food over to his table, have the wait staff add it to our tab, give Patrice a salute with our raised glasses. He would smile and wave back. It was all very uncomfortable.

. Patrice would take the Land Cruiser out in the evenings to fill it up, returning with it looking polished and clean, and would give Jean-Claude advice on how to get through this town or that roundabout, but for the most part he spent his time either looking out the window, rather wistfully, I thought, or stretched out asleep. He whistled faintly when he snored, much like one of those tropical birds he was always trying to point out to us.

We boomeranged through the outskirts of Gitarama, resisting the pull of the city's gravity—all those taverns, cooing my name!—before veering northward onto asphalt so smooth it could only be described as supple. After the twists and turns and potholes that had preceded it, it was nice to be back on the open highway.

The road north ran through alpine forests, with the thick clay waters of the Nyabarongo River curving through below. The shadows seemed darker up here, the greens greener, the blues bluer. As Patrice slept, Jean-Claude confessed to a certain trepidation about driving this route. Rwanda's northern region had once been the heartland of Hutu Power, and in many ways it remained unrepentant. This stretch of highway had long been considered a dangerous one to drive—not for reasons of traffic or road quality. The asphalt here had always been well-maintained; it was the artery of political power, as I would learn. "It was the people in this area," Jean-Claude explained. "Very aggressive toward outsiders. If your car broke down, if you had an accident, or if you hit someone—you got out and ran. You ran for your life, because they would chase you down."

The theme from *Deliverance* could be heard playing faintly in my subconscious.

"And now?" I asked.

"And now? I don't know now." Jean-Claude hunched forward in his seat, eyes on the road. "You know, they started killing Tutsis out here even before the genocide began. If you were a Tutsi, you couldn't pass through here. There were roadblocks everywhere; they were looking for you."

"Does it feel creepy?" I asked. "Driving through here?"

"Yes, it is very weird."

The road descended into grassy meadows, fields shaded by the hills that surrounded them. *If you didn't know the history, you would think only how blandly beautiful it all was.* We crossed the clouded waters of the Nyabarongo, a name that resonates with Rwandans. The bodies dumped here floated downstream all the way to Rusumo Falls, where they formed human log-jams at times, bloated and bobbing, until they eventually reached Lake Victoria. *"Throw them in the river! Send them back to Ethiopia!"* This was the message of Léon Mugesera, an early propagandist and intellectual architect of the philosophy that would later become known as Hutu Power. He was speaking about *this* river, this valley, and as we began our slow ascent back into the hills, we passed a turnoff for Mugesera's hometown.

"He gave that speech near here," Jean-Claude said. "In the next community. In Ngororero."

At a November 22, 1992, rally, Mugesera—a well-regarded university professor and a vice-president of Habyarimana's ruling party—openly called for the extermination of Tutsis, urging Rwanda's Hutus to send their Tutsi neighbours "back to Ethiopia" by throwing them into the Nyabarongo River, whose waters fed into the Akagera and eventually the Nile. Here was the Hamitic hypothesis, run amok. *"Tutsis are not Rwandans. They don't belong here! Send them back to where they came from!*" Professor Mugesera reminded his audience that "the fatal mistake we made in 1959 was letting [the Tutsis] get out. They belong in Ethiopia, and we are going to find a shortcut to get them there," he said. "Wipe them out! Do not let any of them get away!" He ended this Nuremberg-style rally with the cry "Long live President Habyarimana!" In the run-up to the genocide, intera-hamwe death squads would often chant quotes from Mugesera's speech, and the rivers of Rwanda would indeed be clogged with corpses. The youth of Rwanda had taken his words to heart.

The 1990 RPF invasion may have been the catalyst, and Habyarimana's assassination may have been the signal, but the groundwork was laid along this river, with those words.

By the time the genocide began, Mugesera had slipped away. He arrived in Canada with false travel documents and taught at Laval University happily for years. It was like having Goebbels as our guest. Following nearly *two decades* of protests and petitions from the Rwandan government, Mugesera was finally extradited in 2012, where he currently stands indicted on charges of inciting genocide. Personally? I think they should have thrown him in the Nyabarongo River, seen how he fared.

# 43

NGORORERO IS A PROSPEROUS ENOUGH PLACE TODAY. Metal rooftops, knife-edged in silver, have replaced worn-out tiles and the town
centre is busy with shops and small cafés, even a gaudy discothèque
or two.

Ngororero seemed a natural stopping point, so we pulled over to
buy a Fanta, maybe a couple of goat kebobs, admire the scenery:
the town was perched prettily above a postcard-perfect valley. But we
never got out of the Land Cruiser. Jean-Claude parked the truck, but
didn't turn off the motor. He sat there, quietly, with the engine
idling. We were waiting, though I wasn't sure for what. In the backseat Patrice rolled over, mumbled something about blue-plumed
herons, then fell back to sleep. Jean-Claude still didn't move. After
a moment, I said, "You know what? We don't need to stop here.
Why don't we just keep going?" Jean-Claude nodded, put the vehicle back into drive.

Alpine air. The smell of pine so sharp it seemed like dill. The highway curved through forest and field, putting Ngororero farther behind
us with every turn.

"Did I ever tell you," Jean-Claude asked, "about my practice family? The one I had before I met Christine?"

"Practice family?"

"The children I rescued."

This was back in 1994. Jean-Claude had been making the run
between Kenya and Rwanda, carrying news and letters back and forth
between survivors and their families. In Nairobi, he was accosted by a
distraught young woman barely out of her teens. She was looking for
news about her nephews.

"When the genocide began, one of her nephews was staying with
her at her parents' house. She took the boy and ran with him into the
swamps. She was still in high school I think, nineteen maybe. Her

parents, her brother, all were killed. But this little boy and her, they made it through alive."

The boy's mother was Hutu. So when the young woman and her nephew finally came out of the swamps, she sent the boy to his mother.

"The village, it's called Miyove. It was in the north. They were attacking Tutsis again, and she was panicked when she heard this. All her nephews were in the north."

"How many children did her brother have?" I asked.

"Three. All boys. Ages were, like, five, seven, and three. When I spoke to that young woman, she was crying so much, saying it's the only family she had left."

Hutu insurgents were attacking the outlying communities, were still waging a rearguard campaign, and the people in Miyove would be hostile toward the children. Their aunt knew that.

"In that village," Jean-Claude explained, "every Tutsi had been killed. Every Tutsi, except three."

"But those kids were only *half*-Tutsi," I said. "Their mom was Hutu, right?"

"If your father is Tutsi, there's nothing half-Tutsi about you, you are Tutsi 100 percent. Was only a matter of time they were going to kill those children too, leave no survivors. No witnesses to what has happened."

"No witnesses? Even if it's just a seven-year-old child?"

"This is why their auntie was frantic to get them out of there. I was making another run back to Rwanda, so I said, 'Okay, I'm gonna go to the village, talk to your sister-in-law, and bring your nephews back with me.'"

What Jean-Claude didn't realize was that the village in question, as well as being hostile to Tutsis, was located deep inside insurgent-held territory. The RPF had roadblocks on the highway to prevent people entering; it was simply too dangerous. Jean-Claude avoided these RPF checkpoints by chance more than anything, turning down a secondary road before he reached them.

"I knew a quicker way," he said. (Which didn't surprise me; Jean-Claude always knows a quicker way.) "So I passed through this dangerous area without knowing. When I reached the village, everybody was surprised. They were watching me very closely, thinking, 'Who is this guy? He looks Tutsi. Is he with the RPF? What is he doing here?' When I found the boys' mother, I said to her, 'Look, I need to take them with me. If they stay, chance is they're gonna be murdered. Somebody is going to kill them at some point.'"

"And?"

"She said I could take two. The youngest, his name was Oscar, and the middle boy, name was Jean-Marie, they could go. But she wanted the oldest one, the seven-year-old, Xavier, to stay as a kind of hostage."

"A hostage?"

"As a protection. She was Hutu, and those villagers, they thought the RPF is going to come and kill everybody, like a revenge genocide. They thought, 'If we keep a Tutsi child here, they won't attack us, we can negotiate.'"

"What did you do?"

"What could I do? I took the two younger boys with me and left the oldest. I tried so hard, but I couldn't change the mother's mind. It was when I was driving back on the main highway with those two boys that I found out how dangerous that region was. These RPF soldiers came out at a checkpoint, stopped me, said, 'Are you crazy? You came from up there? That is insurgent territory. You have to tell us before you go in. You could have been killed!' Really, I was lucky to get out alive."

The two boys stayed with Jean-Claude's sister in Kigali while he arranged for a vehicle back to Kenya. By the time he got the boys to Nairobi, their aunt was gone. She'd been sponsored by a relative in Canada and had flown out just before they arrived.

"When I called her to say the good news, I thought she would be happy, but she yelled at me! She said, 'What about Xavier? He is the one I was in the swamps with. We kept each other alive. He is the one you have to rescue!' She was very upset. She said, 'Now he is the *only* Tutsi left in that village! They're gonna kill him for sure!'"

"So what did you do?"

"I went back."

"To that same village!"

"I couldn't let this boy die."

Jean-Claude left the other two boys with a Rwandan couple, Peter and Epiphanie, who lived next door and had two boys of their own around the same age as Oscar and Jean-Marie. Jean-Claude then headed back to Rwanda.

"How long a drive would that be?"

"About twelve hundred kilometres, I think. It was like a two-day trip. But this time, I brought photographs of his younger brothers with me, pictures of them in a park in Nairobi, by a pond, smiling, enjoying their new life. You could see how happy they were, how relaxed. When I got to the village, I showed those pictures to the mom, and she said, 'Okay. I changed my mind. You're right. Xavier may be killed soon if you don't take him. The whole village is mad at me for letting the other children go. They said that if this oldest boy grows up, he's gonna tell what happened. He will have memories.'"

Once again, Jean-Claude stayed at his sister's house in Kigali till he could find a vehicle for the drive back to Nairobi.

"It was a very long trip. Xavier was a good boy, very polite. But sad. I think he had seen many things. Sometimes he would have a burst of crying and then become very quiet. But as we travelled, he became happier and he cried less. He held onto those photos of his brothers, was looking at them all the time. He could feel they were going to have a good life. And you know what? They did."

"Their mother never joined them?"

"No."

The Rwandan couple next door helped Jean-Claude take care of the children.

"Peter and Epiphanie helped so much," he said.

Jean-Claude enrolled the three boys in a local primary school, arranged for school uniforms, made sure they did their homework every night, and even attended PTA meetings on their behalf. He was just twenty years old at the time.

"I was with those three boys for two years. I called them my practice family."

He was still taking care of them when he met Christine.

"Especially, I had a bond with the youngest one, Oscar. I think he was seeing me as a kind of dad."

The boy's aunt, now in Canada, eventually secured sponsorship for them as well. She brought her nephews to Montreal, where all three children were adopted by a foster mom.

"Their foster mom was French Canadian. She loved them so much. Those boys grew up as Canadian. They learned to skate, to play hockey. But it's funny, even after I moved to Montreal and then to Calgary, any time when there was an issue between the children, I was still the one they would call. They would tell me what the problem was when they wouldn't tell anyone else."

All three are doing well. Two of the boys are studying accounting. The other has his master's degree and is employed with the Department of Health Services, as a social worker at a Montreal hospital. They had escaped a death sentence and claimed an alternative future as their own. And I thought again of what André Sibomana had said, and the lesson it conveyed. *We are products but not prisoners of our past.*

# 44

THE SCENT OF EUCALYPTUS can be as bracing as peppermint, as invigorating as a splash of aftershave.

We were driving through northern green forests with Patrice asleep in the back. I was tempted to wake him up with a shove, shouting, "Quick! What kind of bird is— Oh, too late," maybe filch a peek at his guidebook beforehand and look up the rarest bird in Rwanda, then describe it to him in great detail. "I saw this little bird, really small, looked sort of like a yellow-eyed owlet with striped breast feathers, but I could be wrong. Seemed like it might have been a nocturnal species as well, native to mid-range montane forest canopies, but again—I could be wrong. You didn't see it? It was right there." In the end, and largely due to Jean-Claude's admonishments, I chose not to disturb Patrice's deeply lathered slumber.

"Welcome to Jerusalem!" Jean-Claude said.

We were passing the turnoff for Gasiza, an otherwise unremarkable village that just happened to be the birthplace of former president Juvénal Habyarimana. Gasiza was referred to as "Jerusalem," or sometimes "Nazareth," because it was—and I quote—the "hometown of God."

Northern Hutu had dominated the Rwandan military under Habyarimana's leadership. Of the eleven military officers who seized power with him in 1973, ten came from this one corner of Rwanda. The men making decisions in Habyarimana's government were almost exclusively Hutu from the north; their southern brethren, though also Hutu, were excluded from almost every key position. It was a geographic divide as much as ethnic. (The only thing the northerners hated more than their southern rivals were the Tutsis.)

"The people who organized the genocide came from these hills," Jean-Claude noted.

Near the turnoff to Jerusalem, a faded, flyblown tavern squatted beside the road. The paint-peeling sign read BAR IBYIMANA, which translates as "God's Bar." Appeals to the deity notwithstanding, the place seemed grim. We didn't stop to find out.

I think we were both looking forward to the end of this section of highway. Tracing my finger ahead on the map, I could see we would come out at a T intersection on the main Congo road. The name of the crossroads town was Mukamira, and as we drew nearer, more and more villages appeared, closer and closer together.

More and more people as well. Men and women, young and old, milling about the roadsides, hashing through the never-ending quiddities of life, laughing and arguing, shopping and gossiping. Children filed by, lugging their water jugs heavy homeward, while others bounced along on the return, swinging empty containers and enjoying the reprieve. Their smaller siblings, some little more than toddlers, were equally weighted down, their bundled kindling stacked high on their heads. A pair of nattily dressed young men, musicians from the looks of it, were dragging a 1970s relic of a keyboard up a hill. "Probably performing at a dance club tonight," Jean-Claude noted. A tumult of younger kids ran past, chasing the wind with homemade pinwheels, and we saw one poor fellow attempting to move a huge wooden wardrobe on the back of his bicycle, thighs straining, feet wobbly on the pedals. We were going to pull a U-turn and offer to help, but we could see the cumbersome piece of furniture would never fit. Too large for a Land Cruiser, but not for a bicycle. That too was life in Africa.

A string of lakes lay on our right, Gishwati Forest on our left. A paint-by-numbers where every colour was green.

Gishwati Forest provided a pocket of calm in an over-cultivated land. During the genocide, thousands of Tutsis fled to these woods seeking safety, only to be set upon by dogs brought in by the interahamwe. No one knows how many died in Gishwati Forest; they don't appear on any census, but even now tree-planting crews will occasionally turn up human bones.

Tea plantations appeared after Gishwati, and we were soon once again in among caterpillar hedges and luminescent fields. A marshy river emptied into an equally marshy lake. And then we were past that, too, as the road brought us at last to Mukamira.

A sprawling town, Mukamira. It sat astride a crucial intersection: turn right and you would be swept back to Kigali along the main highway, left and you would be heading straight for Congo.

We turned left.

As we rattled across a bridge, Jean-Claude shouted to be heard. "The River of Beer!"

That got my attention.

"The what now?"

"The river, it supplies water to— How do you say it, like a factory to make beer?"

"A brewery?"

"Yes. A brewery. This town is where Primus beer comes from. The brewery is over there. And the river—"

"The one we just crossed?"

"The Sebeya. That is where the water comes from. Primus beer is made from the water of the Sebeya River."

Forget Jerusalem! This was my Holy City!

Alas, as we discovered, the Primus brewery didn't offer guided tours, especially to grinning foreigners who showed up at the factory gates asking about "samples and such."

"We'll tell them I'm a journalist," I said. "Here to do a story about Rwandan beer and how good it is, pending a proper taste test of course."

But evening was settling over the town, and the various offices were closing down for the day, making it impossible for me to appeal to a higher level.

The streets of Mukamira (a.k.a. "the Milwaukee of Rwanda") were alive with dusk-lit saloons and patio-lanterned taverns selling Primus as fresh as it could possibly be. We passed the Hollywood Bar, the All-Star Bar, the New Star Bar, and somewhere, I'm sure, the Hollywood All-Star Bar.

"The beer is probably cheaper here as well," I said, dropping the hint like a wet bag of cement. "Seeing as how it's closer to the source."

"Probably," said Jean-Claude, and on he drove without stopping.

*I've really got to get this guy drinking.*

There were other enterprises as well—internet cafés with Christmas lights strung around the doorways, mattress shops, and seamstresses with roadside foot-pedal Singer sewing machines where you could get your clothes mended while you waited. There were bakeries and cafés with French names—La Vie and Est Belle and C'est Belle—but none had the allure of Sebeya River Gold (as I would now call Primus).

The air was cooling down. Clay-packed fields had filled up with impromptu matches and the dust-cloud kicks of homemade soccer balls. Serious old men were playing cards on upturned packing crates. The streets of Mukamira had become a promenade, as the town's young women reappeared in fine dresses to stroll past gaggles of admirers, eye-fluttering the boys into distraction. One group of girls had congregated in front of a church and were exchanging sidelong glances with a coltish group of young men, all under the watchful and disapproving gaze of the Virgin Mary.

A Congolese refugee camp hove into view, overflowing with crowds of undefeated humanity. We drove past endless rows of now-familiar UNHCR tents. A patchwork of laundry was laid out on the grass to dry. Women from the camp moved past, bent forward from heavy burdens held against their backs, kept in place by thick straps drawn taut across their foreheads.

"Congolese," Jean-Claude said. "Rwandese balance stuff on their heads. In Congo they use forehead straps like that. They can carry a lot more that way, but is very hard on their necks, is very hard on their backs."

I could imagine. My own shoulders ached just to see it, and I later learned that Congolese women often suffer from compressed vertebrae in their necks.

Once Jean-Claude had pointed out the difference in how Rwandans and Congolese carried heavy loads, I began to notice it everywhere.

Congolese, overburdened with bundles of sugar cane and root vegetables packed into gunnysacks, backs bent almost ninety degrees, canvas straps across their foreheads; Rwandans, in sharp contrast, moving through with their posture perfectly straight, gourds and baskets balanced atop: smaller loads, carried with confidence. I could identify people at a glance simply by how they carried their cargo— *Congolese, Congolese, Rwandan, Congolese, Rwandan*—and I thought how easy it was to categorize, and what a short step it was from that to isolation, eradication.

The sun was falling, pulling the rest of the sky in with it, and as we began our long slow descent toward the border, Lake Kivu reappeared, looking like gold foil in the last light of day. In the distance we could see a net of lights thrown across a darkening shore: Goma City, on the other side of the line. Goma City, where the fighting had been at its worst.

We'd woken that day to news of war in the Congo. Sadly, there is always news of war in the Congo; at any one time at least a dozen different insurgencies were flaring up in far-flung regions. What made this news significant was the where of it: on the outskirts of Goma City. We were driving directly toward the fighting.

A pitched three-way battle was being waged on the other side of that hill. The FDLR (led by former Hutu Power génocidaires, you may recall) were fighting the M23 rebels (Congolese Tutsi soldiers who'd broken away from the Congolese army), who were in turn facing a full-scale military offensive from the government of Congo backed by UN forces.

South Africa and Tanzania were now thoroughly engaged in the conflict (or implicated, depending on your point of view) as part of the United Nations intervention brigade. More troops were on their way from Malawi to join them. These would be no neutral observers. The UN was fighting alongside regulars from the Congolese army: an army with a well-deserved reputation for depravity against its own citizens. There were no good guys in this fight. It was like a game of Risk played with real armies.

Caught between hammer and anvil, hundreds of thousands of people continued to flee the region, many of them ending up in UNHCR refugee camps. Which is to say, the UN, in perfect bureaucratic fashion, was helping to create the very refugees it was now being asked to house and feed. I believe this is called vertical integration.

We arrived in the Rwandan border town of Gisenyi (now known as Rubavu) as darkness finally settled over Kivu. A heavy moon hung low above the water. We could see flashes of light on the other side of the border.

Two Rwandan villages nearby had been shelled from positions inside Congo, and President Kagame had warned that if these "provocations" continued, Rwanda would send in troops of its own. Gisenyi, however, hardly seemed like a community on the edge of a war zone; the town was brimming with well-dressed night-life celebrants flitting from café to dance club and back again.

Jean-Claude and I checked into the Serena Hotel, beautifully situated on the lake. A string-of-pearl line of lights along the shore curved toward a brighter cluster farther down. That would be Goma.

We ate our dinner on the hotel patio overlooking the water. In Congo, government forces were lobbing mortars at rebel encampments, armoured convoys were rolling in, attack helicopters were hovering like dragonflies, gunfire was ripping through jungle leaves. But over here, all was calm. It was surreal.

After our meal we retreated to the hotel bar to warm up and catch the end of an English Premier League match on the telly. (Something United vs. Something FC. Jean-Claude was more rapt than I—and I don't even think it was live. I think it was a repeat of an earlier match.) It was only when I saw the blond man with the windswept hair stride in that I knew we were in trouble. He ordered a drink, slapped down some money, turned to survey the room with an exorbitant self-regard, as though expecting a buzz of excitement to radiate outward from his presence. His eyes were pale, his face suitably sun-creased; he seemed to be squinting at the far horizon, even though there was no far horizon to squint at. There was only a handful of businessmen milling about, with Jean-Claude and me off in one corner. The fellow with the windswept hair (also odd, now that I think about it, as there was no wind inside the bar either) was wearing a canvas vest with multiple pockets, and he had a telephoto camera slung over his shoulder like a rifle. He was clearly starring in a one-man drama of his own life, and I thought, *Oh shit*. A war correspondent.

# 45

THE NEXT MORNING I DECIDED to walk to the Congo, if only to be able to mention this in future cocktail conversations with a breezy nonchalance. "I say, chaps, did I ever mention the time I ... *walked to the Congo?*" (The italics would be implicit.) But in all honesty, it was less a trek than a saunter, a twenty-minute stroll along the beach and then up onto a leafy boulevard.

I'd woken to the sound of Lake Kivu whispering in my ear. Winds from Congo were pushing waves onto the beach outside my window in a slow, steady rhythm. Early-morning birdsong filled the trees: whistles and warbles, courting calls and sharp rebukes, staccato bursts of maniacal laughter followed by sigh-like coos. One bird was making a loud *chk-chk-chk-chk* sound, oddly reminiscent of a lawn sprinkler. Another, the low *glug-glug-glug* of someone pouring wind-shield wiper fluid into a car. (Funny how conditioned our cultural associations are.) It was loud and joyful and discordantly musical, and a reminder that even in the dry season we were deep in the sodden heart of Africa, amid rainforests rich with life.

I got up and got dressed, then wandered through the lobby, past a sleepy desk clerk and a fully asleep security guard who was, apparently, manning the metal detector. Feeling reassured by his catlike presence, knowing he was ready to awaken and pounce at the first sign of danger, I ambled out the front door and down to the lake.

A shiver of mist lay across everything. Lake Kivu was a clouded mirror. Inlets and islands. Outcrops of rock, like hippos surfacing for air. A large sign, posted outside the hotel's front gate, assured visitors that Lake Kivu contained—and I quote—"no crocodiles." *Yessir!* This lake is completely crocodile free! So go ahead and splash about as much as you like, confident in the knowledge that ABSOLUTELY NO CROCODILES are lurking in the depths, ready to clamp onto your ankles with steel-trap jaws to drag you screaming and flailing into the lake's lower reaches, only to be regurgitated in dissembled form later on. No sir. So you just get that image right out of your mind. (Note to Tourism Rwanda: Some things are better not to call attention to.) I also noticed that the warning said nothing about *alligators*. Alligators don't live in Africa, true, but Kivu is one of the deepest lakes in the world, and who's to say its lower reaches haven't bred some sort of bizarre hawk-eagle-type hybrid: a "crocodile-alligator," skulking about offshore.

In the end, I decided to hedge my bets. I didn't strip down to my boxers and go galloping about, but instead rolled my pant legs up to mid-calf—and didn't I look fetching in my homemade Capri pants—and then waded barefoot along the side of the lake on the assumption that, worst case, you could probably outrun a croc this close to shore.[21]

As I followed the palm-treed beach down to a pier, it became evident I wasn't the only one in the water. I could hear it before I saw it: early-morning children, laughing. They were leaping, bathing, shouting, fanning waves at each other, then coughing and sputtering as they swiped water from their faces.

"Hello, muzungu!" one of them yelled, bobbing like a fishing buoy as I passed. "Hello! Bonjour! Bonjour!"

---

21. I just checked. You can't.

I didn't see any children getting pulled violently under the water in a pinkish froth, which I took as a good sign, so I waded a little deeper into the lake, crimping my pants ever higher and enjoying the cool pull and repeat of waves across my shins.

The real danger in Lake Kivu is more insidious than crocodiles. Impossible to see or even sense, the deep waters of Kivu contain some 60 billion cubic metres of methane (which can ignite) and carbon dioxide (which can kill), fed into them by a nearby volcano. These gases are trapped in the lake's lower depths, more than 250 metres below the surface, making Kivu one of three known "exploding lakes" in the world. A sudden eruption, or "lake overturn," as it's known, can be cataclysmic. In Cameroon, a similar lake erupted in 1986, suffocating more than 1,700 people. Survivors of an earlier eruption spoke of a wave of vile-smelling gas that moved through, killing everything in its path.

The longer the gas is allowed to accumulate, the greater the risks. Warned that their lake would kill again if the methane and $CO_2$ weren't removed, Cameroon began siphoning it off, venting the gas into the air. But Rwanda, with an exploding lake of its own to worry about, saw the potential for something more, something better: a "value added" venture that would turn a potential natural disaster into a plentiful, self-renewing energy source.

One of the great hurdles Rwanda faces is its lack of a national power grid. The vast majority of homes are still lit with kerosene; flying over the country at night reveals pockets of light surrounded by darkness. So a test project was set up to see if they could extract gas from Lake Kivu and, rather than simply releasing it into the atmosphere, pipe it to a plant to generate electricity. By lowering a tube deep into the lake, they were able to suck methane-infused water to the surface, where the gas was captured like bubbles from a flute of champagne. Two megawatts of power had already been extracted, and I could see the platform floating in the distance like a giant raft with a straw on top.

The success of this has led to a far more ambitious project known as KivuWatt. A private venture backed by the Rwandan government and supported with international loans, KivuWatt will extract energy from Lake Kivu on a much larger scale, almost doubling Rwanda's current electrical capacity. It's all part of a wide-reaching plan to bring electricity to 70 percent of the population by 2018. Lake Kivu alone will provide power to more than two million people. It's an incredible judo-flip of a strategy, turning an imminent threat into an energy solution, and it limits the release of greenhouse gas as well, making it a clean energy source.

Rwanda is also planning to build geothermal plants to take advantage of the volcanic furnaces smouldering underground. A utility-scale solar energy plant—the first in East Africa—was already underway in the country's sun-baked eastern province. (The Dutch company that built the solar-panel facilities praised the Rwandan government for its "laser-like focus.") More than 5 percent of Rwanda's energy capacity already comes from solar power, and the country is looking to invest in hydro as well.

Now, if they could just harness the energy of those kids splashing about in the lake, they'd really be on to something …

Searching for a place to sit down and sock-whip the sand from my feet before pulling my shoes back on, I wandered into a small clearing. There I surprised two middle-aged women dressed head-to-trainers in pink velour jogging outfits, right down to matching sweatbands, who were in the middle of their morning calisthenics. They froze, mortified by my sudden appearance. It was as though I'd caught them doing something wrong.

"*Muraho!*" I said cheerfully as I passed, more or less between them.

"*Muraho,*" they mumbled, looking down, avoiding eye contact, and then bursting into self-conscious laughter after I'd departed.

I felt bad. Imagine: you and a friend have decided, "Enough of this! We are going to get in shape. We'll do it together. Every morning, you and me, no excuses, down by the lake." You buy your outfits and your brand-new running shoes and you suit up and you march down with great determination and you find a spot away from prying eyes, and, no sooner do you start in with the jumping jacks than some big pink-faced muzungu shows up. It must have been embarrassing—and funny. I imagine it gave them a shared story to shriek about over the years. *"Remember that time we took up exercising ...?"*

The beach ended at a rocky outcrop. I pulled on my shoes and socks, then walked up onto a boulevard lined with palm trees. This was Avenue de la Coopération, which followed the lakeshore.

In the grassy verge, birds were walking about on stilted legs, picking through the weeds, looking for insects and seeds. Plumed in blue with thin curved beaks, they were probably some sort of hawk-eagle, or maybe a stork-heron or a pelican-goose. Where was Patrice when I needed him?

Avenue de la Coopération changed names, disconcertingly, to Avenue de la Révolution as it neared the border with Congo. The road narrowed and the mood shifted. A military transport plane lifted off from the Congo side of the hill, thunder-rumbling low across Lake Kivu before banking west, as though evading artillery fire. A UN supply plane came in just heartbeats after the transport plane had departed—it's a wonder they didn't collide in mid-air— and it made a similar lake-skimming, chest-rattling approach. The noise was deafening; it made your heart beat faster and left a ringing in your ears as sharp as a tuning fork.

The border crossing was a potholed bottleneck with traffic shoved in from both sides. Uniformed soldiers floated about, serenely calm amid the chaos. At the Rwandan customs office, already crowded this early in the day, I realized—in mid-request for a day visa so that I might stroll over to Congo for my morning repast—that I didn't have my passport with me, or any other identification, for that matter. I hadn't thought to knock on Jean-Claude's door and let him know where I was going, either, so at that moment, nobody on earth knew where I was. If I were detained or spirited away, who would be the wiser? I really should have thought things through.

This "walk to the Congo" jaunt had started as a bit of a lark. But now, wedged in at a teller-like window by a compression of Congolese truck drivers who were working at cross-purposes, waving their papers at the customs officials as if they were bidding at an auction (a Congolese queue is a contradiction in terms, apparently), I realized that it was, perhaps, better not to call attention to myself. I was the only muzungu there at the time, so I was definitely visible. But crossing a border without papers? Not a good idea. So at first chance, I walked off in an apparent huff—"Please wait a moment? *Please wait a moment?* I don't have time for this!"—without having to show my (missing) papers. Short of wrestling a handgun from one of the border guards and shooting my way in, I couldn't see how I'd be able to put one foot inside the Democratic Republic of Congo.

Damn.

A muddy track ran alongside a wall near the customs office. Goma/Gisenyi is really one contiguous city, split down the middle, and this wall was part of the actual border separating Rwanda from Congo. Homes on the other side looked directly into Rwanda. It was a very porous divide, considering the tensions that crackled along it.

Passing a clutch of money traders—*"Dollars américains!* Muzungu, muzungu! Best rates! *Français? Anglais?"*—I turned a corner and ran into an ambush of street sellers hawking items I could have no reasonable interest in buying. (A matching set of toilet seats? Why? Jumper cables? I'm on foot, buddy.) Not that it mattered; I'd forgotten my wallet as well. It was like trying to push my way out of a mosh pit, but I finally managed to writhe through, with the satisfaction of knowing that any pickpockets who might have surreptitiously frisked me en route had come up empty. (Rwanda has very little street crime, but I'm told their pickpockets are of reputable talent.)

On my way back to the hotel, along Avenue de Independence, I passed a slumbering bar called Sky Nevada. Another called Sun Magic. An auto-parts shop was rattling open for the day, the metal slats rolling upward beneath a government billboard urging people to work harder. Harder? How exactly? It was barely past seven, and the entire city was already up and on the go. Streams of people passed. They *appeared* to be walking at a leisurely pace, yet glided by me with ease. Even old ladies burdened with baskets pulled up alongside me ... then past. I picked up my pace—as a point of pride if nothing else—but it was of little use; it was as though I was on a treadmill set at a lower gear than everyone else. It didn't matter who it was. Schoolboys shouting "Morning morning morning teacher! I am fine!" Women with babies wrapped up like plump packages on their backs. Men so thin their suits hung off them as though on clothes hangers. Everyone blew by me, some throwing puzzled glances over their shoulders without breaking stride. They seemed so purposeful, so well turned out. And there's me clomping along in what I thought was a hurried manner with all the vitality of a limp windsock, shirt untucked and hair uncombed, hems of my khakis still sopping wet, yet feeling light-chested and happy nonetheless. I liked Gisenyi. There was a tropical feel to the town—but without any sense of lassitude. It bustled with activity but not impatience. Rwanda in a thimble, it seemed to me.

A clatterfication of bicycles. Minibuses passing in multicoloured blurs. Mosquito-motored scooters zipping in and out. Back on the beach in front of our hotel, waves were sliding onto soft brown sand. Orchestral arrangements of birds once again filled the treetops with song. And then—another transport plane lifted off from Congo with the roar of a lion. A platoon of Rwandan soldiers appeared suddenly, dressed in crisp camouflage, jogging in metronymic formation down the shore, rifles at the ready.

On the hotel's veranda, I found Jean-Claude having breakfast (if you can call seven courses of passion fruit breakfast). He'd been watching the planes taking off too.

When I told him about my aborted attempt at reaching the Congo, he suggested we try again.

"We'll go back," he said, "and tell them you're a journalist."

I didn't think trying to cross an international border between two nations on the brink of war by claiming to be a journalist would help.

He thought about this. "We'll tell them you're an *important* journalist."

And son of a gun if it didn't work. We returned, me with my passport this time—though I was never asked to produce it. Instead,
Jean-Claude spoke with the customs officer and handed him one of
my *Canadian Geographic* calling cards. We weren't permitted to go
into Congo, the situation was too dire, but we could at least stand on
Congolese soil in the no man's land between borders. The Rwandan
customs official walked us over. The only stipulation he made was
that I let him review any photos I took.

His Congolese counterpart, stocky and muscle-jawed, met us
halfway and escorted us into the Democratic Republic of Congo—
or rather, into the strange twilight world between the two. Transport
trucks were everywhere, their cargo stacked this way and that. Goma
City was pushing up against the border, the buildings looking
like stacked crates teetering on a forklift. We could see Congo, but
we couldn't enter. To step through that final barrier would be to
invite questioning, detention. "We would have to bribe our way in
and bribe our way out" was how Jean-Claude put it.

So I wandered about instead, while Jean-Claude chatted with the
Congolese customs officer in French. Or tried to. The man was overtly
circumspect and would give only carefully crafted non-answers to
Jean-Claude's queries. "Has the conflict affected transportation?"
Answer: "The situation is under control." "Is the border busier now?
Are more people trying to come over?" Answer: "The situation is
under control." "Are things cooling down or heating up?" Answer:
"As far as the situation goes, it is under control."

We thanked him for his help (Jean-Claude had the feeling he
was expecting us to slip him a few francs when we shook his
hand), and as we walked back to the Rwandan side, we saw an
American television crew recording a breathless report about the
impending war between Congo and Rwanda. Like the windswept
photo journalist we'd seen earlier, the reporter in question wore a
tanned, multi-pocketed vest—*de rigueur* among the war correspondent set, apparently—and with the Goma cityscape in the
background, he was clutching his microphone with both hands

and shouting into it, as though shells were falling around him as he spoke.

"Why is he yelling like that?" Jean-Claude asked.

Having completed our walkabout in no man's land, Jean-Claude and I returned to the Rwanda customs office.

A sign greets truck drivers and travellers entering Rwanda from Congo. Not "Welcome to the Land of a Thousand Hills!" or "Enjoy your stay!" but rather INVESTMENT YES. CORRUPTION NO. I scrolled through the photos I'd taken, for the Rwandan official to check, and he requested I delete only two: one that showed a soldier's face too closely and another that showed a military licence plate too clearly. Otherwise, it was fine.

"You know," the official said to Jean-Claude in Kinyarwanda, "the main crossing point between Congo and Rwanda is on the north side of the city. That's where most of the trade and foot traffic happens. This crossing is just used mainly for long-distance transport."

The real action was at the other border crossing.

Oh.

"So let's go," Jean-Claude said, and off we went.

We zigzagged our way through the streets of Gisenyi, often along the very walls that delineated the border. On our way, we passed the same throng of money-changers and street vendors I'd squirmed through earlier. The man with the jumper cables watched me go by like the lost sale I was. *So you* did *have a vehicle!* I gave him a sympathetic shrug.

That customs officer hadn't been kidding.

Traffic at the first border crossing was a mere trifle compared to the influx and outflow of people on this wider avenue. Here the two countries ran smack up against each other, with the newly built homes and tidy yards of Rwanda built directly across a muddy stream from the shantytown shacks in Congo.

Even with fighting on the other side of the hill and military planes rumbling overhead, the border was thriving. People were streaming into Rwanda, not as refugees but as merchants, as buyers. Gisenyi was supplying Goma with everything imaginable. It was a decidedly lopsided flow of trade, with the Congolese pouring in empty-handed and leaving laden with goods, loading up and then heading back. Again and again.

This was cross-border shopping as I'd never seen it, a market on the march, a beehive kicked open. Congolese market women were stocking up on cooking pots and kerosene, on yams and cabbages, on gritty sacks of cooking charcoal, on chandeliers of bananas. *Surely they have banana trees in Congo,* I thought. *Why would they need to come all the way here to buy them?* Then I realized that with the fighting raging just outside the city, harvesting any kind of crop would have been dangerous.

These women were carrying commerce on their backs, supply and demand in immediate response. One woman was taking a towering telescope of plastic buckets back with her, another had cornered the market on lime-green flip-flops. Many of the goods were Chinese-made. One lady had an array of brightly coloured Kleenex boxes roped together and balanced on her head. Her burden was the size of a small refrigerator; I didn't know how she managed the weight of it, let alone at such a brisk pace. (Jean-Claude suggested that the boxes might be empty and that she would slyly restock them with coarser, cheaper tissues back home before reselling them.) Raggedy men in stained shirts and tattered shorts were pushing homemade wooden tricycles, the loads lashed down with twine and rope: full-sized mattresses hog-tied, bundles of clothing, even an entire couch in one case. It flowed without end and without beginning, a Mobius strip of people looping back and forth across the border.

Jean-Claude and I spent two nights in Gisenyi. We knocked the dust from our shoes, washed our socks in the sink, strolled among the shops, breathed in the tropical air, and filled our bellies with passion fruit and Primus, respectively. A long drive had brought us here, and our lakeside sojourn felt like one extended satisfying crick of the neck. We finally sent Patrice, our designated but underused driver, home on an express coach, with a generous tip and a warm handshake. It was probably the easiest and strangest assignment he'd ever had.

Before he left, I asked Patrice if it was true there were no crocodiles in Lake Kivu. (I was still considering a dip—would maybe *swim* to the Congo!) He said, and these were his exact words, "Not probably."

I never did figure out what he meant by that.

# 46

TWENTY YEARS AGO, the volcanic plains west of Goma were the site of the largest refugee encampment the world had ever seen.

With the collapse of Hutu Power, a mass migration occurred: more than two and a half million people fled the RPF advance. They were driven forward by interahamwe and Rwandan armed forces who were determined to take the nation with them into exile, denying the victors a people to govern. The first wave went south into Tanzania, the next into Burundi. The rest pushed westward, on foot, into Zaire (as the Congo was known from 1971 to 1997). Most crossed over here, at Gisenyi.

The bulk of the Hutu army, 22,000 strong,[22] crossed over with the refugees, their combat units and command structure intact, bringing with them heavy weaponry, military vehicles, ammunition, and the entire state treasury—more than US$170 million—leaving Rwanda bankrupt.

"The RPF may have the country," one of the Hutu leaders declared, "but we have the people."

It was the largest hostage-taking in human history. Rwanda had been hollowed out. Between the genocide and the exodus that

22. Some estimates put it as high as 40,000.

followed, 60 percent of the population was now dead, displaced, or on the run.

As the génocidaires flooded across the border into Zaire, an Oxfam employee looked on in horror. "They were covered in blood," he recalled. "Not their blood."

The interahamwe quickly took control of the camps. A Hutu Power government-in-exile was proclaimed (including, I kid you not, a "minister of tourism"), and the people were forbidden to return to Rwanda—if the innocent left, only the guilty would remain, after all. And anyway, a "revenge genocide" at the hands of the RPF would be waiting for them if they were foolish enough to go back. That was the warning. That was the fear.

The aims of the government-in-exile were clear: reclaim their country and drive the RPF out, and—implicitly—finish the genocide they'd started. Almost immediately, they began launching raids into Rwanda, terrorizing Tutsis in the remoter rural areas left unprotected and vulnerable. (The Hutu gunmen who killed the students at Nyange Secondary School had crossed over from these camps, and it was into one of these zones that Jean-Claude had so blithely driven when he went to rescue the three boys, unaware of the danger.) In Tanzania, a similar scenario was playing out.

The camps were squalid and dangerous. Cholera and dysentery swept through, leaving thousands dead. International aid, painfully absent in Rwanda during the genocide, now poured in. Armed génocidaires—wanted for war crimes—patrolled the camps unobstructed, confiscating supplies provided by aid agencies, including medicines, and then selling them on the black market to help fund their cross-border campaign. These weren't refugees running the camps, these were fugitives. All the while, French arms continued to arrive, landing in Goma in preparation for the promised counter invasion, aided and abetted by France's long-time ally, Zaire's cartoonish dictator-for-life, Mobutu Sese Seko.

Rwanda had internal refugee camps to deal with as well, among them Kibeho Camp in the eastern region. The RPF had moved through, camp by camp, closing each one in turn and sending the people home. Kibeho was the last. Controlled by génocidaires, Kibeho had become a tinderbox. The interahamwe used it as a staging ground for attacks on the surrounding countryside, targeting both the Hutus who had returned and the Tutsis who'd survived—"killing the evidence," as it was known. More than 250,000 people were entrenched in Kibeho, and tensions were rising. When the RPF arrived to close down the camp, the interahamwe fought back, and what started as a military operation turned into a massacre, with soldiers firing directly into the crowds. The frightened people inside crushed each other trying to escape, trampling over bodies while heavy rains pounded down. Mud and blood, churning together. As many as 4,000 people died at Kibeho. Some estimates put it even higher.

Rwanda issued a warning to Zaire: close down the bases along its borders or face the consequences. Mobutu refused—and even increased aid to the Hutu Power government-in-exile. And so, in 1996, with support from Uganda, Rwanda invaded. The RPF emptied the refugee camps in eastern Zaire and forcibly repatriated more than 700,000 people, who returned as they'd come, on foot, in a bedraggled column that stretched for miles. The interahamwe and Hutu Power génocidaires in Goma fled into the jungle, leaving behind lists of Tutsis in the Lake Kivu region, carefully recorded in ledgers. These were the same people who would later call themselves the FDLR.

With Rwandan-backed rebels having reached the outskirts of Kinshasa, President Mobutu fled the country with only moments to spare and died soon after. Rwanda installed what they thought was a puppet president: a fading rebel leader named Laurent Kabila who had been plucked from obscurity by Kigali as much for his pliability as for any political acumen. But when Laurent Kabila, president of the newly renamed Democratic Republic of Congo (DRC), reneged on his backroom agreement and began targeting Tutsi Congolese and expelling Rwandan military advisers, Rwanda invaded Congo again and toppled him as well.

Two wars in the Congo in less than a decade have left the country reeling. *Millions* have died in the DRC: victims of war, anarchy, ethnic killings, criminal cartels, insurgencies, famine, greed, disease, and malnutrition. It's less a country than an ongoing crisis—one that can be traced back directly to the 1994 genocide against the Tutsis.[23] The apocalypse that Colonel Bagosora and the génocidaires ignited is burning still.

# 47

FOR A BORDER TOWN teetering on the edge of war, the outdoor markets of Gisenyi were surprisingly orderly. Thriving on trade, they were well-stocked and well-swept, with wide tables piled high with goods. Sheaves of fish, alive with flies. Peppers and pineapples. Bibles and yams.

One market was filled with housewares and clothing, and it was here that Jean-Claude and I faced our greatest challenge yet: shopping for our wives. It was sad, really, the two of us relying on each other for advice. "What do you think, do you think she'd like something like this?" one of us would ask, holding up items more or less at random.

The farther we pushed into the market, the more crowded it became; we all but snorkelled through at times, surfacing at intervals to exchange concerned looks before plunging back under.

---

23. The collapse of the Congo and the Great War that followed is beyond the scope of this book, but for a gripping account of this conflict, and the role that Rwanda has played in it, see Jason K. Stearns's *Dancing in the Glory of Monsters*. For a look at Belgium's own brutal history in the Congo, see Adam Hochschild's equally epic *King Leopold's Ghost*. Anyone seeking an understanding of this region of Africa would do well to start with those two books.

Wooden trays were heaped with Allan Quatermain–style treasures: trinkets and talismans, the usual brummagem junk. Unfortunately, after a regrettable incident involving pewter earrings at a marketplace in Mexico, my wife doesn't allow me to purchase jewellery for her anymore, so shiny baubles were out. (My sons were easy. T-shirts at the airport. Done.)

One tout tried to entice me with jumper cables—*"Perhaps m'lady would appreciate some fine automotive accessories as a token of my affection?"*—but somehow I resisted the temptation. (And what is it with Rwandans and jumper cables?) Instead, I decided I would buy my Japanese wife some Rwandan fabric. Jean-Claude chose to purchase a CD of gospel music for his better half. (There were booths in the market that—copyright be damned!—would create a mixed tape for you, to order, from their library of CDs while you waited.) We agreed to meet back in forty minutes and wished each other well, much in the manner of paratroopers about to fling themselves from a moving plane on a moonless night. *"Good luck, it's been an honour serving with you."*

Head held high, striding purposefully into quicksand, I marched off into that labyrinth of stalls.

Well, hell, who knew it was so hard to buy some fabric! The traditional dress of Rwandan women is an intricately patterned, brightly dyed wraparound skirt with matching head scarf, artfully tied. I had assumed these were simply large squares of cloth. But no. There was more to it than that. Much more. The cloth came in different shapes, sizes, colours, and combinations—my head swam as I squeezed past row after row of stalls.

Jean-Claude's parting piece of advice had been "Maybe keep your wallet in your underwear, just to be safe."

I'd peeled off a fat stack of Rwandan francs for immediate use, then tucked the rest into the nested warmth of my nether regions. (I'll give you a moment to get that image out of your head; a shot of tequila should do it.) If someone was going to pick my pocket, I would at least get a free grope out of the deal.

I had money, I just didn't know how to spend it. I didn't even know where to start.

No worries. Several lanky men of dubious intent took a break from selling telephone cards and jumper cables to come to my rescue. They formed a phalanx around me, all talking at once, while the wraparound women looked on, trying to warn me away with their eyes.

The leader of my self-appointed crew, a leather-skinned elder with a chest-rattling catarrhal voice, referred to me repeatedly as "Monsieur," which I thought was terrific. *Monsieur muzungu, that's me!* When I explained, primarily through the art of pantomime, what I was looking for, he held my wrist, almost daintily, as though taking my pulse, and led me farther into the hugger-mugger of the market. With his friends clearing a path, we soon arrived at a large display of men's suits—all of them North American in style. Despite my protests, he discussed matters at great length with the wide-bosomed woman behind the counter. She didn't look happy. I assumed he and his coterie were demanding a large commission on any sales. But no matter how much they badgered and chivvied, she refused, which left us at an impasse. One man gestured one way, another pointed just as insistently in the opposite direction. This was followed by a highly animated and perfectly disjointed discourse with many a passionate digression, none of which brought us any closer to a solution. Proposals were proffered, solutions offered, objections waved aside.

When a dishevelment of grinning schoolboys pushed in, I preempted what was coming with a burst of my own: *"Good morning students how are you I am fine!"* They were under the mistaken impression that I would give them money simply because, well, I was a muzungu, I suppose, and presumably rich. They learned an important lesson that day. Not all muzungus are wealthy or glad-handing in their generosity. Some of us are quite cheap, in fact.

In the end, I thanked the men for their "help" and moved on, though escaping them was a little like trying to disentangle oneself from an overly amorous octopus. They clearly wanted money for their "services," but I pretended I didn't "understand."

"See ya!" I chimed.

When I ended up at a stall that was selling handmade aprons, I decided that what my wife really wanted was a handmade apron. (Memo to any men out there: Turns out, buying your wife an apron is not considered a romantic gesture.) A smiling-eyed woman laughed her way through our mutual language barrier and, mainly with hand gestures, asked me what size.

"Small. Really small," I said, holding my hand out at waist level. (My wife is four-foot eleven, which she insists on rounding up to five.) There was a tag on the apron explaining that it was made by a women's collective. The fabric was certainly beautiful, a mix of geometric patterns suggestive of an African quilt, and when I went to pay, having completely forgotten to haggle, she kindly dropped the price by 10 percent.[24]

Having thus taken care of my spousal duties, I rendezvoused with Jean-Claude, who congratulated me on my selection. Which is to say, he was just as clued out as I was.

---

24. I later discovered that what I'd purchased was a *children's* apron, which was waaaay too small. I didn't even know there was such a thing. My wife did like the patterns, though.

# 48

NIGHT WATERS. SWIMMERS OFFSHORE. Silhouettes emerging and submerging, coalescing and then dissolving back into the lake. The moon was a fisherman's float in a seaweed of clouds, and I thought, *What a beautiful night.*

Jean-Claude and I were on a café veranda with street views and a cooling wind coming in from Lake Kivu. Women in skirts wafted past, and though I know I'm not supposed to notice this sort of thing, let alone comment upon it, it must be said: all that hill-walking does wonders for a woman's calves. (That's right, I'm not just a leg man but specifically a *calf* man.) Even in flip-flops they seemed to be wearing seven-inch stilettos.

I looked over at Jean-Claude, my date for the night (once again), and I sighed.

"Jean-Claude, why couldn't you have been born a beautiful woman?" I asked.

We walked back to our hotel past taverns reverberant with laughter. In the shaded doorways, languorous women swayed to music as jellied-jointed drunks staggered by outside, gloriously insensate. The jangle of Congolese music spilled out of every nightclub, every café. Rwanda sent trade goods across the border; Congo sent back its music. I think Rwanda got the better part of the deal.

It was our final night on Lake Kivu, and the lights of Congo curved into the distance.

"Really," I said to Jean-Claude. "Why couldn't you have been born a beautiful woman?"

Back at the hotel, furtive cabals of Congolese men were hunched around tables, discussing business deals and possible exit plans. Ruddy-faced muzungus milled about as well, NGO administrators with acronymed aides in attendance. And then, sweeping through: the familiar sun-bleached hair and multi-pocketed vests of conflict correspondents. It was strange for me to be surrounded by such a swirl of international intrigue while remaining so oblivious to what was going on. Sort of like Marie Antoinette at the onset of the Revolution, I imagine.

Three weeks after we left Gisenyi, more missiles were fired into Rwanda from the Democratic Republic of Congo. One hit the market we had visited, killing two people. Whether this attack was the work of the Congolese armed forces, the FDLR, or, as the UN asserted, the M23 rebels themselves, in an attempt to draw Rwanda into the fight, remains a point of contention.

I considered telling my wife about our near-miss once I got home—how often can you say you cheated death in order to buy your loved one an apron? But given that I'd assured her I wouldn't be going anywhere dangerous when I was in Rwanda, I reconsidered. Some things are better left unsaid.

# 49

MOUNTAIN GORILLAS DIDN'T EXIST in the European imagination until 1902. That was the year a German captain by the name of von Beringe crossed the remote Virunga rainforests of what was then German East Africa. Near the summit of Mount Sabyinyo, he encountered a troop of what he described as large "human-like monkeys" that were attempting to flee over a ridge. The encounter came as a wonderful surprise—primates were not known to inhabit such high altitudes—and Beringe celebrated the moment by pulling out his trusty rifle and shooting two of the creatures in the back. They tumbled over the edge of the rocky embankment, sliding down the other side. Beringe managed to drag one of the bodies out of the ravine with a rope and had his porters carry it down the mountain in a sling, where he arranged to have it transported to Germany. He had, in fact, discovered a new species—or rather subspecies—of primate, one that would bear his name: *Gorilla beringei beringei*.

Mountain gorillas are immensely impressive animals. Thickly furred and heavily muscled, with males routinely clocking in at 180 kilograms or more (which sounds even more impressive in imperial units: 400 pounds *on average*), they were often depicted by Europeans as monstrous "man-eaters" and were much sought after by big-game hunters. A 1921 expedition by Sweden's Prince William, conducted with the blessing of Belgian authorities, saw him kill fourteen of the Virunga's mountain gorillas in one go; their taxidermy remains are on proud display in Stockholm even now. But their enormous size and alarming canines aside, these animals are gentle giants, peaceful herbivores whose habitat is limited to one narrow chain of volcanoes in central Africa, high in the cool montane forests that straddle the borders of Congo, Rwanda, and Uganda.

American primatologist Dian Fossey spent eighteen years cataloguing the behaviour of these gorillas, often mimicking their cries and grunts—and even belches—until they had become thoroughly habituated to her. As a protégé of renowned paleontologist Dr. Louis Leakey, Fossey was meticulous in her research, discovering intricate social relationships and charting complex genealogies. She began her fieldwork in Congo in 1967, but the country's political turmoil forced her to relocate to the Rwandan side of the border, where she set up the Karisoke Research Center high on a remote hill between volcanoes. Local villagers called her *"Nyiramacibili,"* which Fossey translated, with a great deal of poetic licence, as "the old lady who lives in the forest without a man." (A more accurate rendering would be "small woman who walks really fast.")

Poachers infiltrating the park for bushbuck and duikers would often set traps that snagged gorillas as well. The young ones were especially vulnerable. Even adult gorillas, having easily broken free of the snares, could end up with the wires cutting off circulation to their wrists or ankles, creating wounds that could become infected

*Photos by Will Ferguson*

"When I went to get married, I could see what the genocide had done." A survivor of Bisesero.

The world's most sought-after puddle.

The road, meeting itself on the way back, somewhere above Lake Kivu.

"We are all Rwandans." Students at Nyange Secondary School stand outside the classroom where the events of that night occurred. The school's self-described Master of Discipline is on the left.

Even with fighting on the other side of the hill, trade continued to stream across the border.

A market on the march: the border crossing at Goma.

The forests and hills of Rwanda: layers and layers of layers and layers.

Someone is watching.

King Kong in a more reflective mood. Mountain gorillas didn't exist in the Western imagination until the early twentieth century.

A baby mountain gorilla ponders her strangely denuded cousins.

Our closest living relatives know how to lounge.

The feline grace of Masai giraffes.

The Artful Dodgers of the animal set: the notorious olive baboon.

Akagera National Park. Some sort of bird. Possibly a hawk-eagle.

The banana seller with whom Jean-Claude entered multilateral trade negotiations.

It might have changed everything. Sorghum-stalk homes on the road to Akagera National Park.

Barcode arrangements moving across the savannah.

"My name is Tony, I am a boy." "My name is Asinati, I am a girl."

Jean-Claude Munyezamu in front of the ruins of his brother's home in Rundu village.

The children of Rundu village.

A daughter of the new Rwanda:
Congolese girl at Kigeme camp.

and gangrenous. Buffalo traps—sharp, spiked bamboo hoops set across the trails—were even worse. And when illegal ivory hunters tracking elephants through the forest crossed paths with gorillas, it rarely ended well. A silverback male rearing up to beat his chest, mock-charging and determined to protect the females and children under his care, is in a purely defensive position. But this was usually taken as a threat by the poachers and dealt with as such. The death of a dominant male can be devastating. As Fossey noted, "No gorilla group can exist without its unifying force, the silverback leader." (Something I like to remind my own family of as my hair greys.)

Poachers later targeted the gorillas directly, for trophies (gorilla-hand ashtrays were a popular souvenir at one point) or to kidnap the babies for transport to zoos in Europe and Asia. Fossey tells the horrific story of one band of poachers-for-hire killing ten gorillas just to capture a single infant on order for a zoo in Germany. Fossey worked in vain to have the terrified baby released—only to find that a second baby had been caught in the same manner for the same zoo, with eight adult gorillas killed that time. A French film crew, meanwhile, had pursued a group of gorillas so relentlessly that one of the females miscarried. (The documentary they were filming would later be broadcast in France to great acclaim.) And with growing pressure from farmers and cattle grazers who were illicitly clearing the forest with slash-and-burn methods and steadily encroaching on their territory, the mountain gorilla population plummeted to 242 by the early 1980s.

Fossey was aggressive in her response. She set up wide-ranging anti-poaching patrols. She destroyed hundreds of traps and even arrested intruders—something she had no legal right to do—and would strip them down to their underwear and whip them with nettles as a punishment. Fossey hounded Rwandan authorities until several incorrigible poachers were charged and sentenced to lengthy prison terms. On occasion she would use Halloween masks and firecrackers to raid illegal encampments, scaring off would-be hunters, and her research assistants had several violent clashes with the people they had challenged. Fossey's own life was threatened several times, but she remained fearless in the face of intimidation.

Few people can claim to have saved an entire species, but this is precisely what Dian Fossey accomplished. And although initially opposed to gorilla tourism, she later came to accept it, admitting that limited conservation tours could help the animals "if properly directed." Today, the world's mountain gorilla population is estimated to be 880. Of these, approximately 400 are in Rwanda. They're one of our closest living relatives, and it was time for us to pop in for a visit.

# 50

WE LEFT THE LAKE KIVU SERENA HOTEL before sunrise, driving into darkness.

Even at five in the morning, the roads were filled with people, and our headlights picked up fleeting images of market women carrying goods, of Muslim men going to mosque, of children on their long walk to school. Given how quickly the sun set in Rwanda—much like a lamp chain being given a decisive yank—it was always strange how slowly it rose: a soft wash, a breath of light, a dimmer switch gradually turning up as the mountains formed around us.

It took several hours, but when we passed the Dian Fossey Hotel, I knew we were getting close. The rainforests of the Virunga Mountains (the name is a corruption of the Kinyarwanda word for "volcano") were looming over us, like waves about to break.

These mountains—eight volcanoes: six dormant, two active—run along the northern border of Rwanda as part of Volcanoes National Park. A twisting road took us to the main information centre and muster point, where eighty or so other groggy-eyed would-be trekkers had gathered. There were lots of yawns and early-morning shivers. Urns of coffee beckoned, but Jean-Claude once again declined. Surely this was a morning made for coffee, but no. He would climb the Virungas without the aid of caffeine stimulants, poor man.

Access to Rwanda's habituated gorillas is strictly controlled: eight people per group, with visits limited to one hour, once a day. The gorillas live in extended families, and their populations are clustered in disparate areas throughout the Virungas' misted heights, usually with a dozen or so gorillas under the leadership of a dominant silverback. Some groups were close at hand and others required a treacherous hike to the very top of the volcanoes, so the first order of business was to separate visitors accordingly. Trail guides walked among the assembled guests, sorting us into groups of eight. They put older people and those who looked more out-of-shape in the easiest groups, with the youthful, sporty-looking types assigned to higher, more difficult reaches. It was like a free fitness evaluation, and I was pleasantly surprised to find myself grouped in with a band of healthy-looking hikers. I tapped my hands on my belly, thought to myself, *You still got it, Will.*

Our group would be visiting the Amahoro family of gorillas, and when I thumbed through the guidebook, I almost choked. This was the second most difficult band of gorillas to reach, and some even considered the Amahoro hike to be the *most* difficult, because it went over one side of the mountain and down into the next valley— meaning you had to walk back up again on your return. In contrast, the Suza group, widely considered the most taxing trek, required a gruelling three-hour hike straight up, but once you reached those heights you were done.

I gulped back a bolus of fear and watched as the other members of my hiking group moved about purposefully, strapping them- selves into lightweight aluminum day packs with aerodynamically scientific hiking poles. Several of them had water systems that fed tubes directly into their mouths, so they wouldn't have to break stride to rehydrate. I, on the other hand, had two loose bottles of water *somewhere* in the bottom of my lumpy and decidedly non-aerodynamic rucksack. The entire extent of my prep had been to tuck my pant legs inside my socks to, you know, reduce drag and whatnot.

Jean-Claude and I had been placed in a group that featured a tanned young French woman—a medical student who was travelling with her equally tanned, equally fit mom—and a family of four from Spain: a fit-looking husband (with high-tech water resupply system), an even fitter-looking wife, and two derivatively fit-looking teenage daughters. I was hoping these last two would be of the whatever, eyeball-rolling, stopping every five minutes to take selfies of themselves, "O my god, we are so random!" type of teenage girls, but sadly, they were not. As I was soon to discover, these were the quick-striding, über-athletic, relentlessly energetic type of teenage girls, the kind who scamper fearlessly ahead on steep jungle trails with nary a hiccup, forcing the rest of their group to play an endless game of catch-up. The type who never seem to sweat but only ever attain a healthy pinkish glow.

In a panic, I pulled Jean-Claude to one side. "How the hell did we end up in this group?" I asked.

"It was by request."

Request? *Whose request?* Jean-Claude's of course.

"I talked with the guides," he explained. "They told me the Amahoro group is the best one to visit right now. The Amahoro gorillas have several new babies. It's why they put us in this group."

Turns out, Jean-Claude and I had been slotted to visit one of the nearer, more accessible bands of gorillas, but in his infinite wisdom Jean-Claude had sidled up to one of the guides and explained that I was—quote—"an important journalist" here to do a story about conservation in Rwanda. Which is how a thoroughly sedentary, middle-aged author, whose most strenuous daily activity involves hitting CTRL-ALT-DELETE at the same time when his computer freezes up during a particularly demanding round of Minesweeper, found himself assigned to one of the toughest treks in the forest.

Thanks to my so-called friend Jean-Claude, I now faced a possible (probable) cardiac arrest somewhere on the side of the Virunga volcanoes. Good thing we had a medical student on board!

"You want to see the babies," Jean-Claude assured me. "And anyway, it's too late to change your mind. Everybody's leaving. Look."

We headed out in a convoy of Land Cruisers and jeeps, and as the vehicles peeled off onto different routes, the road climbed higher and the air grew thinner. With every turn, the valley fell away, deeper into the distance. In Rwanda, Point A to Point B is never a straight line, is always a squiggle, and when I looked down I could often see where we had just been, directly below us.

Even in a land as fertile as Rwanda, the rich volcanic soils of the Virungas are exceptionally fecund. We passed tangled plots of green beans and peas, flowering potatoes and thickets of maize: single-family farms carved out of the jungle, their crops embedded among ever-present stands of bamboo and eucalyptus.

On the way, we passed through what had once been a notorious poachers' village. As part of a shared tourism revenue program, the government now plows money from its conservation tours directly back into the villages nearby. The fees paid by tourists have helped build more than a dozen health centres and close to sixty schools. It's an act of strategic altruism, aimed at dissuading poachers and cattle grazers from undermining a source of their community's income.

Formerly among the poorest, most backward regions of Rwanda, the village we passed through now boasted a health clinic and a water-pumping station (sparing the villagers a daily trek up and down the mountain), as well as two new schools, a beekeeping operation, and a small-scale dairy farm, all courtesy of Rwanda's Mountain Gorilla Conservation Programme. Billboards in front of each new facility reminded the populace of this, and the message was clear: there is a direct economic benefit in protecting the gorillas and their habitat. *These schools, this medical clinic, this water? These are courtesy of the gorillas.* Former poachers are now some of the most vocal advocates for conservation, patrolling their areas for intruders. And many of the park's guides were once poachers themselves. After all, they knew the terrain better than anyone.

Our convoy was down to three vehicles. We stopped just past a cluster of mud-walled homes. This was the spot where Dian Fossey used to park her vehicle, our guide told us. The road ahead was too rough for even a 4x4. From here, we would walk.

As we were getting ready to set off, a motley procession of men appeared, walking their bicycles downhill, handlebars and seats overburdened with gunnysacks of string beans and cassava, bundles of bananas, en route to the village market. This too was a legacy of Dian Fossey. There hadn't been a market here prior to her arrival, but during the time she lived in the mountains, Fossey would come down twice a week to purchase supplies. People soon learned to stock up and wait for her. Word spread, and people from other villages began appearing, bringing in more and varied goods, vying for her business. Fossey was by all accounts a tough negotiator. She didn't simply pay the asking price; she wrangled and bargained and selected her supplies carefully. Those items that Fossey didn't want, people traded among themselves. Today, some thirty years after her death, the market still thrives, twice a week like clockwork, on the same days she would have come down from the mountain.

We had two guides assigned to us: Olivier and Placide, a pair of soft-spoken but well-armed park rangers.

"Is that an AK-47?" I asked.

"No. Better."

They gathered us in for instructions, and when Placide showed us where we would be going, he didn't point forward, he pointed *up*.

We set out, single file, beneath the towering indifference of the Virunga volcanoes. A snaggle-toothed trail of volcanic bedrock pushed us past homes that were in various stages of decay and renewal. Some were little more than crumbling piles of clay bricks, others were cement-walled and metal-roofed. Children came running out to holler "Hello! Hello!" as we passed. We nodded, waved, trudged on.

A meadow opened up before us. At the far end stood a solid wall of jungle; we followed a raised trail along an irrigation channel until we came to it. A stone barrier, cobbled together from volcanic rock, ran along the edge of the forest, as though corralling the trees inside it.

"Buffalo fence," said Olivier. "They come out and eat potatoes and flatten the crops. This annoys the farmers too much. Better to keep them away from each other."

We climbed over the stone wall on a rickety stile and began our ascent through the jungle. Almost immediately I was out of breath. Altitude, age, and a dissolute lifestyle were catching up to me, but I'd done enough long-distance hikes to know that I needed to find my own rhythm, and eventually I did. It went like this: *step, stumble, gasp, wheeze; step, stumble, gasp, wheeze; (repeat).*

I quickly dropped to the back. At some point, extra armed guards joined our group (they must have slipped in behind us, ninja-like, while we trundled along), and I ended up, accidentally, with my own personal bodyguard.

"For animals?" I gasped, gesturing to his rifle.

He smiled and nodded as he loped along, easily keeping pace with me the way I might with a toddler. "Sometime is for elephant," he said in halting English. "Sometimes is for buffalo."

Elephants? This was something I always had trouble wrapping my head around: the fact that there were enormous pachyderms hiding in these jungles. Elephants were so bulky, so lumbering, it hardly seemed feasible. I'd always thought of them as a creature of the savannah, lords of the open plains, backlit majestically by rose-madder sunsets, not jungle denizens tromping about on rainforest trails so narrow we required a porter up front just to clear a path.

Running into an elephant on a trail such as this, hemmed in by trees on either side? That was something best avoided.

Sure enough, we soon came upon several knuckles of elephant dung, thick with matted grass. The rest of the group had gathered round to take photos and admire the offerings. Some of the dung seemed fresh, was still moist—to look at, anyway. I wasn't about to go around prodding it with my finger or anything. Instead, I took this as a chance to chug down some water. "How many elephants live in these forests?" I asked with a wipe of my mouth.

Placide hedged. "We aren't certain. I saw one last week, but we don't know how many, not exactly."

*A jungle so big, elephants can hide in it.*

Elephants are highly seasonal animals. They move about constantly. They follow food. They roam widely and on a whim, from Congo to Uganda and back again. There was no telling how many or how near any of them were at any one moment.

I gestured to the dung. "Is there an elephant nearby?"

He looked up at the trail, frowned. "Maybe."

We pushed on, through the mentholated air of the rainforest. For long stretches, all I heard was the sound of my own lungs, panting for oxygen. I could feel my pulse bongo-throbbing in the arteries of my neck as the trail fought its way in and out of the forest, through tangles of greenery, past boulders in a river, furred with moss. Butterflies fluttered by, their wings a deep and abiding iridescent blue, some satin, some velvet, alighting and departing on the faintest whisper of wind.

A break in the forest revealed jungle rolling into the distance, the treetops as tightly bunched as broccoli. Jean-Claude was waiting for me, and he pointed to the hills ahead. We were at the northern border of Rwanda. "Congo," he said, then, pointing the other way, "Uganda." Three nations, converging.

We'd been hiking an hour to earn that view, and it was almost worth it.

With Placide in the lead we headed across a clearing, wading through leafy stands of what turned out be stinging nettles. Layers and layers of stinging nettles. My newly purchased state-of-the-art Mountain Equipment Co-op all-terrain protective hiking pants with patented dry-wick technology™ had failed utterly when faced with a *soupçon* of African nettles. It was like swimming through a tide of jellyfish, each step, each brush a burning slash. And it. Went. On. Forever.

I could see Jean-Claude ahead, in jeans, arms up, threading his way through the lacerating underbrush with an enviable ease. The rest of us didn't fare as well. We emerged on the other side soaked with sweat, legs and forearms embossed in welts. We shotgunned our water, wiped the sweat from our faces, laughed and compared wounds. One of the Spanish teenagers had been wearing hiking pants that ended mid-calf and her ankles were now covered in a web of crimson. She held her feet out one at a time, admired the damage. The French woman's mother, with admirable foresight, had been pushing the nettles aside with heavy-duty canvas gardening gloves, only to find that her exposed wrists were criss-crossed with abrasions. I'd brought antihistamine tablets with me, which I passed out like breath mints. I swallowed a handful just to bring the swelling down; the nettles had somehow passed *through* the synthetic fabric of my trousers, leaving the skin below sliced and brightly pink. Had I dropped my pants, I'm sure I would have won the "Who got it worst?" contest handily. But, inculcated as I am with old-fashioned notions of modesty, decorum prevailed.

"Everyone okay?" asked our guide.

Chastised by nettles, we pushed on with decidedly less verve than we'd started with. The trail gradually levelled off, and I realized with a flick of joy that we'd reached the highest point of our trek.

*Made it!* I thought. And: *Wasn't so bad.*

But of course, I'd forgotten the salient feature of the Amahoro trek: it levelled off—then dropped down the other side of the mountain all the way to the bottom of the valley, which was lower than the hike's starting point. Which meant a second, even tougher ascent on our way back. That first stretch? The one that almost killed me? That was just a warm-up.

Sure enough, the trail fell like a high-diver off an Acapulco cliff: straight down on a ferociously narrow trail. We half-fell, half-ran from tree to tree, bumping into each other at times, then stork-walking wildly, lunging onto vines with a George of the Jungle clumsiness, arms out on every knoll, egg-beating the air for balance. It must have been highly entertaining for the guides.

We kicked up clouds of red clay that gummed our eyes and clogged our nostrils. When we reached the bottom, the wet-nap I used to blot my face with looked like the Shroud of Turin. And as we gulped down water that we should have been carefully conserving (as I would discover on our death-march return), one of the guides came over to tell us that the Amahoro mountain gorillas were just twenty metres away, "on the other side of those trees."

Well, that snapped us awake! We sorted ourselves out, primed our cameras, left our day packs and lunches behind (one of the guides would stay with them to make sure they weren't, I don't know, jacked by monkeys or something).

Now, I should explain that when our guide said the gorillas were on the other side of "those trees," he was using "trees" in the local vernacular, meaning "a thicket of thorns so tightly woven as to appear cross-hatched."

We pushed our way in with grim resolve, scratched and scraped by flagellant thorns, prodded and poked by sharpened branches, lassoed by overhangs of vine—the thought occurred to me that years later they might find our skeletons, still entangled. "Oh, so that's what happened; they tried to go *through* rather than around"—until we found ourselves at last in a leafy clearing, panting and sweating and beaded with cuts.

Our guide held a finger to his lips, and then pointed into the shadows across from us.

Someone was watching.

# 51

SMOKY EYES PEERING THROUGH THE LEAVES. Furry figures, moving through the underbrush.

Gorillas were suddenly all around us. It was as though we'd stumbled into their living room. They were nuzzled in nests of flattened grass, were sitting on haunches, were chewing on wild celery, crawling over each other and shuffling about with harrumphs and hellos. Just a few metres away, a lower-ranked silverback was stretched out, magnificently supine, one long arm outstretched and drooping loosely above him, the other draped over his eyes. Apparently, gorillas spend up to 40 percent of their time "resting." More if it's hot out. Or cold. Or rainy. Or if it's overcast. They certainly know how to lounge.

They were both massive and massively cute, awe-inspiring yet wholly adorable. The younger ones looked like teddy bears with weirdly elongated arms. Ill-adapted to tree swinging, they were giving it their best nonetheless, pulling down thin branches, kicking their little legs, falling promptly off. There was something both poignant and heroic about their dogged attempts at becoming arboreal. Here were the clumsiest of all the great apes, still trying to feed that deeply rooted primate imperative: the desire to climb.

The babies looked impossibly wise, old souls with liquid eyes. Only the moms gave us any heed, keeping a watch from afar as we moved among them. Placide made low greeting grunts to let the moms know we were friends, and they relaxed. Cross-species communication: the females replied with the same low grunt and then went back to grooming their babies.

Under the authority of a dominant male were several younger silverbacks, each with their own group of females, who in turn tolerated the restless, ass-over-teakettle head rolls of the younger gorillas with a paternal patience. The babies were very curious. They would scramble toward us, and then—realizing we were just a boring bunch of grown-ups, albeit weirdly denuded of fur—return to the serious work of playing. Round bellies, stumpy legs, hand-like feet and toes that looked like thumbs. Every now and then, one of the babies would meet your gaze, and you would find yourself transfixed, staring into their eyes: otherworldly, yet strangely, reassuringly *human*. One of the older gorillas peered at me as though over a pair of reading glasses. It was very calm, very quiet, and a far cry from the agitated back-and-forth pacing one sees at a zoo.

Who knew an hour could be so short, or so full?

I spent the first twenty minutes madly taking photographs, then stopped. I had climbed a mountain to get here, and I decided that experiencing it through a viewfinder wasn't perhaps the best approach. Instead, I slung my camera over my shoulder, soaked the moment in.

As we watched our overgrown cousins rummage about, Placide told us a sad story. When a gorilla dies, he explained, the other gorillas will spend at least three days with the body, bringing food to it, nudging it, trying to get it to sit up. If it's a baby that has died—and they often do if they're born in the rainy season, from pneumonia— the mother will carry that baby's body for weeks or more.

"It's very sorrowful," Placide said. "Even though her baby is dead, she won't let go of it, can't. Sometimes the arm will drop off, or the bones will start to stick through the fur, before she finally gives up her child. It's—" Here he switched from French to Kinyarwanda, using a word Jean-Claude translated as "heartbreaking."

The hour was over too fast. Olivier gave us our five-minute warning, and no amount of good-natured cajolery could convince him to extend our stay.

But then, just as we were preparing to leave, we had a close encounter of the gorilla kind. One moment I was standing in the spongy grass, wondering, *Now, where is the big boss, that dominant silverback we're always hearing about?* and the next moment I looked up and right there—crashing through the grass toward us—was King Kong himself.

"Get back," Placide urged. "Everybody. Let him pass. And please! No eye contact."

We complied.

The silverback reared up and beat his chest—not in anger, but just to let us know who was in charge (and truth be told, it was a rather half-hearted, let's-just-get-this-over-with-shall-we? sort of chest-beat, hardly the thunderous kettledrum effect I'd imagined). He pushed past with a shoulder-rolling swagger, forearms reaching out, knuckle-walking with his short back legs hurrying to catch up. A hefty potbelly gave him both girth and gravitas. Musty, too. *Eau de silverback* is a nuanced blend of junior high boys' locker room on a hot day with a dash of bad breath and a sprinkling of fecal funk thrown in. One whiff and I was almost knocked over, which is not the best reaction when a gorilla is brushing by: swooning into his arms. I was so close I could have run my hand along his back as he passed—was tempted to, for one dizzying moment, if only to be able to say, "I ever tell you chaps about the time I *petted a mountain gorilla?*" But I didn't quite feel like getting torn limb from limb just then, so I let him go by, untouched, through the tall grass. He didn't even deign to look at me as he passed.

Placide and Olivier were holding their arms out to keep the Spanish family back (they had strayed perilously close to the silverback's route and, let's face it, if anyone was going to be foolish enough to try to pet a gorilla, it was going to be a teenager).

There has never been a case of a mountain gorilla attacking a tourist in Rwanda. But there's always a first time for everything, right?

I looked at the rifles hanging across the shoulders of our guides, and it occurred to me that if this silverback did decide to tear us limb from limb, there was very little Placide or Olivier could do about it. Before either of them could bolt their rifles, let alone take aim, the silverback would have already been upon them, and the encounter would have ended with Placide and Olivier being flung about like rag dolls while the rest of us tried to climb over each other onto the nearest tree branch with, I imagine, even less finesse than that of a gorilla. That's the sort of image that's hard to shake, once it takes hold.

As we were preparing to push our way back through the Thorn-of-Christ bushes we'd come through earlier, the French medical student's mother spotted something in the grass to one side: a young gorilla sitting on his own, chewing thoughtfully on stinging nettles (gorillas aren't so much immune to nettles as acclimatized; the stalks simply numb their lips).

The medical student's mother pointed out that, as we'd spent no time with this *specific* gorilla, it really shouldn't count as part of our hour. But Placide wasn't persuaded by this. "I will give you one moment," he said. "If you hurry, you can take photographs. But with this gorilla, stay far back. Don't go any closer. He's a troublemaker."

The gorilla equivalent of a surly teenager, our solitary friend had been shunned by the rest of his group because he kept causing problems, starting fights, lipping off, that sort of thing. He now lingered resentfully on the fringes of gorilla society, an outcast eating his nettles, biding his time, and no doubt plotting his revenge.

"Adolescence," Placide said, as though that explained everything, and maybe it did.

Back on the other side of the thornbushes, we ate our lunches—cheese sandwiches and juice boxes, as opposed to stinging nettles and one's own dung—and I thought about the uphill return we now faced: that all but perpendicular trail we'd slid down earlier. I thought about the two-hour, single-file slog back up it, the kickbacks of dust in one's face, the Shroud of Turin clay we'd be inhaling, and I asked Placide, "What do you do if someone can't make it, if they have a heart attack on the trail or twist their ankle or something?" This wasn't an academic question on my part; the prospect of my heart squeezing out its last on the climb ahead was a very real possibility.

"Well," he said, "if someone is in serious trouble we call for a stretcher. But"—and here his voice dropped solemnly—"if that happens, we must charge them *one hundred U.S. dollars.*"

You don't say?

One hundred dollars to be carried over a mountain as you reclined—eating peeled grapes, presumably—whilst enjoying the dappled play of sunlight on one's face? A bargain, I'd reckon. It was all I could do not to immediately clutch my chest in histrionic fashion, declaiming "Alas, I fear I am about to perish! Someone send for the porters!" The air on the way down would have proven salubrious, I was sure, for I would have expected a full recovery by the time we reached our vehicle.

# 52

DIAN FOSSEY NEVER LEFT THE MOUNTAIN.

Having stared down poachers and hunters, and having butted heads repeatedly with corrupt government officials, she was silenced for good on December 27, 1985, hacked to death by unknown assailants at her base camp. She lies buried beside the ruins of her abandoned research cabin, is on the Virungas still.

Fossey's killers were never caught, and rumours remain rife about who ordered her murder and why, but it hardly matters now.

The gorilla tours today are possible because of Dian Fossey. It was Fossey who first habituated the animals. She had no qualms about petting, grooming, or even cuddling the babies—acts that are strictly forbidden now. And although still endangered, mountain gorillas are safer and more secure today than they have been in years—at least on the Rwandan side of the border.[25] And a good deal of credit for that can be given to Rwanda's community-based

---

25. On the Congo side, poaching remains a serious problem. An entire family of mountain gorillas was killed in 2007 in an attempt to capture a single baby. To what end was not clear. No reputable zoo today would accept a mountain gorilla taken from the wild.

approach to conservation and to the ongoing legacy of Fossey herself.

When you finally reach the bottom of the mountain, knees grating, thighs aching, face plastered with sweat, tired and elated, filled with marvel, you feel redeemed by the experience—there is no other word for it. It is the shared humanity you remember best, or perhaps the shared *gorillaness* would be more accurate: their fully rounded personalities, the playful curiosity, the lazy looks, the haughty disdain, the way they cuddle and kiss, lounge and look thoughtfully into the distance. And you realize the debt the world owes to the prickly and abrasive Dian Fossey.

A librarian at my local branch in Calgary had met Dian Fossey many years before. Alina Freedman first went to Africa in 1971 with her husband at the time, an anthropologist named Jim. She was getting her master's in linguistics, and they travelled together to Rwanda on a Fulbright scholarship.

"We were based in the north, in an abandoned Belgian manor with no running water or electricity. The volcanoes were active back then, and at night, the sky would glow."

She met Dian Fossey the following summer.

"It was at the American embassy's residence in Kigali. They rented rooms, and she happened to be there when Jim and I came by."

"What was your impression of her?"

Alina laughed. "She looked like a hippie. She looked like the rest of us. We were all hippies. But her reputation preceded her. She was already kind of a star. She had Leakey behind her. She had Fulbright money. She was a well-endowed scholar. Strong personality. Friendly enough, but quiet. Not a big talker."

The abandoned manor house Alina and Jim were staying in wasn't far from the mountain where Fossey had established her base camp.

"So we went to see her. It was a long hike. Very hot and humid. I passed out at one point, sat down on the trail, I remember. We climbed all day, and when we finally got to Dian's place, we said 'Hi!' And she said, 'I'm going out. Bye.' And she left us there. No tea. No small talk. She just left."

"So what did you do?"

"We climbed back down." Alina thought about this for a moment. "I don't think she was really interested in people."

# 53

JEAN-CLAUDE'S WIFE CHRISTINE had a brother and sister-in-law in Ruhengeri, and Christine had asked us to stop in and see them when we passed through.

I liked Ruhengeri. The town (now known as Musanze) was filled with shops and bustling side lanes, with a scattering of new office buildings plopped down improbably in their midst, yet it didn't feel congested or constrained in the least. Spaced out nicely among the trees, even its "downtown" wasn't choked with traffic or clouded with exhaust—remarkable considering it was the gateway community to Volcanoes National Park and as such was on the main tourist beat.

Muzungus were everywhere, post-trek looking weary but happy, pre-trek looking tidy yet nervous. When Jean-Claude and I stopped at La Paillotte, a bakery café that sold Belgian pastries and suitably murky coffee, it was full of pink faces.

I swirled my cup, finished the last of my croissant. "The coffee's good," I said, prodding Jean-Claude one last time. "You'd be supporting local industry."

We were sitting on the café's shaded veranda, watching a delivery truck loaded with Primus try to back into a space that was physically smaller than the vehicle itself and—in defiance of all known theories of spatial geometry—somehow succeeding.

"Zeyad'za formaldehyde," said the man next to me. "To za bier."

He was South African, with straw-blond hair and a face so sunburned his lips looked white. I wasn't sure I'd heard him correctly, but as I adjusted for his accent it became horribly clear what he was saying. "Primus," he explained. "They add formaldehyde, to help preserve it."

With that he downed his espresso as though from a shot glass, donned a canvas sun hat, and bid us adieu, leaving me with a gurgling sensation in my gut.

I turned to Jean-Claude. "That can't be true, right? I mean ..."

Jean-Claude said, "I don't think so. But look at the positive. If it is true, your insides will be well-preserved." And then, underlining the point unnecessarily, I thought, he leaned in and said, "Very ... well ... preserved."

He was right. Over the previous couple of weeks, I'd downed enough pints of Primus to pickle a pharaoh, *if* what the South African had said was true.[26]

Christine's brother Jackson wasn't in Ruhengeri when Jean-Claude and I came through. A member of the Rwandan Armed Forces, he was away on a peacekeeping mission in Sudan, though this in itself was not unusual; Rwanda is one of the leading supporters of UN missions in Africa and abroad, far surpassing anything Canada provides. When I was there, Rwanda had 5,200 peacekeepers serving in UN missions around the world, the highest percentage of peacekeepers per capita of any country and among the top six *total* contributing nations worldwide.

Jackson was in Sudan, but his wife, Madelene, was in Ruhengeri.

She ran the J Center Restaurant, a buffet-style eatery in one of Ruhengeri's new office buildings. Even then, she'd had trouble finding a space. Vacancies were at a premium in Ruhengeri, and rents were soaring.

She welcomed us in with a quiet grace. Her two-year-old son

---

26. Um, it was, actually. According to journalist Christian Jennings, Primus—like most bottled beer companies in central Africa—adds a derivative of formaldehyde to its product to act as a preservative. Lasts longer on shelves that way. Which means that when archaeologists dig me up a thousand years from now, they'll find me well-maintained indeed. At least on the inside. No wonder Primus gave me such a zip.

Manzi, Christine's nephew, was plump and lovable—and terrified of me. Forget bouncing him on my knee; I couldn't even draw near him without his face scrunching up, his bottom lip trembling, tears welling. If I tried to say hi, he would run for cover into the arms of the nearest non-me adult, bawling.

"He's shy around strangers," Madelene said, unconvincingly.

Manzi had been roused from his nap next door and brought over to meet his uncle Jean-Claude—who was a perfect stranger too, as far as he was concerned. Jean-Claude he had no trouble with. But me? Different story. It was disconcerting to be disliked so intensely by someone so small.

The rest of the staff passed him around like a huggable hamper, as he gurgled and cooed cooperatively ... till he got to me. And then the bawling started.

The staff thought this was hilarious.

Madelene pretended not to know why her son was crying. "C'mon," I said. "We all know why. And it's not because I'm a 'stranger.' Surely other muzungus must come in here?"

"They do," Madelene admitted, "but Manzi isn't usually here. My mother watches him at home."

I exhausted my repertoire—jangly keys, peek-a-boo face, coochie-coochie-coo—nothing. Sigh.

As Jean-Claude and Madelene caught up on family news, I turned my attention to the buffet. As always, it was a Rwandan cornucopia, rich with fresh fruit and trays of savoury fare: stews and dumplings, papa frites and scrawny marathon-chicken legs. As I came back from my third sally, plate dripping, Jean-Claude mentioned to Madelene how we'd noticed the unfortunate lack of restraint shown by his fellow Rwandans when it came to buffets.

"They always pile their plates so high, instead of taking a little bit and going back for more. It's"—he wanted to say embarrassing, but stopped himself—"funny how they do that."

Jean-Claude, I should note, had already made several trips to the buffet himself.

Madelene gave him a pained look. "Well, you see, that's because you are only supposed to go up one time. The price is per plate."

Jean-Claude stopped, mid-chew. He looked shovel-smacked by this. "You mean—you mean it's not 'all-you-can-eat'?"

She clearly felt uncomfortable breaking the awkward news to him, but she had no choice. "Customers are supposed to pay each time they go up."

I looked down at my plate.

"Every buffet is like that?" I asked.

"Yes."

"Every buffet in Rwanda?"

"I think so."

I was mortified, as was Jean-Claude. Here we'd been going cheerfully from buffet to buffet across Rwanda, making multiple sorties every time but only paying once—*and no one had said anything.*

"They were probably embarrassed to bring it up," she said. "We notice it here as well, how muzungus will go again and again. It's very strange."

"But … no one told me," Jean-Claude said.

I looked over at him and grinned. "Face it, JC. You've been gone so long, you're just another muzungu now, like me. They didn't say anything because they figured you didn't know any better."

And here's the thing: he didn't.

Jean-Claude's brow furled, and didn't unfurl for several days.

# 54

A FEW KILOMETRES AWAY from the J Center Restaurant, tucked in behind a school, lies an ancient volcanic cave, complete with a colony of bats and a natural stone bridge formed by prehistoric lava flows.

During the genocide, Tutsis took refuge in this cave and were massacred. The cave, an easily accessible and by all accounts fascinating geological attraction, is also a mass grave. Visitors are allowed in only on a special permit from the RDB, which needs to be arranged in advance—as Jean-Claude and I discovered when we showed up, unannounced, only to be turned away by a security guard with a rubber truncheon.

We could see the opening to the Musanze Cave just below us, down a short flight of stairs. Only a metal fence and that rubber truncheon barred our way, but without a permit from the RDB, stamped in triplicate no doubt, we couldn't enter. The guard hinted, with all the subtlety of a piano dropped from the fourteenth floor, that maybe, just perhaps, he *might* possibly be able to circumvent the rules—we'd come so far to see the caves, and wouldn't it be a shame not to view them?—were we to, oh, I don't know, compensate him for the inconvenience. Say, five dollars U.S.?

Jean-Claude was appalled and refused on our behalf, even as I was reaching for my wallet. I figured, *Five bucks? No problem.* It was the only time we were ever asked for a bribe, and it was such a trifle, on par with what one encounters in, say, Paris or Rome on a daily basis, that I hadn't considered the impact of what I was about to do.

Jean-Claude stayed my hand. "Don't. If you pay, everyone will have to pay and things will begin to break down." Zero tolerance of corruption meant zero tolerance. We shouldn't undermine the struggle Rwandans had made to curtail this sort of thing just for the sake of expediency. I knew that, but ... the caves were *right there.*

"We will go back to Kigali," Jean-Claude told the guard. (Kigali was at least a two-hour drive away, which would make it a four-hour return.) "And we will get the permit. And when we do, I will explain to the RDB that someone—I won't say who, not this time—is attempting to extort money from tourists. If you try this sort of thing again, you will be in big trouble."

The man quickly backpedalled, suddenly claiming it was all a misunderstanding.[27] But Jean-Claude strode off and I followed.

As we walked back along the edge of the school grounds, an epic soccer game was underway: at least, oh, two hundred students or more on either side by my count, with one team in blue pinnies, the other in red, with more students lined up on the sidelines ready to sub in. It was a massive undertaking, and when Jean-Claude asked one of the students watching what was going on, he explained that it was an annual event. Every year, after the final exams were wrapped up, the school's two second-year classes challenged each other to a match.

This was a science school, and these were mathematics and chemistry students for the most part, so not exactly top-drawer when it came to athletics. Let's just say there were a lot of skinny kids with taped-up glasses chasing the ball that day.

Jean-Claude stood watching the match unfold with his arms crossed, frowning. I knew that frown; I'd seen it when he was coaching my son's soccer team.

"No, no, no, no," he said. "That's not right. That's not right at all."

The ball was fired down the field and just as quickly fired back.

"Oh my goodness," said Jean-Claude. "They have no positions, no game plan. Who is coaching these kids?" he asked.

"No one," the student replied. "They arrange it themselves."

The red team was getting pelted. Their blue-pinnied rivals lobbed a long ball past a flailing goaltender to the sound of groans and cheers, respectively. Just a few minutes later, they scored again.

---

27. The RDB has since made it easier to visit the caves, with permits provided at the local tourist office.

"Oh, this is terrible," Jean-Claude said. "Look at that! They're not passing back, they're not crossing over. They are just kicking it as hard as they can."

And next thing I knew, Jean-Claude had vanished. I'm not sure how he did it. One moment he was standing beside me, the next he was gone. I looked around, couldn't find him anywhere—not at first, anyway. I should have known. Jean-Claude had resurfaced on the other side of the field, where he quickly called a time-out (on what authority? his own, I suppose), bringing the red team in for a huddle.

Although mildly confused by his presence, neither side said anything. From where I was standing I could see Jean-Claude frantically carving out angles in the air, explaining to the red-pinnied players how they should come down this way, pass that way, cut across there.

I knew then that we were not going to get to Kigali in time for a cave permit. *The game was afoot!* after all. In every sense. Getting Jean-Claude off a soccer field was like trying to pry a bottle of Primus from my talon-like hands: a doomed endeavour from the start.

Instead, I settled in to watch the game. Jean-Claude's coaching had an immediate impact. The red team scored—finally!—and then rushed to fill in the gaps in their defence as their new coach called out plays from the sidelines. The blue team was still winning, to be sure, but as Jean-Claude would later say, at least now it was a match.

Other students, on seeing me in the crowd, drifted over to say hi, to ask me what brought me to their school, and, just as curiously, why my friend was coaching one of their teams. I tried to convince them that I was a scout for Manchester United, here on orders from me wee fayther, but they weren't fooled in the least.

Their English was excellent. They were tired, though, having just finished writing their final exams, and were waiting now on the results. "We will know how we did on Friday." When I asked if they were nervous, most of them said, "No, no, we will do fine," though one girl admitted she prayed more at exam time than she ever did in church, which roused laughter and agreement from her peers.

She was fifteen and wanted to study industrial chemistry at university.

I didn't miss a beat. "So engineering for chemicals, not for the paint but for the business?"

"Exactly!" she said. Exactly.

# 55

THE RPF INVASION OF RWANDA almost ended before it began. In 1990, the RPF, led by the popular and charismatic Fred Rwigyema, crossed over from Uganda into Rwanda, only to be turned back decisively by a barrage from French paratroopers and government forces. Rwigyema himself was killed within the first forty-eight hours.

President Habyarimana pronounced the RPF "finished." But they weren't. One of Rwigyema's childhood friends had been a serious young boy named Paul Kagame. They'd grown up together in the same refugee camp, were like brothers. Kagame was enrolled in a military training course at Fort Leavenworth, Kansas, as a member of the Ugandan military, when news came of the failed invasion. Kagame immediately flew back, crossed into Rwanda, and took command of a scattered and demoralized RPF.

Kagame made a tactical retreat, not to Uganda—where anger over the RPF's using their border as a staging ground had ratcheted up tensions—but north instead, into the remote and impenetrable rainforests of the Virunga Mountains. There, in the dripping cold, the RPF regrouped. It was a strange, almost surreal moment in history: guerrillas and gorillas, both in the mist, passing each other on jungle trails. Two worlds overlapping.

And it was from those misted heights that the RPF launched an audacious counterattack.

Even Kagame's harshest critics will admit he is a superb tactician. General Dallaire called him "a military genius" when it came to outplaying an enemy using feints, speed, and surprise. Looking down from the Virunga Mountains, Kagame zeroed in on Ruhengeri Prison—the "Rwandan Bastille," as it was known, a notorious holding pen that housed hundreds of political prisoners, many of them Hutu opponents of Habyarimana, with others held on the mere suspicion of supporting the rebels.

Habyarimana's generals were still congratulating themselves on having defeated the upstart RPF (with France's assistance, of course) when the attack on Ruhengeri began. During the night, hundreds of RPF soldiers had infiltrated the forests above the city, slipping silently through the woods ...

At dawn, they struck. The prison's warden, Charles Uwihoreye, called Kigali, frantically asking for instructions. "We are under attack! What should we do? We need the army!"

The orders he received? Kill the prisoners. Kill them all. Don't allow the RPF the satisfaction of freeing any of them.

Uwihoreye was stunned. He couldn't do such a thing, and he said so. He was a warden, not an executioner. "I'm sorry, but I cannot do that." He hung up the phone and sat there, dazed, as the sound of fighting grew closer.

The phone rang. When he answered it, the directive was repeated more forcefully than before. It was an order that came directly from President Habyarimana's office: *Kill the prisoners.* Kill them all.

The warden put the phone down and walked out into the grounds of the prison. Gunfire and panic. Smoke roiling up in the distance.

"What shall we do?" one of his guards asked. The RPF were breaking through the back gates, and hundreds of prisoners were about to escape.

"Let them go," he said. "Let them all go."

The Battle of Ruhengeri lasted throughout the morning, and by midday the RPF had taken control of the town, capturing weapons

and food supplies and bringing several high-ranking Hutu opposition members back with them.

Charles Uwihoreye, the warden who had refused to execute
unarmed prisoners, returned to his office to await his fate. He was
arrested the next day on charges of insubordination and thrown into
prison, but was eventually released under pressure from human
rights groups.

The battle would prove a turning point in the war. It shook the
Hutu Power's inner circle to the core, spread a fear of the rebels that
bordered on hysteria, and demonstrated to the world that the RPF
was a force to be reckoned with. News of their success relit a faltering
fire, and across Rwanda, young men began slipping away in the night
to join their ranks. Under the directives of Paul Kagame, a motley
band of rebels became a hardened, disciplined army 15,000 strong.
It was the beginning of the end for the Habyarimana regime.

Given the pivotal role that Ruhengeri Prison had played in the
war, Jean-Claude and I decided to stop by. It was easy enough to
find, sitting at the end of a long, dirt-packed road. But the prison
itself, a collection of bungalow-slab structures arranged around a
courtyard, was not what I expected.

It was, first of all, surprisingly airy, dare I say well-ventilated. As in,
boasting lots of open windows and low walls, not features one normally
associates with a house of incarceration. Hardly airtight, let alone
prisoner-proof. It must have been the easiest thing in the world to
escape from Ruhengeri Prison, were one so inclined. The boarding
school at Nyange was better barricaded. Hell, the main gate of the
prison was simply a booth with an open door behind it. I don't mean
the door was left open, I mean there was no door at all. And this was
the *main entrance*. It was manned by a single guard with a single rifle,
posted on ground level with his back to the prison yard. I could see
inmates strolling by, just over his shoulder. Had they wanted to storm
him, it would have been the equivalent of a rugby tackle from behind.

"Are you sure this is the right place?" I asked Jean-Claude. It
seemed more like a rundown summer camp than a penitentiary.

It got stranger still.

Directly across from the main entrance was a small shop attached to the prison. The shop was crowded with customers, and when I say customers, I mean, of course, "prisoners." This was, it turns out, the locally run canteen, where inmates in their pyjama-like uniforms came to buy toiletries, foodstuffs, and other small items. The wall of the canteen was completely open—right where the prisoners were queuing.

Let me see if I can convey just how bizarre a sight this was. Jean-Claude and I are waiting to speak with a guard manning the front alcove (it wasn't really a doorway, certainly not a gate) over *here*. And just over *there*, across from us, maybe six metres away, is a building that juts out from the prison (and is, therefore, located *outside* the prison walls; do you spot the flaw in that?). And this building is entirely open on one side, forming a breezy expanse, waist high. ("For the heat," Jean-Claude explained, as though that made it any better.) No iron bars, no wire mesh, no panes of reinforced glass. Just one long open-air window. The "customers" inside could have jumped over and run away before the frazzled woman at the till could've said anything, and anyway, she was so busy making change and counting out allotments of cigarettes and such that she would hardly have noticed.

Several of these prisoners had spotted me by this point and were eyeing us with undue interest, intrigued I suppose by my presence. *"Now what's a muzungu doing here?"* None of the looks were overtly hostile, true, but I felt exposed nonetheless; they could have swarmed Jean-Claude and me in a matter of seconds, and I imagine I would have made an alluring hostage. (More so considering I was Alex Ferguson's son; the ransom demands would have soared.)

"Um, Jean-Claude?" I whispered. "Maybe we should come back later."

The guard we'd been waiting on had been riffling through the papers presented by a visiting family member ahead of us, someone's wife by the looks of it, but now that this was sorted out, he called us forward with a nod.

Jean-Claude explained that I was an important journalist here to do a story on Rwandan prison reform and asked if we might speak with the warden, maybe have a tour of the grounds, meet with some of the prisoners. Did we have an appointment? No, not exactly. A letter of some sort? Ah, no.

The guard rolled his eyes, almost audibly, and said—sighed, really—"Wait here."

And he left!

The only thing now standing in the way of a mass breakout from Ruhengeri Prison was a pair of soccer dads from Canada armed solely with our disarming smiles, indomitable will, and—in my case—a penchant for making children cry. The prisoners inside the main yard were looking at Jean-Claude and me with cocked heads and, to my paranoidally inflamed mind, anyway, they seemed to be inching ever closer. Fortunately, the guard suddenly reappeared at that point, superior officer in tow. I handed this fellow one of my *Canadian Geographic* business cards. *On assignment, baby!* And he radioed someone further up the food chain, and so on, until, eventually, the warden himself appeared.

Attempting to gain access to a federal penitentiary under quasi-false pretenses? Was that an indictable offence? And wouldn't it be deliciously ironic if I ended up being incarcerated at this very prison?

The warden was friendly and courteous. A thin figure with a wry half-smile, he was battling a bad case of laryngitis the day we dropped by, so the conversation was a bit strained.

Because we didn't have clearance from—well, from anyone really, we couldn't go inside the prison grounds, but the warden said he would be happy to answer any questions I might have here at the front gate. He spoke flawless English, having grown up in Uganda.

When he heard "Uganda," Jean-Claude immediately twigged. "You were with the RPF?"

The warden nodded. He had been part of the original invasion, had fought in the Battle of Ruhengeri, had stormed the walls of this very prison. He pointed out the wooded hills where he and the others had crept down, where they had first breached the outer walls and where they had come under the heaviest fire.

I asked him, "Did you lose men?"

He smiled softly. "Of course. It was war. You always lose men. It's unavoidable."

According to the warden, Ruhengeri Prison today held around 1,800 inmates. Only 400 of these were genocide perpetrators, successive presidential pardons having released thousands of the lower-rung members.

"Prisoners grow their own food and are responsible for feeding themselves. They are organized into work groups," he explained. "It keeps them busy."

We could hear the sound of women singing.

"The women's choir," he explained. "We have male and female prisoners, and of course male and female guards. The women stay in separate sleeping quarters, but there are common areas, too." The prison was run on a communal plan, much like a kibbutz.

Under the old regime, Ruhengeri Prison had a dark and fearsome reputation. When the RPF took it over they knocked down walls and rearranged the layout to such an extent that the rear of the prison now opens up directly onto the hills behind it, where prisoners plant crops, tend fields. I could see a line of men, colour-coded, plodding along a distant ridge, hoes on shoulders. Pyjamaed farmers, tilling the ground, slowly paying their debt.

"But," I protested, trying my best to be tactful, "not having a back wall, um, doesn't that kind of make it easy for them to escape? I mean, they can just *go* if they want to."

The warden smiled. "Go? Where?"

I looked at the hills that surrounded us, and he was right: every knoll, every nub, every plot of land, every home was tallied and accounted for. One could run for the Virunga rainforest, I suppose, live among the gorillas or try to cross over to the even thicker jungles of Congo, but who would do such a thing? There really is nowhere to hide in Rwanda. That is what made the genocide possible in the first place, that is what made it so horrifically efficient.

The two most remarkable features of Rwandan society, the two singularities, if you will, are (a) the genocide and (b) the sweeping economic and social recovery that followed. They are equally inexplicable, equally unfathomable, and almost unimaginable in their scale and scope. Standing at the entrance to Ruhengeri Prison, I realized that these two aspects of Rwanda were not at odds with each other, but sprang from the same source, were rooted in the same deeply ingrained national traits. Two sides of the same coin.

As we walked back up the road from the world's most escapable prison, clouds were curling over the Virungas. The sun was trying to come through. I could hear the *kii* of a hawk-eagle above us, but when I looked, the bird was lost in the overcast.

# 56

TIME NOW FOR A CRYPTOZOOLOGICAL INTERLUDE. Cryptozoology, of course, being the study of mythical creatures reputed to exist but rarely encountered, those dwelling in the cusp between folklore and science: yetis, the Loch Ness monster, sasquatches, and their ilk.

Jean-Claude and I were back in the capital again, and Kigali seemed to have grown larger, more hectic in our absence. We were swallowed by the clangour, thrown in and out of whirligig traffic circles, with buses bullying their way through and trucks catapulting past as if fired from a slingshot. It was wonderful.

As we clattered across a teeth-rattling stretch of cobblestone—a rarity on Rwandan roads, thankfully—I spotted a sign that read OGOPOGO RESTAURANT.

Ogopogo?

"Gotta be owned by a Canadian," I said, and we veered over to investigate.

For those of you who may not be familiar with it, the Ogopogo is Canada's answer to Nessie. The creature is said to haunt the cold waters of British Columbia's Lake Okanagan, and legends of the Ogopogo date back further than those of Loch Ness. The Okanagan First Nations told of a malevolent being that would drag people under the water, not unlike the—entirely nonexistent!—crocodiles of Lake Kivu.

If you've been wondering why the Ogopogo hasn't been spotted splashing about in Lake Okanagan lately, I may have the answer. The Ogopogo, it would seem, has pulled up stakes and moved to warmer climes. Even so, Kigali struck me as an odd choice. There were no deep lakes here to hide in, only a shallow and marshy river.

The restaurant's interior was dark and spacious, featuring low ceilings, long tables, and a menu that prominently featured fish skewers—appropriately, considering the restaurant's namesake. I ordered a burger, Jean-Claude had the fish, and when we inquired as to how the café got its name, several explanations were offered.

"It's named after a type of dinosaur," one of the waiters said. "It's extinct now."

The bartender cut in. "Not a dinosaur," he said. "The Ogopogo was never real. It's a myth. Like a dragon."

"No, no," another waiter said. "It's real. The owner's sister lives in Canada. She knows."

Was the owner of the restaurant Canadian? A transplanted British Columbian, perhaps?

"No, he's Rwandan. His older brother owned this place first. It was originally called Papyrus. He renamed it."

And why would Ogopogo move to Rwanda?

"Probably got tired of the cold," the bartender said with a laugh. "I hear there is too much winter in Canada. Let me call the owner. He lives nearby. He can tell you better."

The bench cushions featured African motifs of various stylized monsters, but nothing overly Ogopogo-ish. One would think the menu would have at least boasted "Nessie fries" or "Sasquatch shakes," but no.

The owner showed up soon after, an affable young man with an equally affable smile.

"Hello, my name is Condo Raphael. And you are … Canadian?"

How did he know?

Condo spoke English, French, Kinyarwanda, Swahili—and more. My Swahili being a bit rusty, we stuck with rudimentary English and a smattering of Kinyarwanda, as translated by Jean-Claude.

Condo had indeed taken over the original restaurant from his brother. "That was in 2011," he explained.

His brother had gotten into an argument with the city over parking regulations. He didn't have adequate spaces, the neighbours were complaining, and this being Rwanda he wasn't able to slip someone a discreet payment to make the problem go away, as one might in Italy or Kenya. Instead, he ended up tearing down half the building, almost out of spite. (Condo's brother sounded a bit hotheaded, the sort who, as they say in Northern Ireland, has "ruffled enough feathers to build himself an ostrich.")

Condo, clearly the calmer and more diplomatic of the two, bought out his older brother, added extra parking in front, closed off the noisy open-air patio, and then rebuilt the restaurant almost from scratch, with an indoor deck and a long, inviting bar.

"Around that time, I was watching a National Geographic nature program on television. It was about the Ogopogo, and it talked about how the creature might have endured. The theory was, he survived the ice age in a deep lake and later came back to life. I realized this was like my restaurant. It had survived and been brought back, just like the Ogopogo."

Condo did have a sister-in-law in Canada. That part was true. But the name itself came from a television documentary.

"Rwandese people are puzzled by the name," he said. "Some people think it's a Nigerian word. In Nigerian languages there are a lot of O sounds."

One of Condo's regulars, a flight engineer with RwandAir, was a Canadian—from the Okanagan, no less.

"He told me the images of African monsters I have on the cushions are wrong. He said he's going to bring me back some correct images of Ogopogo next time he goes home."

Condo liked my idea of naming items on the menu after other mythical creatures, yetis and mermaids and such, and I sketched him a picture of the Ogopogo as a possible mascot, dimly remembered from my days in Kelowna as a teenager. He frowned at my rendering. It didn't look particularly fierce. "Maybe add fangs," I said. "Or horns."

The resurrection of this restaurant, like the city, like the country, was a lesson in resilience. Rwanda, in its way, was an Ogopogo nation, one brought back from the brink of extinction, reinvented, reborn. And as evening settled over Kigali, the lights of the Ogopogo grew warmer, and the laughter grew louder. It was a welcoming place, much like its owner, and when Jean-Claude and I finally rose to say goodnight, I asked Condo, "Do Canadians come here?"

"They do."

"How many?" I asked.

He smiled. "All of them."

# 57

WE SPENT THE NEXT FEW DAYS in Kigali catching up on our laundry, cleaning out the Land Cruiser, and making arrangements for the final leg of our journey.

Christine's mother and grandmother lived in Kigali's Ndera district, a warren of homes in the city's west end, and I went with Jean-Claude on one of his visits. Meeting them was like viewing a set of Russian nesting dolls: Christine was taller than her mom and her mom was taller than her grandma, and they all looked exactly the same, just more and more adorable as they got older. While Christine's mom, Hélène, fussed over us, producing snacks and serving the same ginger-laced tea Christine was famous for back in Calgary, the grandmother tutted and fretted, upset that we weren't staying for supper. (She spoke at great length about this, reprimanding Jean-Claude repeatedly over his breach of etiquette, an eloquent and extended discourse in Kinyarwanda that he translated as "She wanted to feed us.")

It took some doing, but Jean-Claude eventually eased us out of their home with repeated promises to return again when we had a "proper appetite." ("Once they start feeding you, they won't stop," he'd warned.) They were wonderful ladies, but in-laws are in-laws wherever you go in this world, and no matter how long Jean-Claude's visits were they would never be long enough, and anyway, why hadn't he brought Christine and the children with him, they hadn't seen their grandchildren in years! When I showed the photographs I'd taken of them to Christine after I returned to Canada, she got tears in her eyes. It had been so long since she'd seen her mom, her grandma, or her siblings that I felt guilty at having made such a breezy visit, one she dreamed of, yearned for, almost daily. Christine's younger brother Jonas lived with their mom, and he asked us, longingly, about Canada—a country he had never visited. There were opportunities in

Rwanda, but he dreamed of a wider trajectory; I'm sure he would have swapped places with his sister at a moment's notice, had he been able to.

Relatives, old friends, former colleagues, future contacts: Jean-Claude had a roll call of people to see over the next two days, and I spent my time sleeping in and occasionally kicking around Kigali. The neighbourhood we were staying in was comfortable, but awfully quiet. There was a definite paucity of pubs, and everything else seemed to shut down at six, so one evening I decided to make the long hike to a nearby hotel. I could see it perched invitingly on a ridge, lit up like the *Queen Mary*, but no matter how long I trudged it never seemed to grow any nearer, at times even seeming to scuttle farther away from me, sideways like a crab. Walking in Kigali is always an act of mis-direction, of oblique angles and coy avenues—the roads are always so decisively indecisive—and I ended up making a long and unfruitful loop down and around, arriving back in the alleyway behind our apartment building, confused as ever. I walked over to the Solace Ministries guest house instead, hoping to catch a late supper.

When I went in, I was surprised to find Jean-Claude there, along with Lorne, the psychiatrist from Toronto, and his daughter Adriana. I'd forgotten that Jean-Claude had arranged a meeting between Lorne and Jean-Claude's niece Clementine, who worked as a psychiatric nurse at Ndera Hospital. Jean Gakwandi, the man who had founded Solace Ministries, was there as well, so I pulled up a chair.

Mr. Gakwandi was a genocide survivor. "For some people the genocide is just a fact of history," he told me. "But for those who went through it, it is a reality that we live every day."

About one-third of those who died in the genocide were children, and many of those children who did survive—men and women now in their late twenties and early thirties—had been exposed to unspeakable acts of violence. Many saw parents and loved ones chopped down in front of them. An investigation by UNICEF revealed that more than 90 percent of the children who survived the Rwandan genocide had witnessed bloodshed. More than half a

million were orphaned. They have been described as "the living victims of the genocide," a generation still struggling to get by, often
plagued by depression, substance abuse, and other mental illnesses.
As one woman told a journalist investigating the effects of these
crimes, "I can't sleep. I'm afraid of dreams."

We know from other genocides—the Jewish Holocaust, the
Armenian—that the effects last for generations, are handed down
from parent to child to grandchild. And yet Rwanda faces a critical
shortage of trained medical staff, not just physicians and surgeons
but therapists as well. In a nation suffering from post-traumatic stress
and other untreated disorders, there are only *six* psychiatrists available for a population of 11 million. Rwanda spends more on health
care than most African countries, but not nearly enough of it has
gone toward mental health. The traumatized often feel abandoned,
forgotten, empty. The use of sexual violence during the genocide was
particularly horrific and widespread.[28]

Jean-Claude's niece was explaining to Lorne the need for therapy.
Lorne was associated with the University of Toronto, and Jean-Claude
had arranged this meeting to discuss the possibility of bringing out an
instructor from Canada to work with Rwandan doctors and medical
staff to provide the specialized training they needed to deal with these
issues, to help people and communities form coping strategies.

A chance meeting during a lighthearted trek to see some chimpanzees had revealed an opportunity to Jean-Claude that many people would have missed. By connecting a psychiatrist from Canada
with a nurse from Rwanda, he'd opened a door to the possibility of
something bigger, something that might have a real and lasting
impact. I'd seen this before, Jean-Claude creating unlikely connections, bringing groups with seemingly unrelated interests together.
Had he put these networking skills of his toward purely financial

---

28. For testimonies from the women who suffered through this, see *The Men Who
Killed Me: Rwandan Survivors of Sexual Violence*. But be prepared; it is a harrowing
and gut-wrenching read.

gain, he would have been a millionaire by now. But nooooo, he had to go around *helping people*.

As we walked back to our apartment across the packed-clay alley, I asked Jean-Claude why he did it.

We reached the back gate, waited for the night guard to let us in.

"Rwanda's doctors and nurses need training," he said. "I thought maybe Lorne can help."

"I don't mean just this," I said. "I mean everything, all of it. You came to Canada with nothing. You had just arrived, were working at a meat-cutting plant, yet you started volunteering at the Calgary Food Bank and Mustard Seed and Inn from the Cold. You set up a free soccer program for low-income families, spent four years running it as a volunteer. Why?"

Jean-Claude had once asked me to help him update his résumé, and I'd counted no fewer than nine different volunteer organizations he was involved with, everything from homeless shelters to youth-at-risk outreach programs to soccer camps for underprivileged children.

I thought he might shrug it off and say something like, "I don't know, Will. It's just something I do. I like to help."

But he took my question seriously. Jean-Claude looked at me—I could hear the guard making his way slowly across the grounds, keys clinking—and he said, "It kind of haunts you, being alive. You always ask yourself why. Why *me,* why did I make it out, when so many others did not? Was this luck? Only that? I was a nineteen-year-old kid. It didn't matter if I lived or not. I didn't have children then or a wife or anybody who depended on me. There were people who were doctors, Will. Who were teachers, who had families, who had something to contribute. And they all died. Why them and not me?" The guard opened the gate, but Jean-Claude didn't go through. He stood a moment at the threshold and then said, "I guess I feel I owe *something,* that I need to give back *somehow.* Otherwise, what was the point of it?"

We stepped into a dark garden on the other side of the gate, started the long walk up to our building.

"I think about that," he said. "I think about it all the time."

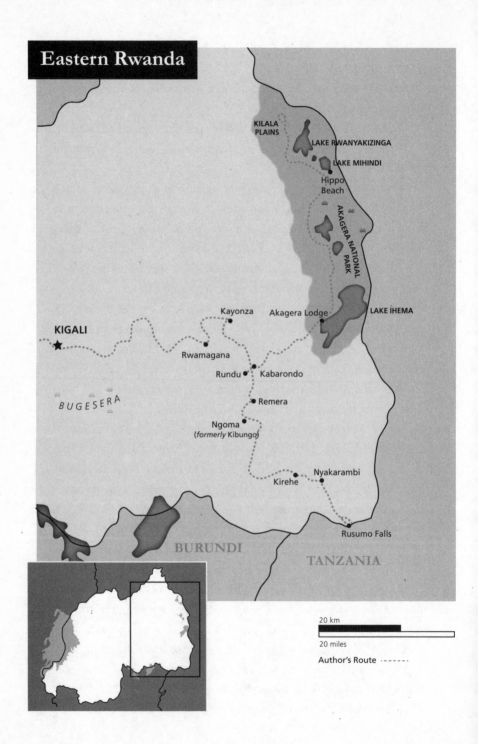

# Eastern Rwanda

KILALA
PLAINS

LAKE RWANYAKIZINGA

LAKE MIHINDI

Hippo
Beach

AKAGERA NATIONAL PARK

Kayonza

Akagera Lodge

LAKE IHEMA

**KIGALI**

Rwamagana

Rundu    Kabarondo

*BUGESERA*

Remera

Ngoma
(*formerly* Kibungo)

Nyakarambi

Kirehe

Rusumo Falls

**BURUNDI**

**TANZANIA**

20 km

20 miles

Author's Route  - - - - - -

# PART FOUR

## THE ROAD TO RUSUMO

## 58

THERE IS A WORD IN KINYARWANDA, *kwihaza,* which means "to be self-sufficient." Kwihaza is the stated goal of Rwanda's long-term development: to end foreign aid entirely and become self-reliant as a people.

Another word, *umuganda,* focuses this idea at the local level. Translated as "communal work," umuganda might involve planting trees, repairing school playgrounds, building terraces to stop erosion. During the genocide, however, the meaning of umuganda changed. Militia death squads began referring to themselves as "work crews," and they considered what they were doing to be a form of community service. The killing of Tutsis and moderate Hutus was referred to as "cutting grass, pulling up the weeds."

Today, the word has been reclaimed. Like the *gacaca* ("patch of grass") courts and the *imihigo* ritual of officials declaring their goals and then being held accountable for their implementation, the concept of umuganda has been revived to fit the current situation.

No one is exempt. On the last Saturday of the month, everyone— government officials, judges, the prime minister, the president, teachers, students, shop owners, day labourers—is expected to show up at their local umuganda project to help out. You will be fined for not taking part, and if you want to receive certain government services, you may be asked to submit a card, signed and stamped, showing you did. (Religious groups such as the Seventh-Day Adventists, who consider Saturday the Sabbath, are required to organize their own projects on alternative days.) It's true that some people just pay the fine and go back to bed, but they aren't allowed to leave their homes until the umuganda is over. You can't go for a morning drive or a casual stroll on umuganda day.

"With politicians, umuganda is like flipping pancakes at the Stampede," Jean-Claude explained, referring to Calgary's perennially co-opted photo-op. "If you are a politician in Rwanda you can make a big production from showing up, maybe just to shovel a few scoops of dirt, shake hands, pose for pictures, talk to the voters."

But most Rwandans take it seriously. How seriously? Allow me to illustrate with the following statistic. Over the course of our three weeks in Rwanda, Jean-Claude and I would travel from one end of the country to the other, up and down narrow roads and broad thoroughfares, on dirt lanes and polished asphalt, through cities and hamlets, hills and plains, and we were never stopped by the police. Not once. The number of police checkpoints we encountered was: zero. Except on umuganda day. The number of times we were stopped by police on this, the last Saturday of the month? Seven.

On each occasion we were pulled over and questioned by gruff police officers who wanted to know why we weren't at our neighbourhood umuganda. Or rather, *Jean-Claude* was questioned. Foreign visitors to Rwanda are not required to participate, and there was something about me, my body language or my accent or something, that suggested I wasn't from around here. Every time we were stopped, Jean-Claude would have to explain that he was a tourist en route to Akagera National Park, and often as not would be asked to show his passport. Only then would we be allowed through.

They never asked for my passport, strangely enough. On occasion, I would try to present it anyway, only to have it waved away.

"This is racial profiling," I grumbled to Jean-Claude as we left the latest checkpoint. "They shouldn't just *assume* I'm not Rwandan."

Jean-Claude, meanwhile, was starting to feel guilty, as though he were shirking his civic duty.

"But you're Canadian now," I said. "You have a Canadian passport, Canadian citizenship. You're allowed to be lazy. In fact, it's positively encouraged."

Umuganda had started early. From our apartment window we could see people gathering in the alleyway below. Women started clearing grass along the edge, moving through with a practised swing of their hand scythes. Men in baggy trousers shovelled dirt into potholes and others tramped it down. Given the size of the potholes in that alley, it was a bit like throwing handfuls of sugar into the sea to reduce salinity, but no matter. I quickly realized that the point was not necessarily the work, but that it was shared.

Jean-Claude and I didn't get a hundred metres in our Land Cruiser before we were nabbed, waved to the side of a roundabout on an angry blast of whistle—so they did have whistles! A young officer demanded to know why *we* (meaning Jean-Claude) weren't volunteering. (Though, when it's mandatory like that, you have to wonder about the use of the word "volunteer.")

"You do know it's umuganda today?" he said. I assumed this was a rhetorical question.

I handed over a couple of my *Canadian Geographic* business cards and we were allowed to continue.

Another hundred metres, another roundabout, and another police roadblock. The cross-examinations began anew. At the next roadblock it was a stern-faced female officer who appeared. She was decidedly unswayed by our dashing smiles and good looks. So much for flirting our way through. She wanted to see Jean-Claude's passport, brushed aside my proffered business cards—and here I'd gone and drawn little hearts on them and everything—then let us pass. At the next roadblock it was an older gentleman, who looked as weary of this as we were.

On it went, like a slow-motion game of Mother-May-I, as we inched our way out of Kigali. Normally, running a gauntlet of police barricades would leave one feeling unsettled, unnerved, even (at the city limits, the roadblock featured a spiked barrier laid across the asphalt). However, when the officers in question aren't checking for contraband goods or illicit weapons but rather asking why you aren't picking up litter or painting the local community centre, it doesn't generate the sense of danger one might expect. We sailed on calmly between checkpoints, resigned to the process. The novelty of it had long since worn off.

We were heading east, into a different Rwanda. And although much of the country is located in the upper altitudes, the eastern region slopes down into endless banana plantations and eventually scrub-plain savannah.

The central mountains give Rwanda a surprisingly temperate climate, even with the country being located on the equator. Daytime temperatures rarely vary, hovering around twenty-seven degrees Celsius year-round—hot, but not oppressively so—and the nights are glorious and forgiving, even chilly at times. And although much of the country is technically within Africa's malarial zone, the higher altitudes are blessedly free of *Anopheles gambiae,* the mosquito in this region that carries the virus. But that changes when you travel east. Here the temperatures creep ever upward as the sun grows prickly and arid.

Rwanda's anti-malaria programs have been very successful. Targeted sprayings and the distribution of millions of insecticide-infused mosquito nets, together with medicine during the outbreaks, have reduced deaths from malaria by 85 percent over the last six years, one of the most dramatic drops and effective campaigns the World Health Organization has ever seen. I took my prescribed dose of Malarone every day, slept under Southern-belle nettings at night, and spritzed my ankles with DEET when I went out in the evenings, but otherwise I hadn't been overly concerned—until now.

Eastern Rwanda was another matter, almost another world. The east was well within the malarial red zone, with the added presence of trap-jawed crocodiles, malcontent hippos, ill-tempered buffaloes, and even a rogue elephant or two. True, these animals were corralled inside the expansive range of Akagera National Park, but it did add a frisson of danger to our travels. And what's travel without a dash of *frisson?* It's like beer without the formaldehyde.

Because this was umuganda day, there was no traffic on the highway. Jean-Claude's foot grew heavier; the speedometer drifted upward and the wind whistled through.

"All we need are flags on the front," he said, "and some motorcycles with their sirens on and we could be a presidential— What do you call it, like a private parade for VIPs?"

"A motorcade?"

"Exactly. It is like they closed the highway just for us."

He was right. It did feel as though we were leading our own motorcade, the sort that visiting potentates and Ruritanian rulers might command, except of course that visiting potentates and Ruritanian rulers are rarely pulled over by the police and forced to pull weeds at a local primary school. Not that Jean-Claude and I were forced to pull weeds, but it came close. We'd barely escaped the capital when an officer popped out of nowhere, from behind a bush, I assume, and waved us sternly to the side of the road. He'd already netted an impressive haul: three different minibuses and two taxis. A passenger from one of the taxis, a beefy businessman in an expensive suit, looked very peeved indeed.

The police officer spoke to us briefly, then waved us through, much to the chagrin of the businessman, who was now being handed a hoe and directed to a nearby field. *If you can't buy your way out of manual labour, what's the point of being rich?* I gave him a "Sorry, but what can I do?" shrug as we passed.

I asked Jean-Claude about the minivan buses that had been flagged down. We'd seen those passengers filing out and being handed farm implements.

"If people don't have good reason to be travelling, for example to a funeral or the doctor's or a far-away wedding, they must get out and help. Women who have young children, or the elderly people or ill people, they don't have to work, but everybody else does." There was an awkward pause. "I still feel bad about not taking part," Jean-Claude said.

"So do I," I lied. "*So do I.* But hey, what can we do?" These were the sorts of sacrifices one makes when one is a Very Important Journalist.

With the road unrolling before us, it seemed to me that the best job to have on umuganda day (other than journalist, of course) was police officer. You got to stride about in a purposeful manner, blowing your purposeful whistle whilst purposefully nabbing layabouts and scofflaws, all without having to dig any actual ditches or pull any actual weeds yourself. And I bet you still got to take part in the picnic at the end, too.

Farther down, we passed rows of motorcycle taxis parked beside an irrigation weir.

"Umuganda is not set up just by neighbourhoods or by villages," Jean-Claude explained, "but also by job and by trade union. Motorcycle taxi drivers have their own association, so probably they arranged their own project."

Man oh man, Rwandans sure do love to organize themselves.

No wonder the public spaces were always so tidy here. They got fully cleaned, pruned, and swept once a month. It was rather inspiring. Not inspiring enough to ask Jean-Claude to pull over so that I might spit in my palms, grab a shovel, and join in. It was more of a low-level, I-doff-my-hat-to-you-in-passing sort of inspiration. The kind that doesn't require any effort. That kind.


# 59


THE JELLY-BEAN TOWNS we'd seen elsewhere in Rwanda were on display in the east as well, with the shops brightly coloured *red, blue, yellow, green; red, blue, yellow, green,* but the landscape around us had grown shaggier, more tangled.

We were deep in banana country now. If I'd reached out through the window I could have run my fingers through the landscape. Layered leaves swayed in the wind, with entire communities playing hide-and-seek among them. As we drove, Jean-Claude explained the correlation between topography, bananas, and teenage pregnancy.

"When you have flat ground," he assured me, "you have more babies."

Say what?

"It happens like this," he said. "Flat land is better for growing bananas, and banana farms are easy to take care of. You have a lot of free time, and with the extra bananas, you can make banana beer. The more banana beer, the more get-togethers. The more get-togethers, the more relaxed feelings you have. The more relaxed feelings, the more unexpected pregnancies. A lot of children are raised by their aunts out here."

A persuasive syllogism, though I'm not sure how much of it was supported by clinical research, and I daresay the people of the region might take exception. But I did hear from other Rwandans as well that the east was considered more, how shall we say, *lax* in its moral stringencies.

"Didn't your wife come from around here?" I asked.

"No," he said sharply. "Much farther. In Tanzania."

Given that Christine was a teetotaller like Jean-Claude, I didn't imagine she could have grown up on a diet of banana beer.

We were approaching Rwamagana Town and with it the Dereva Hotel, a personal landmark of Jean-Claude's.

"We would stop at the Dereva on our way back to Kigali. I would order an omelette and french fries. Was very tasty. This was with the Japanese nurses."

The first time Jean-Claude met my wife, he had surprised her by greeting her in Japanese.

"I learned Japanese when I was, like, fifteen, sixteen," he'd explained, "from nurses who were living in Kigali."

The nurses were in Rwanda as volunteers with JOCV (Japan Overseas Cooperation Volunteers), which also included a major telecommunications project. The Japanese engineers had given Jean-Claude a summer job minding their office equipment (people had been pilfering fax machines and telephones), and he was later hired to help out at the women's dormitory. He was asked to learn Japanese so that he could help interpret.

"I went to live with them in the fall. Was wonderful! There was six girls in the house, they were like, nineteen, twenty, twenty-one, that age. I was in heaven! One was x-ray technician, one was lab technician, one was a teacher, others were nurses. On the first day, when their supervisor was not there, they asked me, 'Can you drive?' I said, 'Sure.' They asked, 'How old are you?' I said, 'Eighteen.' They said, 'Okay, you're going to sneak us out tonight, okay?' Three of them were a bad influence on the other girls, I remember. They said, 'Okay, here's the plan ...'"

On Friday nights, Jean-Claude would shuttle them around the city, from nightclub to nightclub, and sometimes all the way to Akagera, several hours away, to a hotel discothèque.

"It was booming! Was a very popular place. The nurses would stay up all night dancing. Coming back they would be hangovered, and we would stop at the Dereva Hotel for omelettes and french fries. It is one of my strongest memories—those Japanese nurses, so tired but happy, eating omelettes at the hotel."

Jean-Claude might have gone on to become a Japanese–Kinyarwanda interpreter—he was just starting to get the hang of the language—but on October 1, 1990, the world changed.

"The RPF invaded and Rwanda, it went into a kind of panic. A few nights later, there was shooting in Kigali. All across the city. But the RPF was far away, in the east. The soldiers were firing at shadows. The next day, they started picking up Tutsis."

Japan decided to pull out of Rwanda.

"They were ordered to evacuate. The situation was too dangerous for them to stay. One of the engineers, he gave me a pair of running shoes. It was those Mizunos I was wearing that were robbed from me near Somalia. Was very good shoes he gave me. I didn't know then, but it was a goodbye gift."

The nurses closed ranks around Jean-Claude.

"They told me, 'We're gonna take you with us. Don't worry.' But their boss, this older man, he was called Omomi, he just stood there with his arms crossed, shaking his head, kind of sucking on his teeth. He said, '*Taihen.*' I knew that meant 'difficult.' The nurses were shouting at him. One was crying. I could understand some of their Japanese now. I could hear them saying 'My family, they are going to take care of him.' 'My family is going to do this or that.' 'He is Tutsi, do you understand that? Do you understand what's gonna happen to him?' But Omomi wouldn't even look at them, not in the eye. He just shook his head and said, '*Taihen.*'"

They might have been arguing with a stone Buddha.

"These nurses were very upset. They told me, 'It's gonna be okay, go to your house and wait for us, we're gonna send for you.' But they never did." There was a long pause. "Would have been a very different life, if I had gone with them."

On October 5, the Japanese mission to Rwanda was shut down and all staff, volunteers, and other Japanese nationals were evacuated.

"I never saw them again," Jean-Claude said. "I didn't even get a chance to say goodbye."

The Dereva Hotel and Restaurant was a collection of villas in garden-like grounds. The restaurant was airy and open—and largely empty, this being umuganda day. By odd coincidence, the only other customer at the restaurant that day was Japanese. Not a beautiful young nurse, alas, but rather a balding, middle-aged engineer from Nagasaki named Hiro who clearly wasn't expecting to be addressed in his native language. "*Jōzu desu ne!*" he said to me in breathy wonderment, meaning roughly, "Your Japanese is very good!" A blatant mistruth, but one I happily accepted, insincere flattery being a hallmark of Japanese politeness, after all. (For the record, I speak Japanese the way a bear dances; people aren't impressed that the bear dances *well,* just that it dances at all.) Hiro was working on an infrastructure project with the Rwandan government, and when Jean-Claude spoke up, Hiro assured him that his Japanese was pretty darn *jōzu,* too.

After chatting with Hiro, Jean-Claude and I sat on the patio eating beef brochettes and grilled plantain, standard fare and deftly prepared, but as we rose to leave I stopped myself with a jolt.

"We blew it!" I said. "We should have ordered omelettes and french fries!"

Jean-Claude smiled. "I thought about it. But it wouldn't have been the same. They wouldn't have tasted as good as they did when I was fifteen."

And he was right. The omelettes of our youth are always so much sweeter.

# 60

THE LAST POLICE CHECKPOINT of the day wasn't—a checkpoint, that is. It was more of a holdup, albeit a very well-mannered one.

Just east of Rwamagana we were stopped not by the shrill trill of a whistle but by raised hands and apologetic smiles from a pair of police officers. Umuganda had ended and vehicles had begun to reappear on the roads—we'd already passed several communal picnics in the fields and villages—so this was unexpected.

The officers spoke with Jean-Claude softly, almost shyly, and then Jean-Claude turned to me. "They want to know if they can catch a ride back to their police station. It's in the next town, Kayonza. Usually there is a minibus that picks up police officers at the end of umuganda, but it hasn't arrived and they have been waiting a long time. We're going in that direction anyway."

I looked at the automatic rifles the men were carrying. "Do we have a choice?" I joked.

Jean-Claude was puzzled. "Of course we have a choice."

"Okay. Sure. Why not?" I moved our bags around to make space for them in the back.

"An armed escort," I said as we pulled onto the road. "I like it." Now it really was like having our own presidential motorcade.

Having a pair of armed police officers in the backseat, AK-47s at the ready, certainly gave us some extra swagger. It was the only time on this, or any road trip really, that I actively hoped for an ambush, if only to see the bandit's face when our tinted rear-view window rolled down. *What's that you say? Stand and deliver? I think not.*

Jean-Claude dropped the two officers off at their station: a small brick bungalow shaded by palm trees.

On our way out of town, we passed a tavern named Imararungu, which Jean-Claude translated as the "You Won't Be Bored" Bar (it was doing a roaring trade, post-umuganda), and soon after that the Pretty Beauty Salon (which seemed a tad redundant to my mind) as well as several roadside chopping blocks, busy with customers, which apparently sold only the outer extremities of chickens: feet and heads and other indeterminate bits. The people had a bounce in their step, were gathering on street corners to laugh and exchange greetings in that festive spirit that comes at the end of a shared day's work.

There was a breeze at play here, but after Kayonza we took a hard turn south, heading for hotter climes.

This was still banana country, but the earlier claustrophobia had eased. The broad-leafed plantations had stepped back, the valleys had opened up, and the villages had come out of hiding. Spandex-clad cyclists fired past like Luftwaffe dive-bombers in tight formation, helmets sleek as teardrops, legs chuttering, wheels spinning.

"They're in training," Jean-Claude explained, "for Tour du Rwanda," a 910-kilometre multi-stage race modelled on the Tour de France.

The roadsides were thick with avocado and mango as well.

"Is this a nostalgic landscape for you?" I asked.

"Oh my goodness, yes. I have strong memories from this place."

We had entered the Kabarondo district of eastern Rwanda, and although Jean-Claude had been born and raised in the capital, his family's ancestral village was out here, near Akagera National Park.

"My older brother, Jean-Baptiste, he was living in our family village, taking care of our grandfather's land. The village is, like, nine kilometres from Kabarondo Town. Its name is Rundu. When I was in grade four my father sent me away to stay there. I was maybe nine or ten years old."

Jean-Claude had been roaming the streets of Kigali, sneaking into soccer games and dodging the consequences with a cocky sense of impunity, sometimes crouching behind the sedans of government officials entering through the side gates and then sprinting past the security guards.

"I could sneak into any stadium in Kigali," he said with a certain misplaced pride. "I could always find a way in, around, or under that fence. Sometimes they would chase you, but if you could get into the crowd, you could escape. You could disappear and they would never, never find you."

Jean-Baptiste had come to the city to talk to their father.

"He said to my dad, 'You are getting to be an older man now. Is hard to keep a watch on Jean-Claude, and there is too much destruction in the city.' Remember, one of our brothers already was kidnapped. Jean-Baptiste said, 'In the village it will be a quiet life. Jean-Claude can focus more in school and it will be good for him.' And my dad agreed. We had many extended family in that village. Aunties, cousins. Would be very hard to get into trouble there."

Jean-Claude's brother owned one of the only vehicles in the village.

"Was a Toyota HiAce minibus. Very sturdy. People from surrounding villages were hiring him like a taxi to drive them to appointments. He was like an ambulance, too. If someone was sick or a woman was going into labour, my brother would drive them, wouldn't charge. He was doing very well, was leasing our land and driving the minibus, and was building a new house—a very nice house. Was for his wife, his children. It was made of bricks, not mud or clay."

As a prominent figure in the community, Jean-Baptiste was called upon to settle disputes as well, including one with a neighbouring village that occurred soon after Jean-Claude arrived.

"It was over a girl," Jean-Claude said. "The other villagers showed up ready to fight, with bows and arrows and long spears. I was from the city, I never saw such a thing before! What happened was, a boy from our village had damaged a girl's reputation very badly and he needed to be punished. The other village demanded it. It was gonna be a war between the two towns, and my brother spent the whole day speaking to both sides, back and forth, and eventually they came to an agreement. My brother told them, 'There are laws. You can't just kill him. We will surrender the boy to the police, okay? But not to a bunch of angry people who are gonna kill him.' So that boy went to jail, and there was no war. I was very impressed with my brother in that moment."

Jean-Claude attended classes in Rundu during the school year and returned to Kigali for school breaks, holidays, and various weekends.

"I was there from grade four to grade nine. Was a kind of culture shock for me. I was a city boy, and they could tell."

"How so?"

"First off, I had shoes. Everyone else was barefoot. So when I went to school the first day, the teacher made me take *off* my shoes! Second, I was like a soccer superstar, because where other kids listened to games on the radio, for me, I had watched it live. I had met many of those players personally. Some were even from my neighbourhood in Kigali. When I told the kids in the village this, they couldn't believe it. For kids in a village, life in the city is like a kind of fiction."

But as Jean-Claude discovered, the village had its own way of ascribing status.

"In Kigali, I was street smart. I could cross busy roads even at the age of five. I knew which intersections were dangerous, which ones were safe, how to time it, when to go. In the village, there was no traffic—there was no cars!—so these skills were not of any use for me."

In Rundu, the cool kids were the ones who could grow or tend to something that would earn them money, even if it was just a few francs.

"One kid would boast he had a chicken, was gonna sell the eggs, another one would say she grew beans to sell them, another one, he had a goat. I had to do something about this, so I went to my brother and I said, 'I need a place to plant something.' He said, 'Okay, look around. Pick the place.' I bought some beans from a guy, and I planted them. Next morning I woke up early, ran and looked. Was nothing! So I dug up my beans to see what was the problem. I thought maybe this guy, he sold me defective beans. I was mad, and I threw them away, went and got different beans. Better beans. Again, nothing. Next morning and the next, nothing. I didn't know beans don't grow overnight! When I was about to dig up those beans too, I noticed that the first ones—the beans I threw away—had started to sprout. They were growing! I was amazed."

As we passed lowing cattle of the non-royal variety grazing in a field surrounded by banana plants, Jean-Claude recalled how there had once been lions here as well. Hundreds of them had lived in Akagera, and they would often come out of the park to hunt cattle— though "hunt" is perhaps not the best word, cows not being known for their gazelle-like fleetness.

"A lion came into our village one time. Was maybe 1982. That was the last time, I think. The men hunted it with sticks—"

"Spears?"

"Not even that. Sticks and a dog is enough. The man who killed it, I think he used an arrow. It gave him a lot of prestige after that. He kept the skin, the mane, even the fat of the lion—he kept it in this clay bowl, and if anyone was injured, they would go to his house and they would put lion oil on it. He became famous for killing that lion."

Hyenas were even worse, I learned.

"My village was kind of like a hyenas' capital. That was long ago. The hyenas are gone, but even now, women don't walk alone on the road to my village. Hyenas are more dangerous than lions. If a lion is full, it will just sleep there. I find lions are very lazy. If something is hard to catch, the lion will forget it. But a hyena? A hyena will never be full. They are always hungry. They are like walking appetites. When a hyena attacks, it will never leave empty. That's why, if you throw a boot at a hyena, he will go for the boot. And whatever a hyena catches, if it's your arm, your foot, he's going to take it."

We came into the clay streets of Kabarondo, a town that was dusty and green at the same time.

Jean-Claude slowed down. "That's the church," he said, referring to a simple Catholic chapel made from bricks as red as the soil. "This is the place. This is where my brother Jean-Baptiste ran to when the killings started. He got separated from his family and had to find shelter. So many people were in that church. They thought they will be safe there. Then the interahamwe came." Jean-Claude pulled the Land Cruiser over across from it, paused for a moment. "They were watching. They were waiting for everyone to be inside so they could kill them more easily."

When the attack came, it was ferocious, with the military firing mortars from across the street and then lobbing grenades through the broken rafters as the interahamwe militias waited outside, prowling the perimeter. In the madness, Jean-Baptiste managed to escape, breaking through the circle of machetes and fleeing into the forest.

"He went to his friend's house, but they said, 'No no no no. You can't stay here!' Nobody would take him in. Some of these people he had driven to the emergency clinic without charge."

Jean-Claude sat looking at the red-brick chapel across from us.

"So many people died in there. But my brother, he escaped. He made it out. He was going north, trying to get to the RPF lines, is what I think, trying to reach the safe zone. And he almost made it, was very close. Was almost past the last barrier. Then someone he knew saw him and shouted, 'I know that guy! He's a Tutsi!' I always wondered why he was walking in the daylight. I wish I could ask him. Maybe he was so close he decided to take a chance, but you know, if he had just waited until night ..."

Trucks rattled by. Women with baskets moved past us on the side of the road. Children chased a bicycle rim.

"We know who killed him," Jean-Claude said. "We know his name."

A silence settled over us.

"Would you like to go in?" I asked. "Take a moment?"

Jean-Claude shook his head, almost imperceptibly, then put the Land Cruiser into gear and pulled us back into traffic, leaving the church at Kabarondo behind. He watched its departure in the rear-view mirror.

The lions that once hunted among these villages are gone, but their ghosts are not.

"No," Jean-Claude said when I made the comparison. "Not lions. Hyenas. My brother was killed by hyenas."

# 61

THE CHILDREN LOITERING AROUND the gas station at Kabarondo seemed listless and tired. They asked me for money, and when I said no they stood staring while Jean-Claude filled up the Land Cruiser.

Although we were in one of the poorest regions of Rwanda, Jean-Claude still noted how much the town had grown. New banks and electronics shops had opened. Fresh paint and new rooftops were everywhere in evidence. "Kabarondo has improved so much!" Jean-Claude had said as we drove through.

He was oblivious to the sullen glare the children were giving us as we pumped the gas—and then it dawned on me.

"This is where the tourists stop, isn't it?" I said. "This filling station. This must be where they fuel up before heading into Akagera National Park."

"Probably," Jean-Claude said, topping up the tank. "I think this is the last service centre before the park. People going on safari, they must stop here."

That was why the children were so sullen. Muzungus came and muzungus stopped and muzungus gave them money. I was a muzungu, therefore I was supposed to give them money. This was why they were loitering around the gas station instead of chasing bicycle rims down the street or planting beans or lugging pails of water home to their mothers, and it seemed in that moment that this unremarkable gas station on a dusty intersection in eastern Rwanda embodied the entire misguided, well-intentioned but devastating impact of Western aid on Africa. I recalled the signs that greeted truck drivers entering Rwanda from Congo: INVESTMENT YES. CORRUPTION NO. I thought perhaps a similar sign should be posted for visitors at Kigali's international airport and along the main tourist routes: *Investment yes, handouts no.*

Jean-Claude gestured with his chin to a packed-clay road that disappeared into an overgrowth of banana leaves. "My village is that way, on that road."

Kabarondo had been the nearest shopping area to Rundu, so Jean-Claude had come here often, walking for hours to escape the bucolic boredom of village life.

He laughed. "It was worth it. Kabarondo was like Paris to me."

Jean-Claude returned the pump to its cradle, stood for a moment looking down the road he had walked as a boy. Had he pointed the truck west, we would have reached his childhood village in about twenty minutes. Instead he turned east, and we drove toward Akagera National Park, picking up speed on every hillock, every turn. I noticed Jean-Claude looking in the rear-view mirror again, as though we were being followed. But when I turned around, all I saw was our own rolling cloud of dust pulled behind.

I'd been looking forward to the savannah, picturing broad plains and open vistas, but we were hemmed in by thornbush thickets and barbed scrub verges on either side as we rolled down a road that bobbed and weaved. It was as constricting as the banana plantations we'd driven through earlier, and I realized what I had found so disorienting about this whole journey: the lack of a discernible horizon.

The long-distance road trips of my youth had been in North America, and you can't spend three weeks there without eventually ending up on an open landscape, driving toward the vanishing point of a highway. It's inevitable. In South America, I'd ridden in drunkenly top-heavy buses along the Amazon watershed; in Japan, I'd hopscotched across the country's island archipelago by ferry and by thumb; in Ireland, I'd bloody well walked (not recommended); and in Europe I'd taken trains and trams and prams and lorries and lollies, or whatever the hell they call them over there. But this was the first long-haul, endless-hours-on-an-open-road trek I'd taken outside of North America, and it was strange never having a long ribbon of highway to look down. Even here in the savannah the landscape was near at hand, shouldering us in, funnelling us through; the route was forever dropping behind hillocks of tussocky grass and then popping up again. Rwanda was all curve and corner, swerve and slide, with sudden heart-catching panoramas revealed on a magician's flourish. In Rwanda, even the plains are hilly. In Rwanda, there is no vanishing point.

We passed through the derelict shell of a mining town, a tin-ore boomtown gone bust, with buildings broken-backed and falling down. Mud-walled homes were scattered among this dereliction of warehouses and factories, and a congregation of children had gathered around the communal trickle of a water pump, were slowly filling jerry cans and plastic pails for the day's cooking.

Red-earth roads, and red-clay homes. A haze of dust. It was a landscape you breathed in unaware; at the end of the day, I would find reddish mud gummed on the corner of my mouth, the rim of my nostrils. The deep blues and luminescent greens of the forest and field were gone and in their stead, earthen tones: tawny yellows, burnt-orange browns, and a red deeper than rust. It could easily have been the clay from which God had fashioned Adam.

When we saw a lone banana seller pushing his green-laden bicycle up a hill, Jean-Claude pulled to the side of the road. We came to a rolling stop and watched as the man plodded toward us.

"Those are cooking bananas," Jean-Claude whispered. "Very, very delicious. Much better than those we get in Kigali. The soil is better for bananas out here. The price is much cheaper too. Now, because of my accent, he will know I am from Kigali and he will certainly raise his price, but it will still be much less than what we pay in the city. I will run over and buy some of his bananas, bring them back to Kigali as a present for Christine's mom. So get down quickly, hide before he— Too late! He saw you."

Turns out there was the Kigali price and then there was the muzungu price. Jean-Claude sighed. He waved to the man and then crossed the road toward him as though only vaguely interested, made a casual offer on two bundles. But with the banana seller having spotted me in the vehicle, the price jumped by 600 percent.

Jean-Claude stood his ground, demanding a mere 400 percent markup instead. Our purveyor of plantains took this as a personal affront. He shook his head woefully, wiped his face with a hand towel, fought back tears, and after great deliberation, said the best he could agree to was a mere 399 percent markup—and clearly he would be losing money on the deal, but as it was late in the day he was willing to do this even if it meant his children would go hungry. Why, he would practically be giving the bananas away! But Jean-Claude replied no, no, no, this would not do, for there were surely other banana peddlers along this road who would be more than happy to part with their wares, and here we were, willing to relieve this fellow of the burden of his bananas at the end of the day. We were doing him a favour!

While the two of them haggled and sparred, I got out and per-formed one of those stiff, poorly executed shoulder-turning stretches middle-aged people do in the mistaken belief that this somehow "limbers us up." It was a dust-choked road we were travelling down, and my teeth had a texture to them. My hair was gritted with coarse powder; rubbing it free was like raking sand from your scalp after a day on the beach.

Jean-Claude had now made his absolute final offer. The third so far, by my count.

A clutch of clay homes huddled nearby, doorways and windows leaking smoke. Several of the residents had come out to watch, entertained as much by my presence as by the increasingly intricate debate underway between Jean-Claude and our stubbornly resistant banana seller.

A pair of boys watching from the sidelines pushed each other forward, smiled when I said *"Amakuru?"* ("How are you?") They scrambled off in what I thought was a case of the giggling jitters, but soon reappeared carrying model homes they'd constructed out of—I checked with Jean-Claude, interrupting the arcane minutiae of his banana valuations to ask—dried sorghum stalks, a plant similar in texture to sugar cane.

The boys held their creations up for me to see, went solemnly quiet when I took their photo, beamed when I congratulated them on their handiwork.

"Are they trying to sell these to me?" I asked, calling out again to Jean-Claude, who was now entering the final stages of what was apparently a multilateral trade deal.

"What? No. They just want to show them to you."

For one surging moment, I wanted to pull out my wallet and purchase their sorghum-stalk homes, wanted to take them back to Canada as a gift for my own two boys. I thought what a marvellous connective line that would draw across an ocean and between two worlds. I would offer the boys five dollars each, a huge sum for a kid. Their models would make a wonderful memento, and I was sure the two boys would be thrilled. But I couldn't do it. I couldn't because if I did, they would surely waylay the next muzungus they saw and try to sell them small homes as well. They would, I imagined, start to manufacture these models not for fun but for sale—built specifically for passing muzungus. This was the road to Akagera National Park, after all. Tourist convoys rumbled through here all the time. Perhaps these two young boys would set up a roadside stall, try their best to flag down vehicles. Perhaps a small cottage industry would take root, prove semi-lucrative. Or perhaps no one would stop. Perhaps these boys would build their sorghum-stalk homes for nothing, would sit by the road watching

Land Cruisers roll past as they waited in vain for wealthy whites to alight.

Whether my actions would foster a local craft or taint their boyhoods with a sense that life was a mere lottery, I couldn't say. But I did know that if I offered to buy their hobby-work it would change things—maybe for the better, but I couldn't be sure, and I couldn't take that chance. All I could do was hope that somehow, through their pride in this work and the words of encouragement from a passing stranger, the seeds of a future architect, a future builder, might be nurtured. Wishful thinking on my part, perhaps. But since coming to this country, I'd met future chemists in refugee camps, future engineers on dusty soccer pitches. This was Rwanda. Anything was possible: the very worst things you could imagine and the very best.

As these thoughts rattled around in my brain, a bent-backed elderly lady with a walking stick appeared, shuffling slowly toward us. She wore a wraparound skirt, the fabric threadbare and long faded by sunlight and time, reds and purples now pastel pink and pale blue. She had rheumy eyes, and her face was as crumpled as gift-wrap. When she saw me she smiled—smiled as though she'd been expecting me all along. She offered a greeting in Kinyarwanda, chortled at my reply. (There was something about the way I pronounced *"Nimeza"*—"I'm fine"—that caused no end of amusement among Rwandans.) Then, having taken an interest in the ongoing trade negotiations between Jean-Claude and our bicycled banana vendor, she made a loud snorting noise, part protest, part disbelief.

And that's when the balance of power shifted decidedly in Jean-Claude's favour.

The old lady was appalled at the price the man was trying to wheedle out of us. Why, that was many times more than what you would pay at the market! She scolded the man for being so greedy. He, in turn, suggested—politely and with all due respect—that she piss off. But the old lady was adamant. Charging visitors that much for bananas! It was unconscionable!

Jean-Claude had wisely stepped back to let her do the negotiations for him, giving me a running update on her progress. Before we knew it, the price was plummeting. The lady had pointed with her walking stick to the next farm, where she would guarantee a better price, and with that, it was all over.

The man, outplayed and outflanked, settled on a much, much lower price—though still far too high for the old lady's liking, and she continued to scold the seller even as Jean-Claude counted out the money for the bananas. She then wished us well and toddled off, but Jean-Claude ran after her to say thank you—and to pay her a small commission. Just a few hundred francs, but she refused. He insisted. She laughed and kept walking, but Jean-Claude was adamant, saying he would be very sad if she didn't take it. So she did, clasping his hand in hers and laughing, saying she was happy to still be useful and telling Jean-Claude to be more wise in the future. He said he would try. She waved away my camera, saying she was too old to be photographed, and then hobbled away, chuckling to herself as she went.

The banana seller watched her depart with a cold look—he didn't find the old doll quite as endearing as we did—and then untied two large bundles from his bicycle and loaded them into the back of our amazing! ever-expanding! Land Cruiser (it really is astounding how much you can stuff into the back of one of those). He allowed me a single photograph and then, with a nod and a sigh, he too was on his way, pushing a much lighter load uphill with a heavy step.

There may have been a Kigali price, and there may have been a muzungu price, but as we'd learned, nothing beats a bent-backed lady with a wagging finger.

# 62

THE TOURIST LODGE IN AKAGERA NATIONAL PARK was a rambling collection of corridors and hallways with angles that didn't add up. Set amid the scrub brush above Lake Ihema, it had the air of a duchess who'd lost everything yet insisted on dressing up in satin gowns and pearls for dinner. At $100 a night, it was overpriced by approximately $98. Still, I liked it. There was an amiable feel to the place, with its open verandas and bug-speckled swimming pools, its unkempt gardens and airy grounds. More to the point, it was the only option available. The only one that included indoor plumbing, anyway. There was one other spot: a campsite where one could bed down in open bush for half the price and twice the inconvenience. But Jean-Claude had earlier put the kibosh on any notion that we might go camping at any point in our trip. That was one of his preconditions for coming to Rwanda with me: no camping.

"This is something refugees will never understand," he'd said. "Why Canadians love to camp so much." It was a concept he had struggled to explain to the immigrant parents he worked with at Soccer Without Boundaries. "We tried to organize a camping trip for the families one time. And when I explained it to the Somalian and Ethiopian parents, the ones from Sudan or Afghanistan, they couldn't believe it! They said, 'You want us to sleep outside in little tents with no electricity or running water, cooking on a fire? Are you crazy? That's what we left behind in the refugee camps! Why would we want to do that here?'"

So the tourist lodge it was. We'd arrived in early evening, making it through the park's southern gate just before it closed as a bored-looking guard waved us through. With our 4x4 loaded with bananas, I'd half-expected to gather a following en route, to arrive at the lodge in grand style, a Pied Piper of primates, leading a victory procession of monkeys behind us, but no. The only cousins there to greet us were a mangy clan of olive baboons slouching about like the dissolute pickpockets they were. "Windows up," Jean-Claude advised. These baboons were of the grab-and-dash variety, and warnings had been posted. Olive baboons: the Artful Dodgers of the animal kingdom.

We checked in at the front desk. Night was falling, and as Jean-Claude went in search of passion fruit, I wandered down a series of hallways, key in hand, until I eventually stumbled upon my room. It was very dark inside, with blackout curtains drawn as tightly as a state secret. The light switch by the door was, apparently, of a migratory nature, playfully moving up and down, then sideways, depending on where I was slapping my hapless hand at the time. In the end, I groped my way across the room mainly by echolocation, stubbing a toe here, a finger there, using the reverberations of my elaborate invective to chart further obstacles until I bobbled head-long into a dangling cord—which, to go from the shriek I emitted, I initially mistook for some sort of rafter snake.[29] Realizing my mistake, I gave the cord a tentative tug and flooded the room with the crackle and buzz of fluorescent tubes warming up ... slowly. Flickering details emerged. Clearly, I was standing in some sort of antechamber or walk-in closet. This shoebox adorned with a pair of sagging cots couldn't possibly constitute my actual room.

Oh, wait. It *was* my room.

No matter. Time for a bath. I wanted to wash the dust from my face, the road from my scalp. I wanted to soak the stiffness from my back, the weary from my bones. But the faucet in my attractively rust-stained tub was more audible than aquatic, releasing a series of wheezy gurgles as it sputtered out a few slugs of brownish-green water. Ah well, I could skip the bath. I strode across the room and flung open the curtains with a lavish gesture (the lavish flinging of curtains being a forte of mine) and was faced with a jarring spidercrack of glass, fissures radiating across the window from a single violent point of impact. I examined the glass with a

---

29. If there's such a thing as a "hawk-eagle," I'm sure there's space in the menagerie for "rafter snakes" too.

Columbo-like determination but was unable to decide whether the crack had come from something outside trying to get in or—worse, to my mind—something inside trying to get out.

I schlepped my bags back to the front desk, arranged for another room, and then tramped down another meandering hallway. Inside my new room, I groped my way again to another slow flood of fluorescent light. Faced with a slightly less brown gurgle of water and no evidence of violent flight, I decided this room would have to do.

Flopping backward onto one of the cots (I almost bounced over onto the other one), I lay awhile, staring up at the rafters. No large snakes were dangling above me, true, but I could easily imagine spiders rappelling down from the ceiling beams during the night like Tom Cruise in, oh, name a Tom Cruise movie; he usually rappels at some point. I was too tired to care, although I did make a mental note not to sleep with my mouth open. When Jean-Claude and I had charted our course over an opened map on a kitchen table back home, with me jotting down the words "safari lodge," I'd pictured myself stretched out beneath the lazy breeze of a ceiling fan like a Persian king recumbent. Instead, I found myself lying pallid under the incessant buzz and excessive clarity of fluorescent tubes. The mosquito mesh, when I finally succeeded in unknotting it, dropped down like a tattered fishing net from days of yore. There was nothing even remotely "Southern belle" about it. There were gaping holes so big they wouldn't have kept out bats, let alone mosquitoes.

Sigh.

Clearly, I wasn't going to be presented with trays of glacier-chilled strawberries and festively arranged slices of papaya at *this* lodge. In light of these more rustic environs, I eschewed my smoking jacket and ascot, and dressed for dinner instead in a slightly less aromatic T-shirt than the one I had been wearing. (There was a bundle of freshly washed shirts sitting crisply on the bedside table of my room back in Kigali. I had, of course, forgotten to pack them—much to Jean-Claude's chagrin.)

Keenly aware that we were now deep in malaria country, and faced with such a capaciously aerated mosquito net, I doused myself with DDT and PCB and DEET and XYZ, then strolled out in search of sustenance.[30]

It was a calming night. The air was cool and fragrant with a scent reminiscent of lilacs, underlain with just a hint of DEET and—*sniff, sniff*—a touch of baboon feces. I cut across a leafy courtyard, feeling light-chested and content. A flap of wings. The dry-husk rattle of insects, unseen. Something large and clumsy was floundering about in the underbrush, and a waning moon, tangled in the branches overhead, cast a forty-watt light on the matter. Life was good.

Going for a stroll is always about embracing serendipity, so imagine my delight on finding myself right back in front of the door to my room. Dammit. How one goes about getting lost in a lodge with only two hallways, let alone completing a perfectly executed circular route, is best left for a later date. Instead, noting a shallow cement trench that ran along the perimeter of the hotel and recalling, with an observational prowess worthy of a Livingstone heir, that this same trough ran past the lodge's front entrance and restaurant patio, I followed it through the grass with unerring instinct, around to the main building. I'd done my forebear proud! (I later learned that this was a *snake-catching* trench I'd been traipsing along, one that encircled the hotel grounds to keep black mambas and other mood spoilers from coiling through the corridors.)

Fortunately, no serpents had fallen into the trough that night, and I arrived at the dining hall unpunctured and unperturbed, only to find Jean-Claude digging into his fourth plate of passion fruit. He was starting with dessert, apparently.

This being a tourist lodge, the buffet was of the proper Western-style, all-you-can-eat variety, and we worked our way through several

---

30. I may have gone a bit overboard with the DEET; everything I ate that night tasted like insect repellent.

stacks of brochettes and roasted bananas, stewed plantains and ugali dumplings.

Over dinner, Jean-Claude came up with a way for us to get rich. It involved passion fruit.

"I have been thinking," he said. "We could sell Rwandan passion fruit in Canada for less than what they charge at Safeway—and we would still make a profit. And it's better fruit! Much tastier, much juicer. People will line up to buy them!"

Better in every way, I agreed. "Only problem," I pointed out, "is that I'm pretty sure you're not allowed to import tropical fruit into Canada."

"Yes, but the seeds?" He smiled.

"Well, you'd have to smuggle them in."

"Exactly. So here is what we do. The day before we fly out, we fill up our stomachs with passion fruit. We eat and eat as much passion fruit as we can, and then"—his smile became a grin, grew wider, took on a positively demonic glint—"when we get home, *we wait* ... Soon we will have all the seeds we need. We just have to clean them off and plant them. Trust me, if we grow Rwandan passion fruit in Canada, we will make a lot of money! A lot!"

Much like belling the cat, it had to be asked: "And who exactly is going to, ah, clean this bounty of ours?"

"Alister and David!" he said, naming my youngest and his oldest. "We'll pay them!"

Oh, I'm sure they'd love that. *C'mere, son, I have a job for you.*

Funny thing is, I think Jean-Claude was only half-joking about having us smuggle a trove of seeds out of the country in our lower colons. He was already mourning our return to the land of the fibrous papaya and the shrivelled four-dollar passion fruit; you could see it in the wistful way he scooped out the pulp of just one more, the way he sadly spooned it into his mouth.

# 63

THE AKAGERA LODGE, as noted, was located on a rise of hill above Lake Ihema. These were the same shores Stanley had once tried to cross into the Kingdom of Rwanda, only to be met with a less than enthusiastic welcome. By which I mean, "arrows."

In the early morning, I went for a long walk through the hotel grounds, passing several buildings in a state of ... ruin? Repair? Renovation? Demolition? It was hard to say. The bamboo scaffolding looked as though it had been standing for some time; several poles had sprouted leaves.

Birdsong matinals filled the treetops like the first morning of creation. There are more than 500 species of birds in Akagera National Park, and every one of them seemed to be out in force that day.

Low above the lake, the sun hung like a swollen orange.

Time to pull on the ol' pith helmet (figuratively speaking, of course; I don't think they even make pith helmets anymore) and stride forth once more into adventure, although admittedly, when there is a lunch box with an apple and a sandwich waiting for you at the front desk, it does take the edge off one's impending exploits.

Rwanda is not considered a prime safari destination, certainly not on par with Botswana or Kenya, say. Of the Big Five safari animals—elephant, lion, leopard, rhino, and African buffalo— Akagera is understocked in one (only a handful of leopards haunt the park) and clean out of two: the aforementioned lions of Jean-Claude's youth and the black rhino, once plentiful but wiped out by poachers in the early 1980s. True, Akagera does feature an abundance of sproingy deer-like creatures and flurries of birds, but no lions and no rhinos.

In reference to her country's penchant for branding itself as a "boutique tourist destination," Rica Rwigamba at the RDB office in Kigali had joked that Akagera offered "boutique safaris" as well.

Which is to say, a "boutique" population of elephants, along with some "boutique" giraffes imported from Kenya. Given Akagera's lack of large predators, zebras and antelopes were thriving, and the park boasted a lakeshore known as Hippo Beach, but the sexier big cats were either rarely spotted or nonexistent. This was going to change, though, as the park's success in introducing Masai giraffes had sparked plans to reintroduce lions as well. (No word on how the zebras or antelope felt about this, or whether they were even consulted. I imagine the first zebra to be taken down by a lion in Akagera will die with a perplexed look on its face.)

In the final years of the Habyarimana regime, the park had reverted to anarchy, with poachers killing elephants for their tusks, rhinoceroses for their horns, and the few remaining lions just for the sport of it. (By that point most of the lions had already been killed off by cattle herders, who regularly planted meat laced with poison in their pastures.) The larger animals fled into neighbouring Tanzania during the turmoil, but were now returning, and their numbers were growing every year: a distinct diaspora of its own, coming home.

Poaching remains a problem. Akagera National Park lies along Rwanda's eastern border, which forms a maze of inaccessible wetlands and marshes, but the western side opens directly onto farmland and pastures. Following the genocide, the area allocated to the park was greatly reduced to make room for returning refugees, but it's still an impressive swath of protected wilderness. An electrified fence runs down the western length of the park now, mainly to keep the animals in. Harder is keeping the poachers out. More than 2,000 snares had been gathered in the previous year alone.

Jean-Claude and I drove down to the park's interpretive centre, where it was recommended that we hire a guide, which we did. The Akagera bush is interlaced with trails, and the animals could be hard to find, although the staff had provided us with an admirably optimistic checklist of wildlife to tick off as we went (leopards, spotted hyenas, elephants, unicorns, leprechauns, etc.). I was keen to see an elephant up close; I was tired of being teased with tantalizing glimpses of dung. Several elephants had been spotted roaming nearby, among them—pause here for dramatic effect—a rogue pachyderm by the name of Mutware.[31]

Strange thing was, Jean-Claude knew Mutware, had met him on a family trip years before.

Mutware was the most famous elephant in Rwanda. Airlifted into Akagera National Park as a baby in 1975, he quickly asserted himself among the other young ones.

"His name means 'boss,'" Jean-Claude explained. "The park rangers called him that because even as a baby he was bossy." As Mutware got older, his attitude only got worse. As with many of us, his teen years were particularly disruptive.

"He would chase vehicles and smash things for no reason, and he would even steal beer from trucks and drink it."

"Really?"

"Really. Elephants can curl their trunks, pick things up. Mutware would grab plastic jugs of banana beer and squeeze until the tops popped off, and then he would drink it. He liked beer too much."

My kind of elephant.

"When I lived in the village, my brother took me on a drive through the park and we ran into Mutware, with his ears out. This was very scary, because we knew Mutware was angry. He was always angry."

Nor had Mutware mellowed with age. Just a few weeks before we arrived, he'd rolled a vehicle into Lake Ihema as the passengers scrambled for cover. During the genocide, the park staff explained, members of the militia had gone hunting in Akagera, driving around in a jeep and whooping it up. When they came upon Mutware, one of them fired off a round, hitting the elephant's flank. Mutware fled, wounded, into the bush, where he nursed a grudge—*for nineteen years*. As people who work with these creatures will tell you, the long

---

31. Let's skip ahead, shall we, and end the suspense. Our final tally for the day was leopards: zero; spotted hyenas: zero; elephants: zero—dung notwithstanding; unicorns and leprechauns: ditto—though minus the dung, of course.

memory of elephants is in no way apocryphal, and when the man who'd shot Mutware showed up on a retirees' tour to visit his old hunting grounds, Mutware recognized him. Trumpeting wildly, the elephant charged, sending the driver and passengers running as the animal pushed their vehicle end over end into the croc-infested waters of Lake Ihema. Crazed elephant on one side, crocodile eyes on the other: How fast do you figure those tourists ran? Fortunately, no one was injured, and Mutware, having made his point, padded silently back into the bush. The retired military man left the park that same day.

"They were driving a Land Cruiser," the staff said pleasantly. "Same as you."

The story of Mutware's nineteen-year-long grudge smacked of urban legend to me, but it certainly was in keeping with Mutware's famed temper. Tuskless and weighing in at six tons, he was only a mid-sized male, but his fearsome reputation had accorded him a greater stature. The park staff was genuinely afraid of him, and warnings were posted everywhere. Nor was he predictable in his travels. Our Mutware was a ramblin' man; he roamed far and wide across the park and was a good swimmer, too.

"He swims across sometimes," the staff told me. "To Tanzania." When he was away everyone relaxed a little.

Mutware was given to radical mood swings as well. He would pose for photos with tourists, even be considered "semi-habituated," but then during the period of *musth,* when the sides of his head throbbed and his testosterone levels spiked, he would go on a rampage. In 2006, he escaped the park entirely, trampling nearby fields and terrifying villagers. The year before that, after a musth-enraged Mutware wrecked several vehicles in the park, the American embassy issued a travel alert, making Mutware the only single animal to have triggered a security warning from the U.S. government.

"Most elephants live to be about seventy. And Mutware is in his forties," Jean-Claude explained. "So he is having his mid-life crisis."

The younger females no longer wanted to mate with him, and short of buying an expensive sports car, donning shades, and getting a comb-over, Mutware was not handling it well. He'd been spotted just a few hundred metres from the main office, so I was happy to have our guide steer us clear.

Marcel was a trim, impeccably uniformed young man. He offered to drive, was gently rebuffed by Jean-Claude, and, with a shrug, had crawled into the back of our vehicle. He gave us a concerned look on seeing the mountain of bananas that filled the back.

"You know that you can't feed the animals, yes?" he asked.

I turned around and looked at him with a hurt expression. "But everybody loves bananas," I said. "Elephants. Antelopes. Hippos. Buffaloes. Baboons. Zebras. I was told that they all liked bananas."

Horrified at the prospect of us toddling around Akagera National Park flinging bananas out the window in the manner of Luigi in a round of Mario Kart, he protested, "No, no, no, visitors are not permitted to—"

At which point Jean-Claude cut in to explain that the bananas were for his mother-in-law back in Kigali, not the local wildlife, and that I was only "joking."

Marcel nodded slowly, eyed me with an understandable caution. *Ah yes, muzungu humour.*

I grinned back at him. "Everybody loves bananas!" I said.

He was having his doubts about me, you could tell.

A farrago of vehicles and visitors had gathered at the interpretive centre, including a family from Kigali crammed into a single hatchback; a sunburned South African couple in a jeep; a spacious safari-style vehicle with seats lined up on either side, as though the guests were riding an elephant; plus—this is true—a minivan full of nuns. Many of the visitors to Akagera that day were Rwandese, which was always nice to see.

We set off in a ragged line, vehicles fanning out along various routes depending on the interests and inclination of the guides. With Jean-Claude at the wheel, we headed for Lake Ihema. The road was cratered with potholes, and as we rocked back and forth across them in low gear it felt as though we were riding an elephant, too.

"Mutware," the guide said, pointing to a bend in the bush.

He was referring to fistfuls of grassy dung rather than the actual elephant.

"Nearby?" I asked.

Marcel nodded.

As we came over a rise in the road, Lake Ihema opened up in front of us. A wind wrinkled the surface of the water and a clamour of birds lifted off, wings winnowing the air. Jean-Claude brought us to a stop beside Ihema's reedy shores, where we got out to admire the view.

Several gazebos stood back from the water, for picnics and rainy day rest stops, I imagined, and we saw further evidence of Mutware's presence: one of the pavilions had been attacked, its metal roof peeled back like the top of a tin can.

"He is in the rutting season," Marcel explained. "He tried to mate with the females but they chased him off, so he became very angry and he smashed this building."

Not popular with the ladies, our Mutware.

"So," I said. "He's like a guy, goes to a bar, tries to make a move on a girl, gets rejected, and then beats up a phone booth on the way home."

"Yes," said Marcel. "It is exactly like that! I will use that example next time. Mutware will be in a very bad mood, so we must be careful." He looked over his shoulder. "Sometimes he comes here to drink water."

Like an idiot, I was secretly hoping to run into Akagera's famous elephant, maybe have him push our vehicle into the lake as well, just for the conversational trove that would provide later. *"Say, chaps, I ever tell you about the time ..."* Not sure how the vehicle insurance would cover it, though I'm fairly sure elephants are considered Acts of God.

But as I was about to learn, there were other perils nearer by that day. I had wanted to get closer to the lake, but the shore was squelchy so I was standing on an upjut of rock instead. A large monitor lizard was digging up eggs from a hollowed-out pit nearby, its tail whipping back and forth in excitement. When I stepped closer, the lizard scrambled away, a fluid ripple disappearing into the grass.

"What kind of eggs are those?" I asked, thinking they seemed awfully large for a heron or a flamingo.

"Crocodile."

I froze, felt ice forming in my arteries.

Marcel pointed toward the lake and there, floating offshore, was an armoured log—with eyes.

"Maybe we should get back a little?" Marcel suggested.

I heartily agreed.

As soon as we moved, the crocodile dropped below the surface.

"Oh no," I said. "We scared him off."

"No, not scared," said Marcel. "Waiting. Just there. See?"

I looked again, saw a log drifting slowly toward the shore ...

Back in the Land Cruiser, panting, out of breath, pulse throbbing in our ears, we congratulated ourselves on not getting eaten. I reconsidered my earlier desire to be playfully rolled into the lake by Mutware. If nothing else, I'd gained an instant respect for monitor lizards: imagine the type of chutzpah it takes to steal eggs from a crocodile. And these weren't your run-of-the-mill crocodiles, either. These were Nile crocodiles, among the largest of their species.

"Lake Ihema is very peaceful now, and the crocodiles here can live to be one hundred," Marcel said. "So they are able to grow very, very big."

Jean-Claude told me there was a legend among the local people that if a crocodile licks your shadow, it can pull you under. I could see several dugout canoes lined up along the shore. Hard to imagine, but Ihema was a working lake with fishermen who regularly paddled out onto these waters to bring in catfish and tilapia.

"Even with crocodiles nearby?" I asked Marcel.

"Yes, even with the crocodile. They do die sometimes, the fishermen. It happens, some accidents. But there are also hippos in Lake

Ihema, and those are much worse for boats. With crocodiles, we just make sure not to fall into the water. But a hippo will charge you, a hippo will tip boats over and attack you. Hippos kill many more people than crocodiles. Very dangerous animals." Then, with a smile: "Shall we go to see the hippos next?"

# 64

FROM LAKE IHEMA, the road wound through a sea of tall grass that moved on the wind. It had the same sun-golden hue as a lioness's hide, which was surely no coincidence.

"This area, it is very much a lion's habitat," Marcel said.

Flat-crowned acacia thorn trees opened up like umbrellas above the heat, creating pockets of perfect shade for future prides to lie beneath, panting and waiting. But the lions were nowhere to be seen, and their absence resonated.

We came upon a magnificent waterbuck, head held high like a stag on royal heraldry as we passed. It is one of the largest and certainly most impressive of the Akagera antelopes. The smallest, a tiny fawnlike creature called the oribi, appeared out of the grass as well, tiptoeing daintily over the road in front of us. It was followed by a slew of impalas who herded themselves across in such numbers that they brought our vehicle to a halt. Ever observant, I wrote in my journal: *Lots of impalas.* I thought a moment, then underlined "lots" forcefully. I also ticked *impala, oribi,* and *waterbuck* off my list.

Apparently this was some sort of impala crosswalk, because they cantered by with a confidence that comes from having the right of way, wholly unconcerned about our idling 4x4. They were looking awfully relaxed, these impalas, and who could blame them? With no lions slinking about, there was no need for them to remain spring-loaded, ready to bolt at the first hint of susurrations in the grass.[32]

As the Land Cruiser rolled north over rutted trails, the open savannah was swallowed up again by thickets of thornbush wilderness. When we came around a bend in the bush, a man with a rifle lunged out at us. He was a twitchy-looking fellow in a stained undershirt, and he signalled for Jean-Claude to pull over and roll down the window. Ambush? Poacher? No. There was a road crew farther ahead, Jean-Claude explained, and this poor soul had been posted to keep watch for Mutware, armed only with a single-bolt rifle—something that would surely have just pissed the animal off had he actually fired on him. (And given Mutware's long memory, if the man did shoot Mutware, he'd probably have to leave Akagera for good and change his name and assume a new identity, all the while waiting in fear for that fateful knock on the door. *"Hello there. Remember me?"*)

"Did you see him?" the man asked. "Mutware? Was he on the road? Did you pass him?"

The man's face was beaded with sweat, and I didn't think it was entirely from the heat. When we told him we hadn't crossed paths with the elephant, only his dung, our reluctant sentry stepped back, staring down the road again as we passed.

"Mutware can be hard on the road crews," Marcel told us. "During the last rainy season, he got in a shoving match with one of the graders."

"And?" Jean-Claude asked.

"The grader lost."

I asked Marcel what was the biggest danger tourists faced in Akagera National Park. I expected him to say black mambas or pythons (the park has both). His answer surprised me.

"Buffaloes," he said. "And if they are alone, it is even worse. A solitary buffalo can be very aggressive. They will charge vehicles for

---

32. Lions would return to Rwanda in July 2015, with a pride of seven sedated and then transported from South Africa, where they were released into the wild. I imagine the impalas of Akagera National Park will be a little more wary now.

no reason. We park rangers? We don't like buffaloes. They give us too many problems."

And sure enough, right on cue, we came around a corner to see a lone buffalo standing at the side of the road, glaring at us from under heavily curved horns. African buffaloes always look like they're on the brink of 'roid rage, with their thick brows and muscle-knotted shoulders.

Marcel grew tense. He leaned forward, whispered to Jean-Claude, "Don't slow down, but don't speed up. Go carefully, carefully … And if he charges, drive—drive very fast."

We rolled by, just metres away, with the brute scowling at us all the while. It was the tensest moment of our trip.

Jean-Claude was clutching the steering wheel tightly, foot nursing the accelerator. He may have been reconsidering his offer to drive. I know I was.

# 65

THERE ARE NO HIPPOS AT HIPPO BEACH.

The hippopotami of Akagera National Park, being of the free-range variety, had the inconsiderate habit of moving. But at one time, they'd stayed long enough on the southern shores of Lake Mihindi that a beach had been named in their honour, with maps duly updated and road signs posted, just to have the hippos—in what can only be considered an abject display of bad manners—decamp. Rather than chase them across the map, rechristening bodies of water every time the hippos moved on, Rwanda's cartographers decided to let the original name stand, although with more ironic overtones than intended.

"They should probably put quotes around 'Hippo,'" I said as we stood, looking out at the hippo-less waters of Hippo Beach.

Lake Mihindi forms a pool of reedy wetness in the dry scrublands of the savannah, with bright mossy greens near shore and feathery stands of papyrus islands floating farther out. Amid the growing heat of mid-morning, the waters of Mihindi beckoned to us, but latent dangers were lying in wait. On a marshy lump of land: the low waddle of a crocodile sliding into the water.

"They should probably put quotes around 'Beach' as well," I said after a moment.

I looked at my shadow, stretched by the sun, extending to the water's edge, thought about crocodiles licking at it, pulling me under, pulling me in …

As we drove along the marshy shores of the next lake, we startled one of Akagera's roving hippos—which in turn startled us; my heart pinged like an elevator at the sight of this overinflated creature running across our path. It hit the water like a ship being launched: a crash followed by silence. It had vanished as cleanly as a magic trick, disappearing into what looked like shallow waters. The waves it left spread outward, then settled, grew calm. And then, just as suddenly, the hippo resurfaced farther down with a loud *pfffft*. More hippos surfaced and more, an entire pod, and we watched them, spellbound: underwater blimps appearing and disappearing, as hypnotic as a lava lamp. One hippo would sink, another would rise. One would hiss, another would dive.

One of the larger hippos sported fresh wounds: strips of reddish pink, showing through his hide.

"Because of the crocodile," Marcel explained. "Hippos don't have good relations with them."

Crocodiles attack but rarely win, and isn't it funny how we always root for the mammal? Scaly, cold-blooded crocs vs. the soft and fleshy, all-too-human plumpness of the hippo: was there any doubt where our loyalties would lie?

"A hippo will stay and fight," Marcel said. "Every other animal runs away."

They like to wallow in swamp water, but hippos will roam far inland as well, as much as seven kilometres from the nearest marsh. Bumping into a hippo deep in the leonine grasslands must come as a shock.

"But it's mainly at night," Marcel explained. "When it's cooler out."

A family of warthogs trotted past next, chugging across the trail in front of us. How something that ugly manages to reproduce is a mystery; I suspect banana beer is involved. I'm guessing also that the lovemaking doesn't involve a lot of eye contact. Even the name, "warthog": are there any two uglier words in the English language you could put together? The papa was easy to spot because of his tusks, and he held his tufted tail up like a flag for the children to follow. I imagine the mama warthog justifies him to her friends over tea, saying, *"He's not much to look at, I know. But he's good with the kids."*

The warthog family disappeared one after another into the grass, until only the papa's tail could be seen bobbing above. And then, not even that.

Suddenly: zebras.

From Lake Mihindi, we were heading north between ecological zones: swamps on one side of the road, savannah on the other. The Mutumba Hills pushed in from the south; the Tanzanian Highlands rose in the east: sharp blue silhouettes in the shape of axe heads and anvils.

We had entered the vast bowl of the Kilala Plains, and mud-built termite mounds punctuated the emptiness, forming weirdly sculpted, Gaudí-like creations. Everything was sticky with sweat; I felt as though I were poaching from the inside out. Although set at a lower altitude than the rest of Rwanda, Akagera *feels* closer to the sun. It was a heat so heavy you could see it. The distant hills wavered and shimmered in a hazy mirage. Here was the savannah of my mind's eye. Here was what I had imagined all along. The endless sere grasslands, the vaulted skies, the drift of zebras across an open plain.

We had been distracted by dung (yet again!) and almost didn't see them approaching. Having pulled over beside a particularly fascinating mound of droppings, our guide was explaining the varieties one might encounter in Akagera. This inky-black pile was buffalo (hopefully long gone); hyena poop was crusted with white from the calcium in the bones they ate; the impalas' were rounded pellets; and the balled bundles of straw were, of course, elephant. And then, when we looked up, zebras were all around us: bar-code arrangements moving past, trotting round-bellied out of the grass, tails flicking, hooves kicking up dust.

Above us, birds of prey were tracing Olympic flags in a sky bleached of colour. Even with sunglasses on, I had to squint. Then, like a cool breeze, giraffes appeared, unhindered and unhurried. They loped past us on glided stride. Compared to the harrumphing of hippos or the Zoetrope trot of the zebras, the giraffes were positively liquid in their movements. It was striking, and instructive, how much sheer *space* animals in the wild require to feel at home.

Marcel tapped me on the shoulder, pointed to the horizon.

Cauliflower clouds were boiling up. We could hear thunder on the far side of somewhere, like the rumble of an empty stomach. We were now above Lake Rwanyakizinga, having crossed almost the entirety of Akagera National Park. Time to turn around.

We climbed into the Land Cruiser and began reeling ourselves back across the landscape. Birds swooped and whistled, lifting off above the lakes, leaving concentric circles in their wake. A heron hitched a ride on the back of a crocodile, as unperturbed as an empress atop a royal litter.

It was the end of the day, and a buttery sun was melting in the pan. But the warm glow didn't last. Dark clouds slowly sealed off the sky, lowering the ceiling. Loud bone-cracks of thunder. Sultry air, cool and muggy at the same time. A falling drizzle that hastened the arrival of evening, wipers smearing the dust.

Baboons had sought shelter under thorn-tree canopies, both from the coming downpour and, one supposes, the sheer weight of the sky. And then—bullets of rain hitting the windshield, the wipers flailing, the view in front of us liquefying. The road thickened into mud, and just as quickly the storm broke, lifting as surely as birds off a lake, leaving only bruised skies and wet grass behind. It had been a rainstorm almost without rain.

I'd enjoyed our sojourn in Akagera because Akagera had provided a reprieve. Here in the savannah was something older, something stronger, something beyond the purview of human history. But as evening settled upon us, the past reasserted itself. In Rwanda, it always does.

We had taken a short detour onto a bluff of land above Lake Ihema, where an abandoned manor house stood, catching the last light of day. Doors boarded. Windows as empty as eye sockets.

"President Habyarimana," Marcel said. "This was his summer house."

We got out, walked nearer. The manor overlooked a brackish bay. In the grass a sibilant snake appeared, sleek black, moving in mis-directions, tasting the air with its tongue. Or was it just the shadow of a snake? A thin question mark uncurling?

Habyarimana's summer home had once echoed with the laughter of cousins and cronies, with the clinking of glasses, the murmur of conclaves. This had been the holiday retreat of a president who, lifted on a rising tide of Hutu Power, would eventually be consumed by it. His death was the signal to unleash hell, and the 1994 genocide remains the Big Bang of Rwandan history, its effects always present, always evident—even here.

"Not too close to the lake," our guide advised. "Stay back, just in case."

We could discern no eyes in the water, but we knew there were crocodiles nearby, seldom seen but always present, lurking in the murky waters.

After we returned to the lodge, I lay sprawled under the lack-lustre breeze of a ceiling fan that not so much cooled the air as stirred it. I thought about a land so green, so brittle. That night I dreamed we were being chased by faceless people trying to kill us.

# 66

WHEN JEAN-CLAUDE MUNYEZAMU was fourteen years old, he got swept up in a failed coup d'état. Imprisoned and interrogated, he was threatened with torture at the hands of the Hutu regime, all because he knew how to drive a motorcycle. Jean-Claude told me this story—which he thought of as funny—during our long drive back to Kabarondo from Akagera National Park.

We'd woken to grey skies and damp toast, and a family of insufferably chirpy Americans at the next table. They'd been on the night tour of the park and, taking my wan smile as an invitation, set about regaling us with details of how they'd seen a leopard with its kill, hippos flouncing about in the open, elephants riding a unicycle, a zebra playing the banjo—that sort of thing. This did not surprise me in the least. I had long since come to accept, indeed embrace, the fact that I will always be on the Wrong Tour. You would do well, on seeing me at a muster point in an art gallery or before a nature walk, to head in exactly the opposite direction.

Even worse, this family had met the illustrious Mutware.

"He was blocking the road. He wouldn't let us pass, so finally our guide had to throw a papaya or something into the bush, and when Mutware went to investigate we beat it right past him. It was *so* exciting! Wasn't it, honey?"

Honey: "Yep."

Sigh.

As we dropped off our keys, I was disappointed to hear from the desk clerk that a full-scale renovation would soon be underway at Akagera lodge, to bring it up to a four-star standard.

"The next time you come, it will be completely redone," I was assured. "Like new!"

But I liked how it was now, cracked glass and all. I'd grown to appreciate its weathered charms, its old-sweater coziness, its bands of disreputable baboons hanging about the entranceways chewing toothpicks and keeping a sly sideward eye on the tourists. Even without the glacier-chilled strawberries, I enjoyed our time in the lodge, and felt sad at having to say goodbye.

We drove into a bleary-eyed dawn under dishwater skies. A damp day, but the sun soon baked away the wet, and with one last sighting of Mutware's mighty dung, we were gone. By the time we reached the lake, the clouds had thinned to near nothingness. Splinters of light on deep waters.

The road took us back over the same hills, past the same tin-ore mining town gone bust, the same clutch of homes where I'd met the children with their sorghum-stalk models. I looked for them as we passed, but they were nowhere to be seen.

"Did I ever tell you? The time I was almost executed? It was because I knew how to ride a motorcycle. Just for that!"

Those laps he'd taken around the soccer field had paid off. Jean-Claude became known in his neighbourhood as someone who could drive, which is when the military came calling. Or rather, when one particular officer came calling. A low-ranking NCO with a delicate problem.

"His name was Fabien Birori. He was a friend with one of my neighbours, and he was often having a beer with them. One day he was saying how he wanted to learn to drive a motorcycle. He couldn't even ride a bicycle! In Rwanda at that time, many kids, if they grew up poor, they never had a bicycle. This guy was from the south. Maybe it was a poor area, I don't know. But my neighbour, Vincent, he pointed to me and said, 'Jean-Claude knows how. He can teach you.'"

It was summer, and Jean-Claude was free from schoolwork, so the officer hired him. Feeling embarrassed, and not wanting the other officers to see, Birori would practise with Jean-Claude on a borrowed motorcycle along the side streets, far away from the barracks.

"Was a big motorcycle. Red. Very powerful. Yamaha DT-125, I think. The officer would be sitting in front, I would sit behind and hold the handlebars, and he would learn to pop the gears with his

foot. We went two times, three times, four times. Next day, he held
the handles, I worked the gears. Slowly, he got a sense of the balance,
how to drive it."

What Jean-Claude could not have known was that this officer was
part of a military clique planning to assassinate key members of Rwanda's
armed forces as part of a coup d'état against the Habyarimana regime.

"One day, Birori told me he was going to Belgium for military
training. When he came back, he was a sergeant. There was something different about him. You could see there was an optimism now.
When he left, he didn't have it. When he came back, he came with
optimism. And he promised me so much stuff! He said, 'I will get
you a proper driver's licence, you're gonna be my personal driver, I
will give you this and that.'"

But what Birori didn't realize was that he was being set up. The
coup was largely fictitious, staged mainly to remove a certain Air Force
commander, a colonel who had grown too close to the president for
the inner circle's liking. Habyarimana had been planning to make this
colonel his minister of defence, perhaps even vice-president. It would
prove to be a fatal offer.

"The colonel was already commander of the Rwandan Air Force,
and what happened was, Birori killed him."

The sergeant's role, Jean-Claude later learned, had been to assassinate the commander so that the co-conspirators could seize control
of the Kanombe military base and adjoining airport. They told him,
"You do that, we'll take care of the rest."

So Birori strode into the Air Force commander's office, shot
him point-blank, and ... nothing happened. Where were his
co-conspirators, the hue and cry of a revolution? Nothing. Just a
stunned secretary looking on in silence.

"What did he do?" I asked.

"He ran. He hijacked a motorcycle, then a car. They captured
him near his village. He was trying to get to his family home. They
arrested him, took him back to Kigali. He was beaten very badly."

And then came the crackdown. Any military personnel that the inner circle wanted to eliminate were quickly rounded up on the pretext of national security. Also caught in the dragnet was a confused young man who'd been labelled a "known associate" of the accused.

"I remember hearing that Colonel Mayuya had been assassinated, but I didn't think it had anything to do with me. Stanislas Mayuya, that was his name, the air commander that Birori killed. When my dad heard the news, I saw the fear in his eyes. He said, 'This is not good, Jean-Claude. When anything happens, the first thing they do is kill Tutsis. Anything at all, they kill the Tutsis.'"

Soon after, an unsmiling man in civilian clothes, an intelligence officer most likely, called out to Jean-Claude on the street.

"He knew my name. He said, 'Do you know this man Birori?' I said 'Sure, he's my friend.' I didn't know at that time it was Birori who had killed the Air Force commander. He asked, 'When did you see him last?' I said, 'Oh, it was on Saturday. I took him to the barracks on this motorcycle he rented for me.' I still didn't know I was in trouble. He said, 'Come with me. There is someone wants to talk to you.' So I got in his car. That's when I realized where we were going."

The presidential compound had a formidable reputation, and as they drove through the gates, Jean-Claude felt panic clawing its way up inside him. He turned around, saw the gates close behind them.

Inside the compound dwelled one of the most infamous torturers of the Habyarimana regime: a wheelchair-bound sadist named Pascal Simbikangwa. A distant cousin and close friend of the president, Simbikangwa had been made a high-ranking member of the Presidential Guards and head of the Rwandan Central Intelligence Agency. Paralyzed below the waist in an auto accident, he'd found other ways to spend his time, and when it came to interrogating prisoners, he was known to be a hands-on type of administrator. He enjoyed drawing out a person's final agonies.[33]

"I knew now where I was going, who I was going to see."

---

33. Arrested in France, Simbikangwa was eventually sentenced to twenty-five years for crimes committed during the genocide.

What Jean-Claude didn't know was why.

Armed men dragged him into a small room, dimly lit. Jean-Claude could hear screams coming from a holding cell somewhere in the bowels of the building. The handiwork of Pascal Simbikangwa, no doubt. Fortunately (for Jean-Claude, that is), so many people had been brought in during the sweep that the man in the wheelchair couldn't get to Jean-Claude right away.

"While we were waiting, they told me, 'Look, just confess, it will be easier. We know you spent time with Birori. We know you rode a motorcycle.' I was scared. I thought this was to do with not having a driver's licence. I was riding that motorcycle without a licence, you see, and I thought this is why I was arrested. I told them, 'But I was very careful! I didn't pass on the highway. I never went on the main roads. I only drove in the side streets.'"

His interrogators wanted to know about Birori, but again Jean-Claude thought this had to do with giving him driving lessons. "I said to this guy, 'I don't have a licence, is true, but I am a good driver. Ask anyone! I didn't know it was against the law.'"

The other man's gaze narrowed. He gestured to dark shapes dangling on hooks in the corner. "Do you know what those are?" he asked. "Those are the testicles of men who lied to me."

When Jean-Claude told me this, he laughed. "Probably it wasn't true. But I was terrified! I thought, 'Oh my goodness, they take traffic violations very seriously!' Of course, I was just a kid at that time. I didn't know anything."

Having spent the night in a dark cell, Jean-Claude was brought back for questioning the next day and the next, each time expecting to be greeted by Simbikangwa, his instruments laid out in front of him like a surgeon's tools, but no.

Sergeant Birori, meanwhile, had been "vigorously questioned," meaning "beaten until brain dead," and a supposed plot to topple the government had been thwarted.

"I was lucky to get out of that place in one piece," Jean-Claude assured me.

"And with testicles intact!" I said.

"Exactly. Usually when you go into the presidential compound, you don't come out again."

It was Jean-Claude's good fortune that a neighbour of his worked in the compound, and as Jean-Claude was being escorted across the grounds he spotted him, called out.

The neighbour came over. "Why are you in here?" he asked.

"I was driving a motorcycle without a licence," Jean-Claude replied.

By this point, it must have been clear that the gawky teenage boy had not been involved in any clandestine machinations, and the next day Jean-Claude was released into his neighbour's custody. He drove Jean-Claude home.

"That must have been a harrowing three days," I said.

"You know, I was so young, I don't think I realized how dangerous the situation was. My arrest was harder on my father than on me. He feared the worst."

The earthen roads of Akagera were rolling under us, and the highway was fast approaching. I didn't know how to broach the matter, but it needed to be asked.

"Um, you did get your driver's licence at some point though, right?"

Jean-Claude threw back his head and laughed, accelerator sinking ever deeper into the floorboards. The Land Cruiser picked up speed, dust and wind whipping through, and I laughed as well—though I couldn't help but notice he hadn't answered my question.

# 67

HERE WE WERE. Back again at the crossroads town of Kabarondo. We filled up our tank at the same gas station, saw the same sullen children hanging around looking for handouts. Again, had we headed west, we would have soon been in Jean-Claude's childhood village. Instead we turned south, heading for Rusumo Falls and the end of Rwanda.

For Jean-Claude, this was a haunted highway. It was the route he'd taken when he escaped. As we came to the town of Remera, Jean-Claude said, "I had a friend here. His father was a well-known photographer. Ran a photo studio."

"Want to look him up?" I asked, but even as the words were coming out of my mouth I knew the answer.

"He was killed in the genocide. His father, mother. Entire family was pretty much wiped out. I think one daughter survived and— I don't remember her name."

We drove down the main street of Remera, a broad boulevard lined with shops, pulled over, and found the photo studio his friend's father had once owned. It was run by a different photographer now, the front room lined with samples of his handiwork: soft-focus families with strained smiles, neckties and plaid vests on the boys, fanned skirts on the girls. You can see these same photos, with the same diffused lighting and awkwardly arranged poses, at any Sears photo studio back home. They even had the same blue-sky-with-clouds canvas backdrop behind them.

Jean-Claude hadn't been to Remera in twenty years—when he'd returned to Rwanda in '94, it was from the northeast, through Uganda—and the people he'd known here were gone. Gone, dead mostly. Sometimes, just gone. Moved, retired, married. Gone. He asked around at the studio and on the street but wasn't able to make any connections, find any links to his younger self. So we drove on.

Goats were on the road, and men were hacking out brush from among the banana trees. Women were hanging hand-wrung laundry on the hedges to dry.

"How does it feel?" I asked. "Driving this route, after so long?"

"My chest is a little tight," he admitted. "Every hilltop, I expect to see an interahamwe checkpoint. We are getting close to that place where—how would you say it?—that place where you can't change your mind, where you have no choice but to keep going."

"The point of no return?"

"Yes, that."

Kibungo Town (now known as Ngoma) was the last population centre of note before the border with Tanzania. After this intersection, there really was no turning back. From here, the road went only south. You had no alibi, no excuse if you were caught beyond Kibungo. After Kibungo, it was clear you were trying to escape, and young Tutsi males caught slipping away would have been assumed to be leaving to join the RPF.

"I felt I was going into a blank map," Jean-Claude said.

His father had passed away the year before. "He was, I think, eighty-two when he died, but it was still unexpected. He was always very healthy, my father. I never remember a time when he was sick."

The end, when it came, came quickly.

"He fell ill and went to a clinic. They transferred him to a big hospital, ran tests, and after one week, he died. He went into a coma and never came back. I still don't know what it was that killed him, what illness he had. Just—he was gone. In our house now it was just my brother Emmanuel and me. Was very quiet."

"If your father hadn't passed away when he did, would you have left Rwanda?"

"No, I would have stayed."

"And when the genocide began?"

"I would still have been there, taking care of him."

"So … you both would have died."

"Oh yes, I'm sure we would not have survived."

In a strange way, dying was the kindest thing Jean-Claude's father could have done for him. "It was for the best, then?"

Jean-Claude thought about this. "Maybe, but it didn't feel that way at the time."

In the end, it was the faded photograph of his brother Saïd, sent from Kenya, that would propel Jean-Claude onto a different path, one that ended not with machetes but marriage, not death but family, not a mass grave but a new life.

"You know, Kenya was like the China of Africa back then. Manufactured goods, clothes, mattresses, everything came through Kenya. It was why my brother was based there. Mombasa was a trade centre, and he was a truck driver. In his letter he said, 'Anything you need, let me know, I can send it. I'm living in the Jomvu district.' This letter, he had sent it many years before," Jean-Claude said. "But I still kept it. I still had it. No address, no telephone number, not even a street. Just this name: *Jomvu*."

That, and the photograph. It showed Saïd looking happy and relaxed, smiling at the camera, and in the background, slightly out of focus, was a sign that read THE ZAIRE BAR. A small clue, but a good one. Based on this single image, Jean-Claude Munyezamu set out across East Africa to track down his brother.

"The first truck driver I approached betrayed me. And he was our neighbour! We knew each other very well. I told him that I was going to Kenya and he said, 'Okay, I will drive you.' I told him it was just to visit my brother. I didn't say to anyone that I wasn't coming back. He said, 'Okay. I'm leaving tomorrow morning. I will take you.' But what he did was, he left that night and didn't tell me."

The next morning, Jean-Claude packed a small bag and went to the truck stop looking for his neighbour.

"But he was gone. Everybody saw me with this little suitcase. They said, 'What's going on?' When I told them what's happened, they said, 'That guy? He left last night.' I said, 'No, no, no. He's leaving today because he's gonna take me with him.'"

Jean-Claude was astonished at the betrayal, even now, after all these years.

"I didn't know what to do. I never thought he would lie to me, never. This guy was a born-again Christian! Another truck driver, he overheard what was going on, and he kind of laughed. He said, 'Oh, man. That guy is a born-again Christian and he left you?' I said, 'Yeah. That's weird, right?'"

The other driver said, "Come on. I'll take you."

His name was Hodali. As they climbed into his cab, he turned to Jean-Claude and said, "From now on, when we come to a roadblock, anyone asks, you're my employee, okay?"

There was someone else in the truck as well: the driver's turn boy. In Africa, there are always at least two people in a truck: the driver and his assistant, a turn boy who helps the driver back up, fit in, squeeze by. Hodali's turn boy was an older man who had a well-stamped passport if anyone asked for it. So they decided they would tell people the older man was another driver, catching a ride to a rig parked at Rusumo Falls. Jean-Claude would be the turn boy.

"When we got near the border, there was this guy, he was running a guest house. He was a friend of this truck driver, they had a kind of business they were doing. The truck driver would bring goods from Kenya, this guy would resell it. In Rwandan culture, it is always about relationships, and these two guys—this driver named Hodali and the owner of the guest house—they had a long relationship. So when Hodali asked him to help, he had to say yes. Even if he didn't want to, he had to say yes."

Jean-Claude stayed overnight at the owner's house. The owner had a young family, a wife, maybe three or four kids, and was risking a lot.

"They made a bed for me, and I slept very deep. And then about three in the morning, the owner, he woke me up. It was still very dark out. I think you know the African night now. It is very dark. We had a flashlight. My bag was still with the truck, and Hodali was still sleeping, so I was by myself. The guest-house owner had a bicycle and he said, 'We're gonna ride it to the border. You sit on the back. I will pedal. When we come to a roadblock, we will say that your truck is waiting at the border and I'm giving you a ride. If they ask you for ID, you say it is in the truck.' This guy, the owner of the guest house, he was a Hutu, and he had a thick northern accent. All the soldiers knew him. If they came to drink beer, they were coming to his guest house. Most of those soldiers, they were from northern Rwanda also, so they kind of had this brotherhood relationship. A Hutu with a northern accent? No one is going to expect he is helping a Tutsi."

"Do you remember his name? The owner of the guest house."

"They never told me. He was nervous. He said to Hodali, 'What you are making me do, if they find out they may kill me.' And now, it was just him and me. I got on the back of his bicycle and I held on. I just hoped that he wouldn't betray me."

"Did you run into any roadblocks?"

"Maybe three. These were twenty-four-hour roadblocks. At the first checkpoint, they said, 'Where are you going?' He said, 'Oh, I'm going to the border. I have this guy from my guest house, his truck is down there. He was back in Kigali to get some documents he needed to cross.' They said, 'Okay, go ahead.'"

"How long a bicycle ride was that?"

"Maybe half an hour. It was going downhill. We were coasting most of the way. I remember the air was cool."

"Why a bicycle, why not go in the truck?"

"This truck driver Hodali, he was Tutsi. It would be dangerous for him to cross the border with me. When they see his ID card says TUTSI, they might check more carefully. So after we passed through the last police roadblock on the bicycle, the guest-house owner took me to a different truck, very big, an eighteen-wheeler carrying maybe fifty tons of coffee. This other driver, he was a Hutu also, and he wasn't happy about having me. He was angry and didn't want anything to do with me. I think maybe they pressured him to take me. Probably he thought I was running away to join the RPF. The plan was, he would drive me across the bridge, and at the next parking area he would meet up with Hodali and I would change trucks. Then Hodali would take me the rest of the way to Mombasa. This other driver, he only had to get me across to the other side after the border opened."

"Could you trust him?"

"I didn't have a choice."

And so, after making sure no one was watching, they pulled open the tarp on the back of the truck and Jean-Claude climbed in.

"They told me, 'Go deep, into the middle. Make a hiding place.' These sacks were high on both sides. I was afraid they were going to fall on me. Each sack was fifty kilograms." He laughed. "At that time, I was weighing probably no more than that."

"It was still dark when you climbed in?"

"It was. And I waited forever for that truck to cross. I couldn't sleep. I could hear truck engines, people talking. Slowly, I could see light poking through the canvas sides, and I knew the sun was coming up. The heat was becoming stronger. Then the engine started and we began to roll forward."

There was one barrier left to cross.

"Just before the bridge, there was a kind of gate. I could feel the truck stop and I could hear the military say, 'Open the back!' The driver said, 'It was already checked. It's just finished to be checked.' But they said, 'Open it again.'"

"What would they have done?" I asked. "If they had found you."

"Oh, they would have killed me."

In Kirehe Town, the plantains had completely taken over, the wind-shredded leaves thick on either side, and I watched as the town appeared and disappeared, overgrown and ongoing, for miles.

Once we got past Kirehe, the topography changed dramatically. You could feel Tanzania coming to meet us, arid and open. The air grew drier. The greens grew thinner. Stubbled fields. The banners of opposition parties. The deep blue of the Tigo cell phone company. The sunflower yellows of MTN.

We passed a café called Taste of Success, and Jean-Claude suddenly pulled over to the side of the road. "This is the place," he said. "I remember it so much! The guest house was near here."

This was the road Jean-Claude had travelled down in the early hours en route to a rendezvous with a cargo of coffee beans. Nineteen years old on the back of a bicycle. Coasting to Tanzania.

# 68

WHEN JEAN-CLAUDE SLIPPED UNDER THE CANVAS and into the back of that truck at Rusumo Falls, he didn't know he was going to be trapped inside for ten hours.

"I didn't have any water or food. I hadn't even eaten breakfast before we left. So I was feeling a little dizzy, when all of a sudden that soldier said, 'Open the back!' I hunched down. I was sure he could see me, but he didn't say anything. He just stood a moment and then said, 'Okay, you're good to go.' Even now I think he knew. Maybe he was paid off, I don't know. Or maybe—maybe it was just luck."

Crouching under sacks of coffee, Jean-Claude was feeling nauseated.

"It was very hot, and the smell was giving me a bad headache. This was not roasted coffee. This was raw beans. I could smell vegetation. Not manure, but something green—like a green branch—which is not bad at first, but when you stay there for so long it becomes stronger. And the sacks they put the coffee in, also they have their own smell, a chemical smell, something they spray on them. It was the worst smell I have ever experienced, the coffee and those sacks in the heat."

We had stopped for lunch at a dusty café in Nyakarambi, a village known for its traditional crafts, particularly that of *imigongo,* or "cow-dung paintings."

Cow dung?

Yes. Cow dung. This was an ancient Rwandan art that mixed natural pigments with dried dung to create intricate geometric designs. I considered bringing one home for my wife, y'know, as a token of my love, but wasn't sure how she would feel about hanging it above our dining-room table. If nothing else, it would have made a terrific ice-breaker/conversation piece. *"Can you feel the texture of the brush strokes? Wonderful, isn't it? What's it made from, you ask? Well, interesting story that …"*

As we waited for our order of skewers to arrive, it hit me.

"That's why you don't drink coffee, isn't it, Jean-Claude? The heat, the smell of those coffee beans, the chemicals, the nausea and fear, the memory of it. That's why."

He tilted back in his chair, started to say something, then stopped. When the woman came by with our meal he turned to her and said, purposefully, carefully, "I would like a cup of coffee also."

"Make it two," I said.

It was served strong, in chipped china mugs. A Rwandan brew, rich and dark. If night has a flavour, it tastes like Rwandan coffee.

After he finished, I asked him what he thought.

"Bitter. Very bitter. But good."

I never did get Jean-Claude to try beer, but he does drink coffee now—though usually only when he's with me.

A wedding was pouring into Nyakarambi that day, and as we left the café the streets were alive with colour. A procession of women in bright wrapped dresses passed by, accompanied by the usual men in ill-fitting suits. It was like a slow-moving fashion parade. Hundreds of women, and I don't think any two were wearing the same patterns. They carried gifts on their heads in large woven baskets, the type we had seen at the royal court weeks before.

"Big wedding," I said as the guests filed past. Their numbers stretched down the road, in both directions, as far as we could see.

"By African standards, this is usual." Jean-Claude had been to weddings in Canada, was always surprised how small they were— even the big ones.

"Are you ready for Rusumo?" I asked.

He was.

Beyond Nyakarambi, the road grew heavy with transport trucks, passing on angry blasts from their air horns, hand-painted slogans beseeching Jesus and all the Saints to protect them. *Never mind them, what about us?* The increased traffic was inevitable, I suppose. This narrow two-lane strip of highway was, after all, the main trade route south to Tanzania and Kenya beyond.

We climbed higher. And higher still.

Here was a dry season worthy of the name. A haze of chalky dust hung over the fields. Parched sunlight filtered through. Saffron-coloured clouds. Clay-baked villages scattered across the hills. And in the distance, the flat-topped mountains of Tanzania, rippling in the heat.

We passed the Dar American Saloon amid a cluster of taverns and chophouse cafés that were filled with truck drivers, and then we dropped down, suddenly, toward Rusumo Falls.

Jean-Claude parked across from the Rwanda Customs and Immigration office. We walked to a knoll of grass above the river, construction going on all around us. The raised roadbed of a new highway curved around; judging from the artist's rendering posted out front, it would be four lanes wide and emblazoned with street-lights. We could see the cement pylons of this Bridge of Tomorrow already marching across the river, billboards proclaiming it a joint venture of Rwanda, Tanzania, and Japan. And I wondered if Hiro from Nagasaki was somewhere in among the many earthmovers and bulldozers that were rumbling about.

The falls themselves were hidden from sight, and when we approached a pair of Rwandan soldiers, a young man and woman, faces sheened with perspiration, automatic rifles slung over their shoulders, they gave us a shrug and a wave of their hand. If we wanted to walk onto the bridge and take some photographs, that was fine with them. Just don't go past the middle of the bridge, they advised, because after that we would be Tanzania's responsibility. Oh, and try not to get clipped by one of the trucks that were constantly roaring across. It was a tight squeeze.

I was about to walk out when Jean-Claude stopped me.

"We should check in with the immigration office first," he said, referring to the cement building set farther back. "Just to let them know we are here."

"Are you sure? The soldiers already said it was okay."

"Don't worry. It will take only a moment. I promise."

# 69

TWO HOURS AND ONE ARTFULLY CALLED BLUFF LATER, we finally ended up on the bridge above Rusumo Falls.

"Define 'moment,'" I said to Jean-Claude.

He noted, wryly, that it had almost been easier for him to cross twenty years ago than it was today.

Transport trucks from Tanzania rumbled by, the bridge bouncing under their weight. Jean-Claude remembered the sound of the waterfall as well, the muffled roar of it as they passed over. But he had never seen it until now. "I could hear the water," he said. "Then it just faded away ..."

On the Tanzania side of the river, we could see the adjoining ramp where the new bridge would be built, and I said to Jean-Claude, "It's good we came now. Next time, the bridge you crossed will be gone."

He nodded. "I'm glad I finally saw it. This is where the rest of my life began."

The waters at Rusumo continued to fall. A few scribblings of cloud uncurled above us like the absentminded doodles of a distracted god. As we walked back to our vehicle, I asked Jean-Claude, "Where to now?" We'd run out of Rwanda to drive across.

"There is one last stop," he said. "At my village."

# 70

AFTER CROSSING THE BRIDGE under a cargo of coffee and being tossed about like a castaway on high seas, Jean-Claude had waited for the signal. The truck he was in lurched uphill, then came to a shuddering halt. The driver cut the engine. Three short raps on the side of the truck told him it was all clear. Hodali had come to collect him.

So began Jean-Claude's long, elated journey across Tanzania to Kenya and the sea.

"Hodali fed me. He paid the police at roadblocks. Paid for my room at the guest homes we stayed at. I gave him just five thousand francs, which didn't cover very much. He even helped me track down the Zaire Bar."

Using the photograph Jean-Claude had of his brother, they threaded their way through the port city of Mombasa until they found the Jomvu district and eventually the bar.

"Was very small and smoky. They were roasting meat outside. Goat meat. You could smell it. People were drinking beer, and they were playing Congolese music. The bar was Kenyan, but the music was Congolese. This is famous music in East Africa."

Rwandans who knew Jean-Claude's brother sent word down the line, from truck driver to truck driver, to find him.

"I stayed with them while I waited to hear what's happened."

"How was Mombasa?"

"Hot. In Rwanda we don't have heat like that, or such humidity. It was very congested, very crowded. And Kenyans are different. Modern. They don't care about you. Everybody goes about their business. It was a kind of culture shock. I felt like a foreigner for the first time. But there was also a sense of freedom. And"—Jean-Claude smiled—"I saw the ocean for the first time. It was so huge! I saw those container ships passing. I think that was the biggest thing I had ever seen."

Jean-Claude would finally meet up with his brother Saïd, would join him on a run to the Somali refugee camps. Jean-Claude would travel on his own to Sudan, where he would see the desert for the first time, and eventually to Montreal, where he would see snow.

"What a long, strange trip it's been," I said, and Jean-Claude nodded.

"It has."

"Did you keep in touch with the truck driver, the one who took you to Mombasa?"

"Hodali? I did. He came to see me in Kenya. He was very happy to know I was okay. He passed away in 1997 or '99, I think. He lost his entire family in the genocide. His wife, his children. Everyone. He only survived because he was not in Rwanda at that time. He was outside of the country, driving truck. So he survived."

"He was lucky, then."

"Lucky?" Jean-Claude thought about this. "I don't know if that's the right word."

# 71

OVER THE COURSE OF OUR TRAVELS in Rwanda we'd been shedding our supply of soccer gear—team uniforms, goalie equipment, hand pumps. There was only one duffle bag left, and one destination: Rundu village, where Jean-Claude had lived as a child and where his brother Jean-Baptiste had once built a handsome home.

Jean-Baptiste had been killed by Hutu militias, but his scattered children had survived, and among them was his daughter Odile.

"We call her Fifi, it's like a nickname," Jean-Claude said.

Odile was the superintendent of schools for the region, and we stopped in to see her on our way back through Kabarondo.

"How did she survive the genocide?" I asked Jean-Claude as we drove down a narrow residential lane.

"In Rwanda, you never ask that. You don't ask what someone did to survive. If they want to tell you, they will, but you never ask. I have friends I have known for many years who lived through it, and they have never talked to me about it." He put the vehicle in park, looked at me. "So maybe don't ask."

His niece lived in a tidy cement-walled home alongside other tidy cement-walled homes on an equally tidy well-swept lane. We sat in the dimly lit softness of her living room around a low table adorned with a doily and a sprig of flowers in a vase.

Odile's husband, Hussein, was an agricultural engineer. He was away, but their four-year-old son Tony was on hand, along with his elfin-like cousin Asinati. Odile had a new baby as well. He was sleeping on a woven mat in the next room; I could see his chubby legs and twitching toes through an open door, cooled by the cross-breeze.

While Jean-Claude and his niece discussed various matters concerning their family's property, I chatted with the little ones. They were learning English at their local kindergarten and had proven to be attentive pupils.

"Hello," I said. "How are you?"

Odile's son piped up immediately. *"Hello teacher, my name is Tony, I am a boy, I am four years old."* This was delivered in one extended breath. Impressive.

As Tony beamed up at me, his cousin launched into her own version of the same: *"Hello teacher, my name is Asinati, I am a girl, I am four years old."*

"So, do you like school?"

*"Hello teacher, my name is Tony, I am a boy, I am four years old."*

Followed by: *"Hello teacher, my name is Asinati, I am a girl, I am four years old."*

"Do you like sports?"

*"My name is Tony, I am a boy, I am four years old."*

"How about you? Do you like sports?"

*"My name is Asinati, I am a girl, I am four years old."*

Putting this down on paper makes it seem repetitive, even annoying, but it wasn't. Not in the least. I was absolutely charmed by their chimed recitals of English; they were clearly so proud of what they'd learned.

When we got up to leave, I shook their hands solemnly and said, "Goodbye, Tony. Goodbye, Asinati. It was very nice to meet you."

To which they replied— Well, you know what they replied.

Odile accompanied us to Rundu; there was paperwork to sort out and documents to review at the village office. Jean-Claude followed a roughly hewn road past tumbledown farms and tattered banana plantations. A road that had once seen hyenas and lions, but no longer.

On the way, we stopped for a mother who was standing by the side of the road with a swaddled baby on her back. She climbed in beside Odile and held the baby on her lap as we bounced along, carefully draping a scarf over her child's face to protect it from the nasal blast of our air conditioning. When I noticed, I gave Jean-Claude a nudge and he turned it off. A narrow lane led us to her farm, hidden in the undergrowth, where she softly thanked us and got out.

During our time in this country, I'd grown fascinated with the spice box of Rwanda's earth, from the gritty cinder dust of the Virungas to the talcum-powdered heights above Lake Kivu, from the terra-cotta clays of the Bugesera to the blood-rust soils of Akagera. But here, in Jean-Claude's childhood village, lived a shade of vermilion that was richer than I'd seen before. It was a colour almost tactile, with its own texture and warmth.

Rundu itself was hard beset, a reminder that despite the impressive strides Rwanda has made, the country has a long way to go. There were a thousand hills yet to climb, and the way was often steep. Rundu itself seemed to lie in a half-forgotten realm. The area was once reputed to harbour malevolent spirits and apparitions unholy. It was said to be the dwelling place of witches and necromancers, but today its most striking feature is simply the poverty that marks it. It's a poverty that lacks the optimism in other reaches of Rwanda. Here, you have the feeling of a people passed by, left behind.

There are no fibre-optic cables connecting Rundu to the outside world, no billboards exhorting the citizens to greater heights; there isn't even electricity. The homes are dark and lit by lamp oil; the shops are drab, lacking the brightly painted facades you find else-where. No phone companies are sponsoring Rundu's shops. Most of the buildings are crude wattle-and-mud arrangements, with the plaster falling away at times to reveal the woven-branch framework underneath, like bones through an animal's hide.

We visited one home—dirt floors, clay walls, soot-filled interior—where Jean-Claude spoke with an arthritic old lady and her twelve-year-old grandson. They lived alone, just the two of them in a crumbling house the size of a shed. Jean-Claude and the grand-mother were discussing the possible cost of having her grandson board at his school.

Rather than attend the local school, the boy, who had shown real academic potential, walked two hours every day to Kabarondo. A small stipend from Jean-Claude would allow him to remain at his school during the week, where he could study under electric lights and be spared the exhausting back-and-forth daily trek. Jean-Claude agreed to help on the condition that the student keep his grades up. It would be a small amount of money, given twice a year, but one that would have a huge impact. Odile and Jean-Claude would work out how the funds would be sent, who would keep tabs, and how the student's progress would be evaluated.

"Odile told me about this boy," Jean-Claude explained as we stepped back outside. "A good student, trying hard. She thought maybe I could help."

Jean-Claude's next meeting was not so convivial. It was with a sinewy man in a frayed shirt, the cloth patched over many times, who'd been encroaching on Jean-Claude's family property for years. Jean-Claude confronted him, and there was a terse exchange with warnings of legal action. The sinewy man hung his head, avoiding JC's gaze as he mumbled something ineffectual in his defence. Once a member of the feared Hutu militia, free to chop whomever he liked, he was now required to follow the rules like anyone else.

"That man," Jean-Claude told me later. "He looted my brother's house after my brother was killed."

As Jean-Claude dealt with these and other matters, I wandered among the mud-walled homes of Rundu, past scuttling chickens and tethered goats. I soon had a mob of children, assorted ages and sizes, accompanying me. Not as brash as the kids in the cities, but equally amazed at my existence. They'd heard about muzungus, now they were seeing one firsthand! I felt I should do something entertaining—maybe turn a cartwheel or juggle some gourds—if only not to disappoint them. Instead, I said *"Amakuru?"* which caused them to scatter, regroup, and then tiptoe back in. More than one child, egged on by his peers, snuck up, poked me, and then ran away. Others hung back shyly. Several smiled with a heartbreaking lack of guile. One of the older boys, having been to the city and therefore clearly more cosmopolitan than the rest, was selected by the other children to act as their spokesperson. A smiling beanpole of a kid with a natural confidence, he was, I imagined, what Jean-Claude must have been like when he was young.

"How are you, America?" he asked and then, voice dropping to a whisper, he confided: "I am fine."

# 72

JEAN-CLAUDE'S BROTHER had been a prominent member of the village, and his house had been among the finest in Rundu. Made of brick, with glass windows and a metal roof, it featured a new latrine in the backyard as well. When the genocide began, Jean-Baptiste's home was torn apart, brick by brick, down to its foundations. Following that, the Tutsi boys in the village were rounded up.

"They kept the women and younger girls for themselves and killed the men. The boys they tossed into our latrine."

"Alive?"

He nodded. "One of the little ones, maybe five years old, they could hear him crying for days and days until his voice gave out. Other boys were pushed on top of him. Then they filled it in."

Years later, these bodies would be exhumed. The excavation left behind an open pit, overgrown but clearly visible.

We stood beside it awhile.

It hit me. "Your family home is a genocide site."

Jean-Claude looked over at me and said, "All of Rwanda is a genocide site."

From the ruins of his brother's house, we walked out into nearby fields. Jean-Claude wanted to show me his family's land, banana plantations mainly, some of it leased, some of it surreptitiously encroached upon, much of it lying fallow, awaiting crops.

Of the adults who came out to watch, holding back, eyeing us warily, many were undoubtedly killers. And yet I could sense no anger on Jean-Claude's part, no simmering rage, no eye-for-an-eye thirst for vengeance. Instead, we climbed back into the Land Cruiser with Odile and then drove our final bag of soccer equipment and uniforms out to the local elementary school, where we lugged the bag onto the field.

The Rundu girls' soccer team was particularly strong. They'd beaten many of their opponents from larger towns while playing in bare feet with their school uniform skirts hitched up. Their coach, a friendly young teacher, was thrilled with the shining jerseys and soccer gear Jean-Claude had brought with him for both the girls' team and the boys'.

"They will feel like superstars!" he said.

I looked at the children crowding in around us, and I turned to Jean-Claude. "You know, a lot of these kids will be the children of murderers."

He nodded. "That's true. Many of the parents killed people in the genocide. But their children did not."

It's a fine line, isn't it, between honouring the past and reaching out for a better future, between fixating and forgiving. It would be so easy to succumb to bitterness. Or to rush forward into selective amnesia, to pretend none of it ever happened, to wish the past away. I thought about the many roads that had taken us here. It was a journey that began on the bridge that carried Jean-Claude away from Rwanda, and ended on a schoolyard soccer field, with a visit and a parting gift.

The children ran headlong down the pitch, kicking up dust and trailing laughter behind them.

# SOURCES

THE STATISTICS CITED in *Road Trip Rwanda*—from reports by UNICEF, the World Health Organization, Transparency International, the World Bank, Human Rights Watch, Reporters Without Borders, the Committee to Protect Journalists, Gallup International, the World Economic Forum, and Democracy Watch—as well as the articles quoted from *Economist* magazine, *The Globe and Mail,* and *The New York Times* are all readily available online.

For the historical and cultural background on Rwanda, and the genocide, I relied on the following sources:

Adekunle, Julius O. *Culture and Customs of Rwanda.* Greenwood, 2007.

Anyidoho, Henry Kwami. *Guns Over Kigali: The Rwandese Civil War—1994 (A Personal Account).* Fountain, 1997.

Berkeley, Bill. *The Graves Are Not Yet Full: Race, Tribe and Power in the Heart of Africa.* Basic, 2001.

Berry, Carol Pott, and John A. Berry, eds. *Genocide in Rwanda: A Collective Memory.* Howard University Press, 1999.

Briggs, Philip. *Rwanda: Bradt Guide, 5th Edition.* Bradt, 2012.

Carr, Rosamond Halsey, with Ann Howard Halsey. *Land of a Thousand Hills: My Life in Rwanda.* Plume, 2000.

Chu, Sandra Ka Hon, and Anne-Marie de Brouwer, eds. *The Men Who Killed Me: Rwandan Survivors of Sexual Violence.* Douglas & McIntyre, 2009.

Crisafulli, Patricia, and Andrea Redmond. *Rwanda, Inc.: How a Devastated Nation Became an Economic Model for the Developing World.* Palgrave Macmillan, 2012.

Dallaire, Roméo, with Brent Beardsley. *Shake Hands with the Devil: The Failure of Humanity in Rwanda.* Vintage, 2004.

Des Forges, Alison. *Leave None to Tell the Story: Genocide in Rwanda.* Human Rights Watch, 1999.

Dugard, Martin. *Into Africa: The Epic Adventures of Stanley and Livingstone.* Broadway, 2003.

Feil, Scott R. *Preventing Genocide: How the Early Use of Force Might Have Succeeded in Rwanda.* Carnegie Commission, 1998.

Fossey, Dian. *Gorillas in the Mist.* Houghton Mifflin, 1983.

French, Howard W. *China's Second Continent: How a Million Migrants Are Building a New Empire in Africa.* Knopf, 2014.

Gourevitch, Philip. *We Wish to Inform You That Tomorrow We Will Be Killed with Our Families: Stories from Rwanda.* Picador, 1998.

Grant, Richard. *Crazy River: Exploration and Folly in East Africa.* Free Press, 2011.

Hatzfeld, Jean. *Into the Quick of Life: The Rwandan Genocide: The Survivors Speak.* Serpent's Tail, 2005.

———. *The Strategy of Antelopes: Rwanda After the Genocide.* Serpent's Tail, 2009.

———. *A Time for Machetes: The Rwandan Genocide: The Killers Speak.* Serpent's Tail, 2005.

Hochschild, Adam. *King Leopold's Ghost: A Story of Greed, Terror, and Heroism in Colonial Africa.* Houghton Mifflin, 1998.

Jennings, Christian. *Across the Red River: Rwanda, Burundi and the Heart of Darkness.* Phoenix, 2001.

Kapuściński, Ryszard. *The Shadow of the Sun.* Vintage, 2002.

Kinzer, Stephen. *A Thousand Hills: Rwanda's Rebirth and the Man Who Dreamed It.* Wiley, 2008.

Mamdani, Mahmood. *When Victims Become Killers: Colonialism, Nativism and the Genocide in Rwanda.* Princeton University Press, 2001.

McCullum, Hugh. *The Angels Have Left Us: The Rwandan Tragedy and the Churches.* WCC, 1995.

Melvern, Linda. *Conspiracy to Murder: The Rwandan Genocide.* Verso, 2004.

————. *A People Betrayed: The Role of the West in Rwanda's Genocide,* new updated edition. Zed Books, 2009.

Peterson, Scott. *Me Against My Brother: At War in Somalia, Sudan and Rwanda.* Routledge, 2000.

Prunier, Gérard. *The Rwanda Crisis: History of a Genocide.* Columbia University Press, 1995, 1997.

Rittner, Carol, John K. Roth, and Wendy Whitworth, eds. *Genocide in Rwanda: Complicity of the Churches?* Paragon, 2004.

Rusagara, Frank K. *Resilience of a Nation: A History of the Military in Rwanda.* Fountain, 2009.

Sebarenzi, Joseph, with Laura Ann Mullane. *God Sleeps in Rwanda: A Journey of Transformation.* Atria, 2009.

Severino, Jean-Michel, and Oliver Ray. *Africa's Moment.* Polity, 2011.

Shaw, Martin. *War and Genocide.* Polity, 2003.

Stearns, Jason K. *Dancing in the Glory of Monsters: The Collapse of the Congo and the Great War of Africa.* PublicAffairs, 2011.

Thompson, Allan, ed. *The Media and the Rwanda Genocide.* Fountain, 2007.

Wallis, Andrew. *Silent Accomplice: The Untold Story of the Role of France in the Rwandan Genocide.* I.B. Tauris, 2014.

# ACKNOWLEDGMENTS

I WOULD FIRST like to thank Jean-Claude Munyezamu. Without Jean-Claude, *Road Trip Rwanda* would not exist. His friendship, good cheer, help, and encouragement—to say nothing of his steady hand behind the wheel—were instrumental in bringing this book to life. I would also like to thank our respective spouses, Christine and Terumi, for allowing their wayward husbands to go toodling about central Africa while they stayed back and managed the households.

Support from the Alberta Foundation for the Arts made this project possible, and I thank the Foundation for this.

I would like to thank Publishing Director Andrea Magyar, Publicity Manager Trish Bunnett, Senior Production Editor Sandra Tooze, copy editor Karen Alliston, and everyone at Penguin Canada for their enthusiasm and support for this project, and editor Barbara Pulling for her fine work, as always. It's been an absolute pleasure.

In Rwanda, Jean-Claude and I relied on the kindness and assistance of many people, from the staff and students at Nyange Secondary School to the ever-patient trail guides we encountered along the way. We would especially like to thank Rica Rwigamba and Vivian Kayitesi at the Rwanda Development Board; Yvette Rugasaguhunga at the Rwandan Embassy in Washington; Jean de Dieu Mucyo at the National Commission for the Fight Against Genocide; Jean Gakwandi at the Solace Guest House in Kigali; Urooj Saifi, Deo Ntirenganya, and Clementine Kayirangwa at the UNHCR camp in Kigeme; Alice Kampire and Jerry Were at Nyungwe Forest Lodge; Duncan Lewa at the Lake Kivu Serena; and Manzi Kayihura at Thousand Hills Expeditions, who also hosted Jean-Claude and me at his home in Kigali. Thank you!

A big thank you as well to Brian Carnduff and the entire Calgary Foothills Soccer Club for the uniforms and gear that Jean-Claude brought with him to Rwanda, and to my next-door neighbour

Jacqueline Ford for once again transcribing endless reams of notes for me. I would also like to thank my son, Alex Ferguson, for creating the templates for the maps that the designers used.

In Canada, several people shared with me their stories and experiences—and even personal contacts—from their own travels in Rwanda, and I would like to thank Margaret McQuiston, Alina Freedman, Christine Magill, and Lynn Gran. I would also like to thank Kirsten Olson for connecting me with Lynn. (Sadly, Lynn passed away while I was writing this book, and I wasn't able to thank her properly for her help.)

The Rwandan community of Calgary has been very kind to me, and I thank them for their support, in particular Andy Amour, President of the Rwandan Canadian Society of Calgary, and Melchior Cyusa, the Secretary General. Andy and Melchior were in Rwanda while we were there, and it was a pleasure to meet up with friends from back home while we were travelling. (Melchior was getting married as well!) I have warm memories of the laughter and food we shared with Andy at Chez Lando—the liveliest eatery in Kigali.

*Murakoze!*

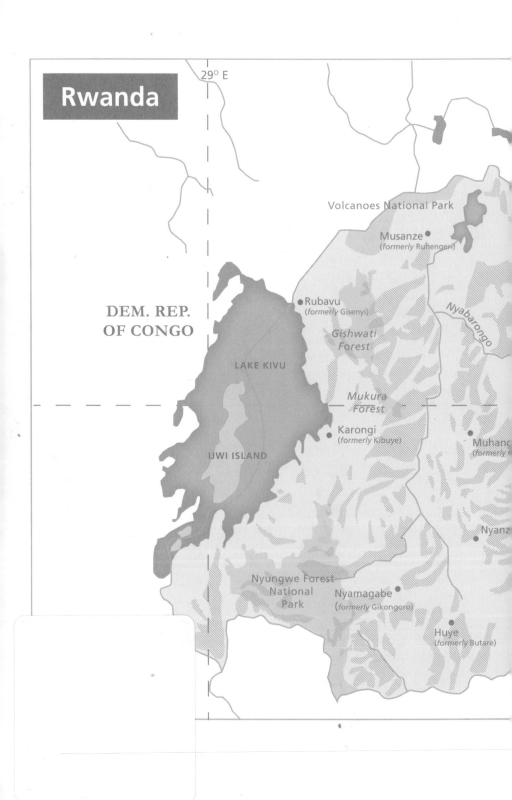

**Rwanda**

29° E

Volcanoes National Park

Musanze ●
*(formerly Ruhengeri)*

DEM. REP.
OF CONGO

●Rubavu
*(formerly Gisenyi)*

*Nyabarongo*

*Gishwati
Forest*

LAKE KIVU

*Mukura
Forest*

Karongi ●
*(formerly Kibuye)*

Muhan
*(formerly*

IJWI ISLAND

●Nyanz

Nyungwe Forest
National
Park

Nyamagabe ●
*(formerly Gikongoro)*

Huye ●
*(formerly Butare)*